For Rup

THIS IS A CARLTON BOOK

Text copyright © 2006 Marcus Fairs
Design copyright © 2006 Carlton Books Limited

This edition published by Carlton Books Limited 2006
20 Mortimer Street, London W 1T 3JW.

All rights reserved
A CIP catalogue record for this book
is available from the British Library
ISBN-10 1 84442 269 0
ISBN-13 978 1 84442 269 2

Printed and bound in Dubai

Executive Editor: Lisa Dyer
Senior Art Editor: Zoë Dissell
Designer: SMITH, Karl Shanahan
Copy Editor: Diana Craig and Nicky Gyopari
Picture Researcher: Paul Langan
Production: Caroline Alberti

CARLTON
BOOKS

Twenty-First Century Design

new design icons, from mass
market to avant-garde

Marcus Fairs

Foreword by **Marcel Wanders**

Contents

Foreword
The Contemporary Renaissance of Humanism

Marcel Wanders

I remember my first design years in the early 1980s. I was studying design, totally enthusiastic and ready to change the world! According to me, design was a deep and refined cultural medium, able to touch humanity in a subtle and caring way and guide it to new unprecedented heights. I looked for all the little and bigger philosophies and ideas to support my growing knowledge and dreams. Reacting to my endless enthusiasm, my teachers and my other design heros used to give me their "more realistic" view and told me, "Marcel, it's terrible, the people in the street are ignorant, stupid and traditional. They're not interested in the great future designs we try to realize. They have no sense of taste and are unwilling to follow us." I was shocked and couldn't understand why we, being the heroes of the future, were so incredibly misunderstood and left alone.

Later I started understanding that, in fact, our point of view was outdated and that our works were conceptually as well as visually based on a design theory and sense of style that was created for the first years of the industrial revolution and the baby days of industrial design. Throughout the twentieth century, architects and designers strived to produce products that could be made by machines and that would help create welfare, equality and a political foundation for democracy. They created works that celebrated the poor possibilities of the available machinery. In this period bending metal tubes and cutting wood with a machine were considered small miracles. Designers created products that were easy to manufacture, but difficult to communicate to an audience that was used to beautiful, crafted, ornamented objects.

Unfortunately, this once-interesting quest became a stylistic dogma, which is still today controlling the works of design. The industry is far more capable of creating fantastic products, but we still follow this traditional dogma and we don't use the industry's

full potential. We still feel the need to make things easy, economic, functional and simple instead of inspiring and brilliant (just imagine these as the qualities of a gift you receive from your lover). When I finished school, I started understanding that our public perhaps was not so much interested in our so well-engineered works because it wasn't meaningful enough to them and they were looking for more inspirational media. They were just not so interested in our ancient (design) philosophy and they wanted more out of life.

If I look into the hearts of people, sometimes I can sense what they dream of. If I talk to them I can understand their needs: their need for surprise, for security, for contribution and growth, for individuality and familiarity. Humanity creates an endless flow of illusions and hope. So many girls want to be beautiful princesses or flying elves, so many boys want to feel like cunning knights or wise kings. Why don't we make it our goal to realize those dreams,

and contribute deeply to the lives of others and ourselves in the meantime. We are allowed to speak the universal language of design, which can be an inspiration to so many if we find the right words to speak. It is our responsibility to be magicians, to be jesters, to be alchemists, to create hope where there is only illusion, to create reality where there are only dreams.

We cannot work for the company who pays us; we have to work for our public and create great value for them. In the twenty-first century we can no longer use humanity to serve technology; we have to use technology to serve humanity.

Introduction

The twenty-first century is just a few years old, but already it has witnessed a phenomenal surge of creativity across all design disciplines. In almost every field of design – architecture, furniture, graphics, fashion, urban design, homeware – there is a revolution going on. The old ideas and dogmas that dominated the last century are being thrown away and the new century is beginning to look like a very different place.

The change is most noticeable in the way twenty-first century design looks. The predominantly rectilinear and rational forms of twentieth-century Modernism have been swept away in favour of a new spirit of experimentation and sensuality. Modernist slogans, such as "less is more" and "ornament is a crime", are now being wilfully ignored. Decoration is firmly back in favour and designers once more feel confident to create forms for purely aesthetic reasons, rather than justifying them through functional logic.

Architecture, the most visible of all the design disciplines, has abandoned the rectilinear dogma of twentieth-century Modernism and embraced a more plastic approach to form-making that has produced buildings that resemble blobs, gherkins or clouds. A wave of instantly recognizable "iconic" buildings by cutting-edge architects has erupted across the world in the last few years, such as Norman Foster's 30 St Mary Axe building in London, Frank Gehry's Disney Concert Hall in Los Angeles and Daniel Libeskind's Jewish Museum in Berlin. Furniture designers, meanwhile, are creating idiosyncratic, highly expressive pieces that are more akin to art than design. Dutch designer Maarten Baas takes existing pieces of furniture and singes them with a blowtorch, selling the resulting burnt items in art galleries; Swedish designers Front are creating tables by putting twigs into a compacting machine, making chairs by producing moulds of the craters left by explosions, and allowing rats to nibble at plain wallpaper to create patterns. Industrial designers, too, are taking standard banal types such as radiators, DVD players and security fencing and giving them baroque flourishes and intricately crafted details. Marcel Wanders' range of home electronics products for Dutch brand HE is as ornate as an Art Deco radiogram; Joris Laarman's Concrete radiator is as florid as Art Nouveau ironwork.

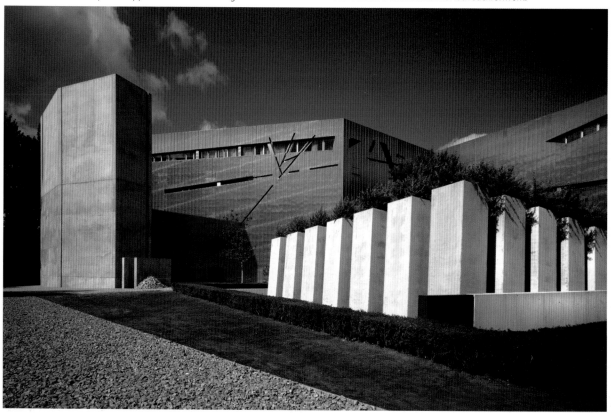

OPPOSITE: Daniel Libeskind's Jewish Museum in Berlin.
RIGHT: The conceptual fashion of Hussein Chalayan.
BELOW RIGHT: Neo-baroque Midsummer light by designer Tord Boontje.

What has brought on this sea change? It's perhaps a coincidence that all this design activity coincides with the start of the new millennium – although the hopes and fears generated by the start of the new century have undoubtedly contributed to the hot-house atmosphere in the design industries. The excitement generated in the run up to the turn of the millennium no doubt explains the rash of blobby, retro-futuristic and overwhelmingly white buildings that sprung up around this time, as architects revisited science fiction classics such as Stanley Kubrick's *2001: A Space Odyssey* for clues as to what kind of aesthetic might be suitable for the third millennium.

Yet this brief flirtation with neo-space age imagery proved shortlived: perhaps the most striking aspect of the current design movement is that it looks nothing like we were led to believe it would by twentieth-century sages. We are not dressing in high-tech fabrics nor living in futuristic pods. Instead, a bewildering array of styles and attitudes have blossomed, from the neo-baroque of lighting designer Tord Boontje to the data-driven architecture of Rem Koolhaas and the conceptual fashion of Hussein Chalayan. One of the main aims of this book is to capture the astonishing variety of design activity happening during what must surely be one of the most exciting periods for design that there has ever been.

Developments in design
The reasons for this feverish activity are multiple and vary from discipline to discipline, but there are common threads that unite them all. First, the incredible technological advances of the last few years – particularly in computing and manufacturing – have given today's designers the tools to create forms that would have been impossible for past generations to even imagine, let alone realize. Computer-aided design (CAD) technology has enabled architects and industrial designers among others to not only dream up extraordinary products – such as Frank Gehry's Guggenheim museum in Bilbao, or Seymour Powell's hydrogen-powered ENV motorcycle – but to actually test them in computer simulations. This removes much of the risk from the development process, with the result that clients and manufacturers have become much braver in the buildings and products they commission.

Second, globalization, the ease of travel and the Internet allow new ideas from every corner of the world to spread much faster than they used to. This has led to an incredible amount of cross-fertilization between designers from different cultures and led to the rise of a much more adventurous type of consumer. The speed at which ideas spread has led to fears of the world being swamped by a bland monoculture, but in fact the opposite seems to be happening: many designers are resurrecting local traditions or drawing inspiration from their own experiences to create highly personal, defiantly local objects

which nonetheless have global appeal. The work of the Campana Brothers, which is inspired by the Brazilian vernacular of their home town of São Paolo, is a good example of this.

Third, design has become democratized: a growing number of affluent consumers care about their clothes, their homes and their possessions. Design is no longer the passion of a wealthy elite, and new affordable brands, such as IKEA in furniture and H&M and Zara in fashion, are bringing stylish products to the masses. Design in all its manifestations is voraciously reported by the media – which is always on the lookout for new ideas and personalities – through "design" publications, such as *Wallpaper** magazine, and its many imitators, the ever-expanding number of lifestyle publications and, increasingly, television and the Internet. In short, design is presented as the sexier, more desirable end of the consumer landscape. And the ubiquity of contemporary media has led to the collapse of the importance of the uber-critic or style dictator: trends and movements are no longer dependent on the nod of a clique of elite commentators, but find their way into the collective consciousness by an infinite number of routes.

Alongside this, the notion of "conformity" (where everyone dressed the same and "standing out from the crowd" was generally considered undesirable) has been replaced by an acceptance of "self-expression" – people now use their clothes, their interior decor and their possessions to send out signals about who they are and what their aspirations are.

These three phenomena have combined to present designers with greater freedoms than ever before. Yet at the same time, the notion of what design actually means is changing. During much of the last century, design was considered a discipline that sought to create industrially manufactured products – be they buildings, bicycles or toothbrushes – that solved functional needs. In a world recovering from two devastating world wars and trying to overcome the inequalities of the nineteenth century, with its bourgeouise elite living in luxury while the majority of the population lived in poverty, architecture and design became tools for social and material progress. Today, in Western societies at least, most of our material needs have been solved. A consumer requiring a vacuum cleaner or a sofa will find more affordable options than they could ever need in their local high street or for sale on the Internet. This glut of cheap consumer products – which are often aesthetically banal, if not downright ugly – might not be viewed as "design" by elite critics, but it has forced designers and design-led manufacturers alike to move into new ground.

Celebrity status and the age of aesthetics

The breathtaking advances in computer and communications technologies means that the role of the designer has changed: rather than working on every aspect of a product, as great twentieth-century figures such as Dieter Rams did, industrial designers today are more likely to find themselves asked by the marketing department of a company to take a product, conceived and perfected in a laboratory, and make it more appealing to the consumer. Thus, in mass-produced goods at least, design has become a branding tool used to give one product the edge over its rivals. A designer's name on a product makes it more exclusive and, by extension, more expensive.

The phenomenon of the celebrity designer, which began with Philippe Starck in the late 1980s, has now become almost ubiquitous: "signature" architects such as Jean Nouvel or Zaha Hadid are called upon to design "landmark" buildings that add glamorous cachet to otherwise unknown towns or districts; leading designers, such as Marc Newson and Jasper Morrison, are invited to work on product ranges for household-name brands in the hope that a bit of designer magic will rub off on the brand. This manifestation of design – where

OPPOSITE: The Campana Brothers' Melissa shoes.
BELOW: Ordinairy Furniture, designed by Ineke Hans.

the designer or architect is selected for his or her celebrity as much as his or her talent, and the resulting product or building is as much a marketing device for the brand or city as anything else – would until recently have been dismissed as superficial. But recent years have also seen a resurgent belief in the importance of aesthetics for their own sake. In her 2004 book *The Substance of Style*, American writer Virginia Postrel argues that we have now entered the "Age of Aesthetics", a period in which the way things look is every bit as important as the way they work.

This debate reached an explosive head later the same year at London's Design Museum when James Dyson – inventor of the Dyson vacuum cleaner and chairman of the museum's trustees – resigned in disgust at the curatorial policy of the then director Alice Rawsthorn. Rawsthorn, sensing that design was increasingly becoming as much about styling, concept and attitude as about creating functional products, organized a series of shows celebrating media-friendly stylists, such as Marc Newson and shoe designer Manolo Blahnik, at the expense of the type of industrial products epitomized by Dyson's own products. But Rawsthorn had correctly identified design's zeitgeist: architecture and design are now in many ways inseparable from marketing and entertainment.

Design has also started to come to the attention of wealthy connoisseurs who would formerly have collected works of art. A whole new industry has grown up in the last few years whereby galleries and auction houses are promoting the work of avant garde designers, such as Ron Arad and Zaha Hadid, as if they were paintings or sculptures – and often with prices to match. This is partly because contemporary art as a commodity has become so expensive as to be almost unaffordable to many discerning buyers; and also partly because tables, chairs and lights by celebrity designers increasingly display as much formal ingenuity and technical brilliance as the work of leading artists, but lack the baffling conceptual hyperbole that usually accompanies art. After all, a chair is still a chair, no matter how complex its manufacture or obscure its inspiration.

Function and concept

Now at end of essay

To many designers, the functional requirement of a product is increasingly taking second place to the concept. The rise of Dutch "conceptual" design in the 1990s, spearheaded by the Droog collective, signified a key break with the past, as designers abandoned the idea of taking form and function as their starting point and instead began with a narrative or a cultural observation. Jurgen Bey's Tree Trunk Bench (see page 162), for example, takes as its starting point the idea that a felled tree trunk lying in a forest is equally useful as a seat to anything a designer might produce; Bey then simply adds traditional chair backs cast in bronze to domesticate the raw log and make its function unequivocal. Dutch design has had a huge influence: Stuart Haygarth's Tide chandelier (see page 228),

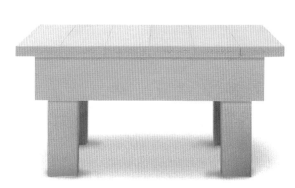

made of plastic items washed up on an English beach, is on one level a narrative about Haygarth's beachcombing activities, on another a parable about today's disposable culture and pollution, but on yet another level, is simply a beautiful light shade.

The emergence of the "art design" phenomenon implies a very different definition of design to the twentieth-century insistence on function and mass production. Indeed, many of the pieces selected for this book are produced in small batches or are sometimes even unique handmade one-offs. Thus design has partially colonized the territory formerly occupied by craft – still a deeply unfashionable term, but one that is again gaining currency as designers rediscover materials and techniques that were sidelined by industrial processes, or apply craft techniques to advanced materials. One example of this is Niels van Eijk's Bobbin Lace lamp (see page 212), which applies fifteenth-century lace-making techniques to fibre-optic materials.

Technology is also providing designers with both new materials and manufacturing techniques to experiment with, and new sources of formal inspiration. As mentioned before, computing power is liberating architects and designers from traditional constraints: they can design almost any shape they want, knowing their software will tell them how to make the building stand up. Architects, such as Rem Koolhaas and Foreign Office Architects, are able to invent extraordinary new forms by feeding data about the site, how a building will be used and how external factors, such as weather and earthquakes, need to be accounted for into their computers, and letting their software suggest how the building might look. This "parametric" approach to design is also happening in furniture design: Kram/Weisshaar's Breeding tables (see page 184) are created by feeding a range of essential parameters (height of top, position of legs, etc) into a computer,

which then generates an endless variety of potential forms that the designers then select from. Thus the tables are both industrial products and unique one-offs, since no two tables are the same. The boundary between industry and craft is therefore blurred.

Designers have always sought inspiration from nature, but advanced three-dimensional scanning technology has allowed Marcel Wanders to produce a range of vases based on an unlikely source: microscopic particles of mucus in a human sneeze (see pages 268). Frank Gehry also uses three-dimensional scanners to digitize the architectural models he constructs from paper and other found materials, reversing the traditional practice of working first with two-dimensional drawings and then moving to three-dimensional models to test the ideas.

Rapid prototyping, a relatively new manufacturing technique that "prints" three-dimensional objects, is also transforming the way designers think. Liberated from technical considerations, such as mould release angles and the shrinkage that occurs when moulded products cool, rapid prototyping allows designers to make objects in any conceivable shape. Interestingly, many of the most successful of these products, such as Freedom of Creation's Lily lamp (see page 196), have adopted natural, rather than geometric or abstract, forms: technology has paradoxically ushered in a return to organic form and pattern at the expense of the clean, minimal lines of so much twentieth-century design.

In fact, the return of decoration is one of the most visible phenomena of the new century. Perhaps as a reaction against the constraints of minimalism, designers are applying flowers, butterflies and other patterns to everything in sight, from dinner services to wallpaper and upholstery. Time will tell whether this is a passing fad, but the fixation with unadorned white surfaces

OPPOSITE LEFT: Niels van Eijk's Bobbin Lace lamp.
OPPOSITE RIGHT: Freedom of Creation's Lily lamp.
BELOW LEFT: Bouroullec Brothers' Algue system.
BELOW RIGHT: Frank Tjepkema's Do Break vase.

now = end

appears to be well and truly over. In part, this chimes with designers' new-found enthusiasm with the emotional content of the objects they create.

Twentieth-century functionalism focused exclusively on how an object performed – the form was the result of the designers' painstaking attempts to achieve functional perfection. This led to objects that were sterile and lacking in personality. In addition, the formal purity of a well-designed object is often all but indistinguishable from the relative formal purity of the vast majority of manufactured objects that are not well designed. Thus many designers today are attempting to invest their work with unique qualities that will endear them to their owners. Frank Tjepkema's Do Break vase (see page 270), for example, is designed to be smashed on purchase. A rubber lining holds the porcelain shards together so it still functions as a vase, but the pattern of cracks is unique and

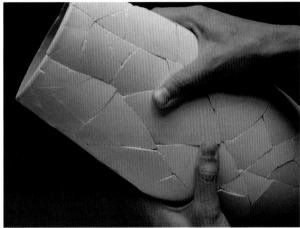

forever reminds the owner of the violent act perpetrated against it. This approach is taken to an extreme by Tobie Kerridge and Nikki Stott's Bio Jewellery project, which produces jewellery grown from bone tissue samples extracted from clients (see page 370). The notion of giving the consumer a role in the life of the object is taking hold across many areas of design. Mass customization – in which manufactured products are individually tailored to their end user – is catching on in fashion (Elena Manferdini's Clad Cuts, see page 358) and homeware products such as the Bouroullec Brothers' Algue system, which consists of clip-together plastic components resembling seaweed that consumers can assemble however they see fit.

Inevitably, of course, there are many designers who are already growing tired of the constant striving for sensation and novelty that characterizes the contemporary scene. From furniture designers, such as Ineke Hans (whose Ordinairy Furniture attempts to produce objects that appear not to have been designed at all), to interior designers, such as Ilse Crawford (whose interiors for Soho House in New York feature eclectic assemblies of antiques and found objects) and Rei Kawakubo of Comme des Garçons (whose Dover Street Market in London eschews architectural perfection in favour of rough finishes and a scrap-yard aesthetic), these pioneer designers are ushering in a new punk spirit.

Developments such as those listed here have caught the imagination of the public and governments alike, with the latter in many countries now focusing their attention on design as a growth industry that could help Western economies cope with the loss of manufacturing industry in the face of competition from low-cost economies such as China and India. In short, there has never been a time when design has been so exciting – or so visible.

Architecture

The start of the twenty-first century will go down in history as the era of the iconic building. Around the world, architects are striving to outdo each other with spectacular and unique landmarks, often commissioned with the express purpose of drawing attention to a particular city, district or institution. Iconic architecture has been around for a long time of course – Gustave Eiffel's (1832–1923) Eiffel Tower has been a marketing device for Paris since 1889, while Jorn Utzon's Sydney Opera House put the Australian city on the map in 1956.

But over the last few years the craze for icons has reached epidemic proportions. Frank Gehry's 1997 Guggenheim Museum Bilbao showed how radical architecture could reverse the fortunes of a declining city, its spectacular rippled-titanium panelling becoming perhaps the first example of architecture as pin-up. The Guggenheim helped generate unprecedented public interest in avant-garde architecture, which in turn further emboldened clients around the world to commission yet more outlandish buildings. To meet this demand, a global cabal of "starchitects" – famous designers such as Norman Foster, Zaha Hadid and Daniel Libeskind – has emerged, each with their own signature style or approach. Yet there is already a backlash against the globalization of the star architect's ubiquitous signature, with more thoughtful designers, such as Jean Nouvel, Rem Koolhaas and Foreign Office Architects, producing buildings that respond to local conditions – although the approach of such firms are often fiercely intellectual.

A number of factors have combined to create the conditions for this explosion of architectural creativity. Globalization and the booming world economy have led to high demand for large-scale projects, both for corporations, brands and cultural institutions who require unique and instantly recognizable buildings: the faceless glass and steel corporate tower is no longer an attractive option. An equally globalized media ensures that new buildings get rapid exposure, with the resulting PR and increases in visitor numbers partially justifying the huge build costs. Architecture has become as much about

providing spectacle as solving functional requirements. On top of this, the emergence of sophisticated new computer aided design packages has made it relatively easy for architects to design and build radical forms that would have been inconceivable a few years ago. This has allowed relatively small avant-garde architectural offices to take on major overseas projects – such as Foreign Office Architects' Yokohama Ferry Terminal – meaning the stranglehold of the huge and largely uninspired international architectural offices has been broken.

Stylistically, "anything goes" seems to be the present mantra. The turn of the millennium saw a rash of blob-shaped buildings, such as Future Systems' NatWest Media Centre and Nicholas Grimshaw's Eden Project, but this trend appears to have been quickly superseded by more idiosyncratic angular forms as exemplified by Rem Koolhaas' Seattle Public Library and Zaha Hadid's Phaeno Science Centre. The current diversity of architectural form largely defies categorization and owes more to the mannerisms of individual architects.

Sustainability is beginning to be taken seriously by architects, many of whom try to persuade their clients take on board energy-saving ideas, often with limited success. Foster & Partners' No 1 St Mary Axe and Behnisch, Behnisch & Partner's Norddeutsche Landesbank are notable attempts to invest glass buildings with environmental systems.

Much contemporary architecture responds to, and reacts against, the Modernist dogmas that were dominant throughout much of the twentieth century. Whereas the International Style eschewed decoration, which was considered bourgeois and frivolous, there has recently been a revival of interest in pattern, ornamentation and colour. A love of raw concrete and acres of glass remains, but this is softened by the use of more organic and expressive forms and playful experimentation with material and light. Yet the idealism of Modernism remains, with architecture largely being the domain of idealistic – and often egotistical – individuals who yearn to make their mark on the world.

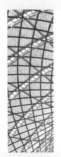

Tod's Omotesando

Date **2004**

Place **Tokyo, Japan**

Architect **Toyo Ito & Associates**

Omotesando is Tokyo's most fashionable boulevard and the location of choice for premier European brands such as Christian Dior and Louis Vuitton. In recent years the boulevard and its neighbouring streets have emerged as one of the most architecturally exciting districts in the world as fashion houses compete to employ the most stylish architects to design their stores.

So when Italian leather goods company Tod's decided to open a flagship store, they selected Toyo Ito, one of Japan's best-known and most avant-garde architects (and whose office is a stone's throw away from the site). Yet the concrete and glass exterior of the striking seven-storey building he designed is founded on an extremely simple concept: the interlocking, stylized silhouettes of the zelkova trees that line Omotesando boulevard.

The L-shaped building fills the irregular corner site, offering a narrow frontage onto the boulevard, but a much larger rear façade. The tree forms, constructed of 30 cm (1 ft) thick reinforced cast concrete, are the building's structure as well as its decorative motif, and wrap around the entire exterior. The 270-odd gaps between the branches – no two are the same – are mostly filled with precision-cut glass, except where it rubs up against an adjacent building, where aluminium panels are used instead.

Ito rose to prominence in the 1980s and 1990s when his architecture – which fused the visual language of Modernism with an interest in high technology and media – seemed appropriate to the frenetic pace of technological advance during Japan's bubble economy. His 1986 Tower of the Winds in Yokohama, for example, features an interactive, illuminated façade that changes colour and pattern in response to weather and sound, while his 2001 Sendai Mediatheque in Sendai expresses the fluidity of data in the information age by having no solid walls: the exterior envelope is entirely constructed of glass and the structure consists of a number of swaying, tubular steel lattices intended to evoke the way seaweed moves underwater.

However, in recent years Ito has returned to a simpler and lighter architectural language based on geometry – evidenced by his Tod's building as well as the temporary pavilion he designed for London's Serpentine Gallery in 2002. This took the form of a simple box, made of glass and steel panels and arranged in an abstract pattern of intersecting straight lines that resembled fractured Islamic tiles.

Kunsthaus Graz

Date **2003**
Place **Graz, Austria**
Architects **Spacelab Cook-Fournier**

Kunsthaus Graz is an arts centre commissioned as the flagship of the Austrian city of Graz's tenure as European City of Culture for 2003. Described by its architects as a "friendly alien", it is perhaps the most extreme example of the "blob" style of architecture that was briefly fashionable at the turn of the millennium (see also pages 61 and 70). It also reflects the contemporary vogue for "iconic" structures, commissioned as much to attract attention as to provide useful new facilities.

Designed by architects Peter Cook and Colin Fournier, the building has its roots in an avant-garde architectural collective created 40 years earlier. Cook and Fournier were members of Archigram, a group formed in London in 1961 and which influenced an entire generation of architects with its pop-inspired fantasies. A reaction against the strictures of modernism and what they saw as the conservatism of the British architecture scene, Archigram – whose other original members were Warren Chalk, Dennis Crompton, David Greene, Ron Herron and Michael Webb – fused a belief in social change with technological advance to produce concepts such as the Walking City (a giant, mechanical city that would roam the earth) and Plug-in City (which consisted of living pods that could literally be "plugged in" wherever their inhabitants desired). Yet despite their profound influence on movements such as high-tech architecture and individuals including Rem Koolhaas and Zaha Hadid, Archigram were ahead of their time and they only built a handful of minor projects.

With the Graz project, Cook and Fournier were able to revisit many of Archigram's themes. The building is replete with both organic and technical references but it is, above all, a spectacle designed to amuse. Built beside the river Mur in the western part of the city, it is intended to bring life to a previously disadvantaged part of town. The 60 m- (196 ft-) wide bulbous structure stands clear of the ground and is clad in panels of blue glass. At night, it is animated by 925 off-the-peg circular fluorescent tubes that are set beneath the glass and which flicker on and off, creating abstract patterns. On the upper surface, rows of nozzle-shaped skylights funnel daylight into the building, while a glazed viewing gallery projects incongruously from one side. Inside, two large exhibition spaces are linked by an inclined travelator.

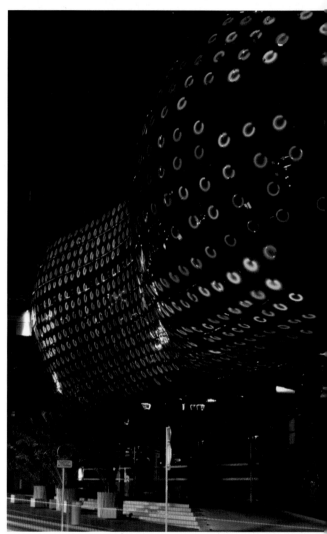

Casa da Musica

Date **2005**

Place **Porto, Portugal**

Architect **Rem Koolhaas/OMA**

Casa da Musica is another example of the almost perverse rationalism of Dutch architect Rem Koolhaas. Koolhaas had earlier designed a house for a private client, which took the form of a shoebox out of which irregular voids were excavated to house different family members. The project was cancelled, but Koolhaas scaled up the voids, stuck them on the outside of the original shoebox and filled the spaces between them with concrete to come up with the strikingly original form of this concert hall.

Thus the building's concept is effectively recycled from a previous project. The shoebox form remains at the heart of the hall, providing an auditorium with a huge picture window that is glazed with a vast pane of corrugated glass – this gives the audience a panoramic view of the city during performances. The hall's remaining functions – such as practice rooms and public spaces – are housed in voids that are cut into its concrete bulk. The modern, stealth-bomber-like aesthetic of the building itself is offset by the idiosyncratic use of traditional Portuguese hand-painted tiles, which are used to clad some of the public spaces.

In the last few years Koolhaas has gone from being considered an avant-garde maverick to something of a Svengali. Besides his architecture, Koolhaas works as a consultant with clients including Prada, publisher Condé Nast and the European Union. He is now working on his biggest project to date, the giant headquarters for the Chinese state television company CCTV in Beijing.

Koolhaas was born in Rotterdam in 1944 and his architectural firm, Office for Metropolitan Architecture (OMA) is based in the Dutch city. He also heads a research and consulting firm called AMO, the work of which feeds into his architecture. Koolhaas studied at the Architectural Association in London and won the Pritzker Prize, architecture's highest honour, in 1999. He is Professor in Practice of Architecture and Urban Design at the Graduate School of Design, Harvard University. Koolhaas has influenced a whole generation of architects, including Zaha Hadid and Foreign Office Architects' Alejandro Zaera Polo and Farshid Moussavi, all of whom worked under Koolhaas early in their careers. He has also inspired many of the "SuperDutch" generation of Dutch architects, such as MVRDV.

Seattle Public Library

Date **2004**

Place **Seattle, Washington, USA**

Architect **Rem Koolhaas/OMA**

Seattle Public Library is an attempt to rethink the notion of the library from first principles. Designed by Dutch architect Rem Koolhaas, it is the result of intense research into the requirements of a contemporary library carried out by the architect and his practice, Office for Metropolitan Architecture (OMA).

Rem Koolhaas is one of the most influential and intriguing figures on the contemporary architectural scene and has pioneered a new, research-driven "programmatic" approach to building that is concerned first and foremost with function rather than appearance.

OMA began by examining the requirements of a library (parking, offices, book storage and so on) and designed an optimum space for each one. The books, for example, are stored in an expandable "book spiral" – a four-storey spiralling structure that is almost 1 km (3,280 ft) long and allows each of the 780,000 books in the collection to be displayed in sequence. The spiral has the capacity to hold double that number as the collection expands.

The same rational analysis was applied to every other function of the building until optimum configurations had been found for each department. These were then simply stacked on top of each other in eight horizontal layers in a way that provided the best circulation routes between them while maximizing views between neighbouring buildings in downtown Seattle to the mountains beyond. The result is a curious, toppling pile of irregular-shaped boxes.

A glass-and-steel skin was then thrown over the heap, shrink-wrapping the building and generating its peculiar external profile. The skin also stabilizes the building structurally, and is earthquake-proof.

Until recently, Koolhaas was known more for his polemic writing than his buildings, which were few and far between. A former journalist, he rose to prominence with a string of seminal books including *Delirious New York* (1978), *S, M, L, XL* (1996), *The Harvard Guide to Shopping* (2002) and *Content* (2004), in which he set out his theories and observations on architecture.

Blur Building

Date **2002**

Place **Lake Neuchatel, Switzerland**

Architect **Diller & Scofidio**

When avant-garde American architects Diller & Scofidio were invited to propose a building for Switzerland's Expo 2002, they came up with the idea of an "architecture-free" building that would attempt to represent the contemporary age of all-consuming digital media in the same way that the Eiffel Tower – built for the 1889 World Fair in Paris – represented nineteenth-century industrialism.

Called Blur, their idea was based on the concept of an artificial cloud designed to hover above the waters of Lake Neuchatel – one of Expo 2002's four waterfront locations, along with Yverdon, Biel and Murten.

To create the cloud, the architects designed a simple steel lattice structure resembling a primitive flying machine and measuring 60 by 100 by 20 m (200 by 330 by 66 ft), which supported a network of 31,400 tiny nozzles, each with apertures of just 120 microns in diameter. These nozzles sprayed atomized lake water into the air, thus creating an artificial fog. A sophisticated computerized control system adjusted the spray according to climatic conditions in an attempt to keep the steel structure hidden beneath the artificial cloud; however, in practice the cloud tended to drift off across the lake when the wind blew.

After donning raincoats fitted with wireless communicators, visitors entered the cloud via a pontoon linking it to the shore and wandered around the structure. The raincoats alerted them to the presence of other visitors in the mist via sounds and lights. The project was intended as an intangible media experience rather than a tangible architectural one: visitors would explore the interior of the cloud, which was a metaphor for the perpetual fog of invisible data that surrounds us today.

Formed by Elizabeth Diller and Ricardo Scofidio in 1979, the practice is now called Diller Scofidio & Renfrew with the addition of partner Charles Renfrew, a collaborator since 1997.

Rosenthal Center for Contemporary Art

Date **2003**
Place **Cincinatti, Ohio, USA**
Architect **Zaha Hadid Architects**

Born in Baghdad in 1952, Zaha Hadid is far and away the most important female architect of her time and the first woman ever to be awarded the prestigious Pritzker Prize – architecture's equivalent of the Nobel prizes – which she won in 2004.

During her career she has pursued a radical brand of architecture that dissolves traditional notions of structure and form, creating fluid sequences of spaces and buildings that merge with the ground or hover above it. Hadid's designs are often derived from studies that extrude mass from the ground and slice, fold or chop it to create flowing, colliding forms. Influenced by the Modernism of Le Corbusier and Mies van der Rohe and the more expressive work of Oscar Niemeyer and the Russian Constructivists, Hadid's great innovation was to break away from the reliance on the drawing-board crafts of two-dimensional plans and sections, and instead design in three dimensions. Even before she had built a single project she became revered in architectural circles for her paintings, which expressed her ideas for buildings and even whole cities in exhilarating compositions of clashing planes and warped grids. Produced by hand long before the advent of powerful computer-aided design packages, these suggested hitherto unimaginable architectural possibilities and pre-empted, by many years, the current explosion of radical forms facilitated by digital technology.

It is only recently, however, that she has began to build on a significant scale. Her 2003 Rosenthal Center for Contemporary Art in Cincinatti occupies a corner block in the city's downtown. The central design feature is the "urban carpet" – a continuous concrete surface that extends the street into the lobby and then folds upwards to form the back wall of the building, drawing both people and light into the centre. The carpet also flows into a series of pedestrian ramps that criss-cross the building's central void, linking the various levels. Externally, the structure reads as a jigsaw puzzle of interlocking, prefabricated concrete and black steel boxes that express the differently scaled galleries within.

Phaeno Science Centre

Date **2005**
Place **Wolfsburg, Germany**
Architect **Zaha Hadid Architects**

The Phaeno Science Centre in Wolfsburg, Germany, which opened in November 2005, is Zaha Hadid's largest and most ambitious project to date. Wolfsburg is a factory town best known for its giant Volkswagen car plant, but with fears over the future of manufacturing in Europe in the face of cheaper Far Eastern labour, the city is trying to rebrand itself as a centre of scientific innovation. Hadid's building is intended to serve as a cultural attraction that expresses the city's ambition. Yet the building itself is intended as a celebration of scientific experimentation, and Hadid was asked to push the technical and aesthetic boundaries as far as she could.

The low-slung, triangular building contains a vast exhibition space on its upper level, which is raised 7 m (23 ft) above the ground on ten huge columns that resemble inverted cones. Each of these cones contains a function, such as a shop, café or entrance hall, one holds a 250-seat auditorium. The entire building, including the cones and the sloping walls, is cast in self-compressing concrete – a new type of concrete that is far more fluid when in its liquid state, meaning it can be poured into highly complex moulds without forming air bubbles.

Hadid sees her work as an extension of the ideals of the twentieth century Modernists, who believed that science and the arts could, together, deliver a better society. Her Phaeno Centre sits very much in the Modernist tradition of heroic architecture built for the common good, albeit with a radically new aesthetic and spatial language.

The project compares to her 2005 Central Plant Building for BMW in Leipzig, Germany, which is the nerve centre of a vast car manufacturing plant. The building's form expresses the trajectories of components and people moving within, the movement of incomplete chassis suspended from overhead conveyor belts providing kinetic drama to the vast interior void.

Born in Iraq in 1952, Hadid – like so many of the figures that dominate twenty-first century architecture – studied at the Architectural Association in London, graduating in 1977. She worked with Rem Koolhaas as a partner at his Office for Metropolitan Architecture (OMA) in Rotterdam before setting up her office in London in 1982. She first attracted international attention with her 1983 competition-winning but unbuilt design for the Peak, a private club on a hilltop in Kowloon, Hong Kong.

Allianz Arena

Date **2005**

Place **Munich, Germany**

Architect **Herzog & de Meuron**

Built as part of Germany's preparations for the 2006 Football World Cup, the Allianz Arena in Munich, is a 66,000-seater stadium designed by Swiss architects Herzog & de Meuron. Headed by Jacques Herzog and Pierre de Meuron, the practice has emerged as one of the most highly regarded architectural firms of the twenty-first century. They are particularly known for the exquisite way they treat the external surfaces of their buildings, employing unexpected materials such as rock-filled gabions (Dominus Winery, California, USA, 1998), photo-printed polycarbonate panels (Ricola-Europe Factory and Storage Building, Mulhouse, France, 1993) and embossed and perforated copper (de Young Museum, California, USA, 2005).

Herzog & de Meuron rose to stardom with their 2000 conversion of London's Bankside Power Station into the Tate Modern – now the world's most popular art museum. Since then they have won two of architecture's biggest prizes: the Pritkzer Prize for outstanding contribution to architecture in 2001 and RIBA's Stirling Prize for the building of the year in 2003, awarded for their Laban Centre in London.

With the Allianz Arena, they have again employed cladding materials to spectacular effect on what is generally one of the most architecturally neglected building types: the sports stadium. The arena is an austere grey concrete bowl on the inside – the football-crazy architects did not want anything to distract from the action on the pitch – but externally it takes the form of a giant, illuminated rubber dinghy.

This effect is achieved by the use of 2,816 inflated pillows of ETFE (ethylene tetrafluoroethylene), a lightweight plastic substitute for glass that was also used on the Eden Project (see page 50). These are lit internally by coloured lights that can turn the entire stadium red, blue or white. The stadium is shared by two Munich football teams, Bundesliga champions Bayern Munich (red) and second division TVS Munich 1860 (blue), and also plays host to the national side (white).

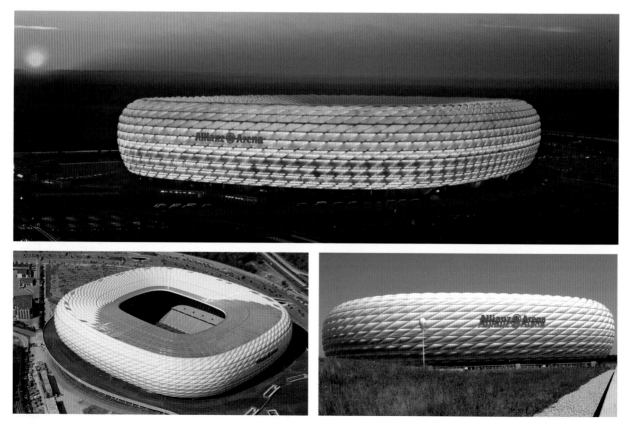

30 St Mary Axe

Date **2004**

Place **London, England, UK**

Architect **Foster & Partners**

The 30 St Mary Axe office building in the City of London is a dramatic reinterpretation of the corporate tower, cross-breeding glass and steel modernism with a voguish organic form and employing a host of green features.

Tall office buildings have become more popular at the start of the twenty-first century, with cities around the world racing to out-do each other with record-breaking skyscrapers. However, many of these buildings are of dubious architectural merit and have little real economic significance. Instead, they are often headline-grabbing symbols designed as instant icons for ambitious municipalities.

Perhaps the most architecturally innovative of this new breed of trophy towers, 30 St Mary Axe, takes its inspiration from natural forms. Designed by Foster & Partners and opened in April 2004, it was commissioned as the corporate headquarters for reinsurance company Swiss Re. Its circular plan and tapering form have earned it the nickname the "Gherkin", although it more closely resembles a pine cone.

The building is constructed around a central concrete service tower from which floors are cantilevered; the external cladding consists of a diagonal grid of steel glazing bars that spiral up the tower, giving the building added rigidity. The spiralling pattern created by the glazing bars is reminiscent of – and inspired by – natural forms such as the arrangement of spurs on a pine cone or the configuration of seeds on a sunflower. Although the building's exterior appears to be a fluid curve, the glazing panels are in fact flat, with the exception of the domed glass occulus that sits on top of the tower.

The site was formerly occupied by the historic Baltic Exchange building, which was destroyed by an IRA bomb in 1992. Foster's design proved controversial, as many felt it was too tall and too modern for this sensitive site close to St Paul's Cathedral and wanted to see the bomb-damaged exchange rebuilt. The 180 m (590 ft) tall building is fractionally shorter than the nearby Tower 42 and is significantly shorter than an earlier Foster scheme for the site that was ironically rejected as being too tall.

Following a lengthy enquiry Foster's tower was approved because it was deemed to be of such architectural quality that it would enhance, rather than denigrate, its surroundings. The acclaimed building is considered one of the most environmentally friendly towers ever built, since rather than relying entirely on air conditioning the triangular glass windows open and close automatically to regulate the temperature. It has also been praised for the way the building narrows as it approaches the ground, creating space for a public plaza rather than occupying the entire site.

Scottish Parliament

Date **2004**
Place **Edinburgh, Scotland, UK**
Architects **EMBT Arquitectes/RMJM**

The Scottish Parliament in Edinburgh, Scotland, is one of the most controversial buildings of recent times. Conceived to serve as the seat of the devolved Scottish government, the project was put out to an international architecture competition that was won by Barcelona practice EMBT Arquitectes, headed by the poetic Enric Miralles, and the Scottish-based RMJM.

Miralles' proposal was for an extremely expressive and romantic building, with a debating chamber inspired by an upturned boat and a covered courtyard with skylights he compared to leaves floating on water. Located at the foot of a dramatic escarpment called Salisburg Crags, the building aimed – metaphorically at least – to link the city to the fabled Highlands via a landscaping scheme of converging paths that represented the routes Scottish chieftains might make to a gathering of the clans.

Miralles' architecture is often compared to that of fellow Catalan Antoni Gaudí, who pioneered a uniquely exuberant variant of Art Nouveau in his native Barcelona in the early years of the twentieth century, and who frequently based his buildings on natural forms such as cliffs and sea caves. With its rich detailing and its use of motifs derived from folklore and mythology, the Scottish Parliament was always going to be a building that bucked contemporary trends. Rather than employ abstract, universal forms, it unashamedly refers to the local vernacular and attempts to express the idea of Scottishness without resorting to cliché.

Unfortunately, however, the project suffered setback after setback. Miralles died of a brain tumour in July 2000 and Scottish secretary Donald Dewar, whose vision the parliament had been, died in October of that year after slipping on a step. Benedetta Tagliabue, Miralles' widow and partner in his architectural firm, assumed control. The project brief repeatedly changed and expanded, which caused the budget to spiral out of control and caused severe delays. By the time the building finally opened in 2004, it was three years late and ten times over budget. Yet it was critically acclaimed upon its opening and it won the prestigious RIBA Stirling Prize for the building of the year in 2005.

Norddeutsche Landesbank

Date **2002**
Place **Hanover, Germany**
Architect **Behnisch, Behnisch & Partner**

This office building in Hanover, Germany is the headquarters of Norddeutsche Landesbank – the North German Clearing Bank – and provides a rare example of corporate architecture and sustainable design coming together.

Designed by Stuttgart practice Behnisch, Behnisch & Partner, it contains a plethora of technologies intended to reduce energy consumption, including computerized blinds that adjust automatically according to the sun, natural ventilation (meaning openable windows instead of air conditioning), solar panels for water heating and a geothermal system that uses water pumped from below ground to stabilize temperatures in the summer.

The flat roofs are planted with sebum and wildflowers that absorb the sun's heat and prevent the building from overheating, and the open-air courtyard is brightened by a bank of "heliostats" (reflective panels that track the sun and bounce light into otherwise dark corners). Many of these elements, such as the green roofs and the heliostats, are somewhat gimmicky and add little to overall performance, but the architects still claim that the building uses half the energy of a typical office building. While many architects are experimenting with such technologies, it is unusual for them to be employed in an office block, since corporate clients usually demand power-hungry heating and ventilating systems. It is also extremely uncommon to find them in a glass building, since these tend to be stifling in summer and freezing in winter.

The unusual form of the building's central tower, which is 17 storeys high and features floors that shift in orientation and cantilever precariously – is partly the result of the designers having some fun – again unusual with corporate clients – but also out of necessity, as German building regulations demand that office workers' desks be no more than 50 cm (20 in) from a window. Thus the narrow "fingers" of the tower shift to give each worker adequate daylight and are angled to maximise the amount of light falling in the courtyard below.

Jewish Museum Berlin

Date **2001**
Place **Berlin, Germany**
Architect **Daniel Libeskind**

Daniel Libeskind shot to international fame with this, his first major project, which opened in 2001 and introduced the world to Libeskind's highly intellectual, and highly emotional, brand of architecture. Situated on Lindenstrasse in the historic heart of the city, it commemorates the history of Berlin's Jewish community and is a memorial to those murdered during the Holocaust. This was an intensely personal project for American-educated Libeskind, who hails from Lodz in Poland – just a few hundred kilometres east of Berlin – and who lost the majority of his family to the Holocaust.

The zig-zagging, zinc-clad building is an extension to the 1735 Kollegienhaus, the Baroque former Prussian courthouse. This now serves as the main entrance to Libeskind's building, which does not have a front door of its own and is entered via an underground tunnel. Libeskind has attempted to express the experience of the Jews through the building itself, rather than through the exhibits it contains, and the design is loaded with symbolism. On entering, the visitor is offered three different routes. The first represents continuity and leads to the museum's main exhibition spaces. The second represents exile and proceeds to an external memorial garden. The third, representing extermination, guides the visitor to a disturbing, empty concrete shaft illuminated by a single lightshaft and called the Holocaust Void. Along this route, a series of empty side chambers symbolise the loss to Berlin society that the Holocaust caused.

The jagged plan of the building is a distorted Star of David that Libeskind generated by plotting lines between the one-time homes of both Jews and Germans in the city, representing the interconnectedness of both groups. Libeskind also cites Schönberg's unfinished opera *Moses and Aaron* and Walter Benjamin's apocalyptic book *One Way Street* as key influences on the building.

Following the Jewish Museum Berlin, Libeskind secured a string of high-profile commissions, many of which had similarly emotive themes, most notably the masterplanning of Ground Zero in New York.

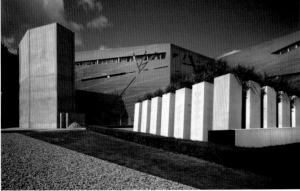

Loftcube

Date **2005**
Place **Berlin, Germany**
Architect **Werner Aisslinger**

With major population centres reaching critical densities, and property prices putting home ownership increasingly out of the reach of many people, architects and designers are constantly looking for new ways to squeeze affordable housing into cities.

Loftcube, developed by German industrial designer Werner Aisslinger, is typical of such approaches. Designed to be placed on the roofs of existing buildings, it provides 45 sq m (148 sq ft) of accommodation – a fairly limited amount of space, making it appropriate, according to Aisslinger, to "nomadic" types who only spend short periods of time in cities before moving on, rather than as a permanent living space.

The 7.25 by 7.25 m (24 by 24 ft) living pod is fabricated in steel and is delivered in pieces in a standard 40 ft shipping container. The shell is then lifted into place by a crane or a helicopter, after which a team of two or three people should be able to assemble the provided kit of parts in two to four days. The open-plan interior can be configured according to the owner's taste. It is not entirely self-sufficient, as it needs to draw on power, water and sanitation from the host building, thus making it a form of architectural "parasite".

Loftcube went into production in 2005 and although there is a fantasy element to it, it is also a serious attempt to address the significant issue of housing shortages, while exploiting under-utilized space on top of existing buildings. Yet architects have long fantasized about the possibilities of prefabricated dwellings being delivered to site and it remains to be seen whether Loftcube will become more than just another exercise in experimental living.

Walt Disney Concert Hall

Date **2003**
Place **Los Angeles, California, USA**
Architect **Frank Gehry**

No architect has done more to change the course of twenty-first century architecture than Frank Gehry. Born in Toronto, Canada, in 1929, during the 1970s and 1980s he was one of the pioneers of the style that grew out of Postmodernism and which came to be known as Deconstructivism. This ignored conventional means of assembling buildings in favour of sculptural, seemingly irrational collages of elements. His titanium-clad Guggenheim Museum in Bilbao, which opened in 1997, marked a turning point, triggering the global demand for iconic cultural buildings as a means of both branding and regenerating cities. It was one of the first buildings to fully exploit advanced computer-aided design software: Gehry borrowed three-dimensional scanning techniques from the aerospace industry that allowed him to sculpt models out of cardboard and other refuse and then digitize their forms. The computer then worked out how the building should be engineered and constructed. These liberating technologies allowed Gehry to concentrate on the sculptural effect of his buildings without worrying about the painstaking calculations that architects previously had to go through.

Since then, Gehry has been one of the most fêted architects in the world and has embarked on a flurry of projects, many of which employ the same essential vocabulary as Bilbao, such as the billowing metal cladding mounted on a lightweight steel frame and the use of external forms that bear no relation to internal spaces.

The best-known and most critically acclaimed of these is the Walt Disney Concert Hall in the Bunker Hill district of downtown Los Angeles, which was designed in 1991 – before Gehry took on the Bilbao project – but which was not opened until 2003 due to funding problems. The hall, named in honour of a donation from the Disney family, was built to give Los Angeles a world-class concert venue with a 2,265-seater auditorium, and is now home to the Los Angeles Philharmonic. Formally similar to the Bilbao building, the hall is finished in stainless steel rather than titanium, its surface clad in 6,100 computer-cut panels.

Dutch Pavilion
EXPO 2000

Date **2000**
Place **Hanover, Germany**
Architect **MVRDV**

Built as the Dutch contribution to Expo 2000 in Hanover, Germany, MVRDV's Dutch Pavilion explores ways of making better use of land, while promoting sustainability in an intensely developed country. The provocative temporary project consists of a number of different, typically Dutch, landscapes stacked one above each other in an open-sided tower and connected by a staircase that winds its way around the edge of the entire structure.

Visitors begin their journey on the upper level, which is called the Windmill Floor, upon which are mounted three slender wind turbines that generate the building's power, while a landscaped pond collects rainwater. Below this is the Rain Floor, where water from the pond above cascades down and is purified. Next is the Forest Floor, a triple-height level planted with oak trees nurtured by water from the level above, which suggests how threatened natural landscapes such as forests could be recreated as public parks within tall buildings. Beneath this is the Pots level. Here, the giant pots that contain the trees on the level above can be seen suspended from the ceiling, reinforcing the artificiality of the forest. These double as screens for displaying information, while other pots contain toilets and storage. The Green House level contains thousands of flowering plants growing under artificial light, representing the Dutch flower industry, while below this the subterranean Dunes level consists of an eerie artificial landscape of undulating concrete, expressing the infertility of the band of sand dunes that protects the Netherlands from the sea.

MVRDV, which is based in Rotterdam, is an acronym of founding members Winy Maas (born 1959), Jacob van Rijs (born 1964) and Nathalie de Vries (born 1965). Prior to forming MVRDV in 1991, Maas and Van Rijs worked for Rem Koolhaas' Office for Metropolitan Architecture. The Dutch Pavilion is typical of MVRDV's approach, which often involves proposing solutions to contemporary problems that are ideologically pragmatic, but aesthetically radical. Another of their (as yet unrealized) projects is Pigcity, a proposal for a highrise pig farm that would dramatically reduce the amount of land required for rearing livestock.

Japan Pavilion, EXPO 2000

Date **2000**
Place **Hanover, Germany**
Architect **Shigeru Ban**

Many contemporary architects are exploring ways of designing more sustainable buildings but Japanese architect Shigeru Ban has gone further than most, pioneering the use of paper and cardboard as structural materials. He began experimenting with industrial cardboard tubes in the 1980s, placing them vertically side-by-side to create partitions and walls and mixing these with more conventional structural systems, in pioneering works such as the Miyake Design Studio Gallery in Tokyo, Japan (1994) and Paper House in Yamanashi, Japan (1995). Ban had to get Japanese construction regulations changed to recognize cardboard as a legal building material in order to realize these projects.

He later produced experimental temporary "log" houses from paper tubes for people made homeless by earthquakes in Japan, Turkey and India. These were completely recyclable, featuring foundations made of used beer crates filled with sand and made watertight with tarpaulin roofs. In the late 1990s he developed a method of employing paper tubes as a structural material by creating giant arches constructed of lattices of short lengths of tubing held together with plywood bracings. His 1998 Paper Dome at Gifu in Japan, the first structure to be built this way, has a 27 m (88 ft) span and supports a roof of corrugated polycarbonate panels.

Shigeru Ban's temporary Japan Pavilion at Expo 2000 in Hanover, Germany, was his most ambitious project to date and the largest paper structure ever built: an arch constructed of paper tubes, it was 74 m (242 ft) long, 25 m (82 ft) wide and 16 m (52 ft).

The complex "gridshell" form of the building, which curves in two directions and has undulating surfaces reminiscent of a caterpillar, is designed to contain the intense lateral forces experienced by the lattice of 12.5 cm- (41 cm-) diameter tubes. Ban worked with legendary German structural engineer Frei Otto – who pioneered the use of steel and timber gridshells – to perfect the highly advanced structure.

German regulations forced Ban to compromise his design by adding a timber substructure and plastic and metal elements to tie the structure together. Otherwise it was a highly sustainable building that featured a paper and fabric membrane roof and sand-filled foundations, meaning nearly every component could be recycled when the pavilion was dismantled.

Eden Project

Date **2001**
Place **Cornwall, England, UK**
Architect **Nicholas Grimshaw & Partners**

As the twentieth century drew to a close, the British government launched a major building programme to mark the turn of the millennium. Under the auspices of the Millennium Commission, funds raised through the new National Lottery were given to projects around the country in what amounted to the biggest cultural building programme in the nation's history.

Many of the projects, including Branson Coates' National Centre for Pop Music in Sheffield and Richard Rogers Partnership's Millennium Dome in London, were embarrassing flops, but the Eden Project, which opened in 2001 near St Austell in Cornwall, England, proved to be the most enduringly popular. With its "space-age" domes, it is also one of the few twenty-first-century buildings that actually looks anything like the predictions of twentieth-century science fiction writers.

Designed by British architect Nicholas Grimshaw, the project is essentially a giant greenhouse set in a former quarry. The aim of the project is to promote an understanding of fragile ecosystems, a concept that is indicative of the wave of interest in environmental issues at the start of the century. It consists of giant "biomes", made up of interlocking partial domes, that contain recreations of biospheres from around the world, including a piece of Amazonian jungle and a North African desert. At 65 m (213 ft) high, it is the largest greenhouse in the world.

The domes are constructed of tubular steel hexagons that are inspired by the geodesic structures developed by Buckminster Fuller in the 1930s and 1940s. But instead of glass, they are clad in triple-skin pillows of a translucent, lightweight and extremely thin plastic called ETFE (ethylene tetrafluoroethylene), which at the time of construction was a relatively new material. These pillows are kept constantly inflated by a system of air pipes, which keeps them rigid and increases their insulating properties.

Grimshaw, who also designed the snaking Waterloo International Station in London in 1993, was associated with the British high-tech movement of the second half of the twentieth century, which emphasized structural elements and services, such as lift shafts and air-handling pipes, to create a distinct aesthetic. The Eden Project marks a late flowering of this style, which experienced a final surge in popularity at the end of the millennium, but has since dropped out of favour in the face of newer, more fashionable styles such as the Deconstructivism of Zaha Hadid and Frank Gehry.

Torre Agbar

Date **2005**
Place **Barcelona, Spain**
Architect **Atelier Jean Nouvel**

Jean Nouvel is one of the most enigmatic present-day architects. Unlike most of his contemporaries, he has no clearly identifiable style, meaning his work is often difficult to pigeonhole. He describes his approach to architecture as a search for "singularities", and he engages in deep research into the requirements of the building and its location in order to develop a solution that is unencumbered by stylistic preconceptions. He claims this is a reaction against the tendency for star architects to thoughtlessly impose their particular brand of architecture around the world, regardless of context. Nouvel made his name with his 1987 Institut du Monde Arabe in Paris – a cultural centre for the Arab world that featured a high-tech façade of motorized irises that opened and closed according to light conditions and which was inspired by the delicately carved screens found in traditional Arab architecture.

Torre Agbar in Barcelona is perhaps his most acclaimed building since then, and it similarly takes its cue from local culture. The tapering cylindrical tower is based on the eroded pinnacles of rock at Montserrat, a mountain near Barcelona that has enormous spiritual significance for Catalans and was often used by the great Catalan architect Antoni Gaudí (1852–1926). The form doubles as a reference to a waterspout – this is after all the headquarters of local water company Aigues de Barcelona (Agbar).

As with the Institut du Monde Arabe, Torre Agbar strives to modulate the effects of the sun, this time featuring a monumental shell of solid concrete (chosen for its heat-regulating characteristics) covered in a sheath of glass and polychrome steel louvres angled to admit, or block out, the dazzling Spanish sunlight, depending on which side of the tower they are on. Beneath this sheath, 4,400 square windows, arranged in pixel patterns, are set into the concrete superstructure. At night the LED luminous devices allow the generation of a kaleidoscope of colour in the façade.

The 34-storey, 142 m (466 ft) high tower is the third highest in the city and is located at the point where the Plaça de les Glories meets the Avinguda Diagonal. It marks the transition between the existing city centre and a huge regeneration area to the north, thereby acting as both gateway and icon for the city's expansion.

Leaf Chapel

Date **2004**
Place **Yamanashi Prefecture, Japan**
Architect **Klein Dytham Architecture**

Located in the grounds of the Risonare resort hotel and set among wooded hills in Yamanashi prefecture, Japan, this small chapel was built in 2004 to host wedding ceremonies. Its jewel-box qualities belie its mechanical function, for the building operates much like a vending machine for rapid-fire nuptials.

Shaped like an eye poking out of the hillside, the structure is covered by two curved, leaf-shaped panels, one of glass and one of steel, perforated with a delicate leaf pattern. Sunlight falls through the acrylic lenses set in each of the 4,700 perforations, pinprick patterns of light on the rows of seats and floor. At night, the canopy lights up like a field of stars.

As the ceremony ends, the mechanized steel panel rotates upwards on bearings in imitation of the way a groom lifts a bride's veil, revealing stunning views across the valley and allowing guests to spill out into the garden. Once the chapel is cleared, the panel descends once more, allowing the next group to take their places.

The Leaf Chapel was designed by Klein Dytham Architecture, a Tokyo-based outfit headed by Mark Dytham and Astrid Klein. Hailing from England and Germany respectively, Klein and Dytham have established themselves as one of the most interesting young practices in Tokyo. Unlike many other architects, their work is entertaining and accessible rather than elitist, happily borrowing ideas from Japanese and Western popular culture and employing visual metaphors that result from their need to explain concepts quickly to Japanese clients when they could not speak the language. They also exhibit a love of novelty that goes down well in trend-obsessed Japan.

Other projects include their wedding banqueting suite, also at the Risonare resort, which resembles a mirror-clad caravan wedged into the side of the hotel; while their 2005 Billboard Building, set on an extremely narrow infill site in Tokyo, is designed as a three-dimensional advertising hoarding. Its glazed façade is printed with a bamboo pattern through which the interior can be glimpsed. Another project, Vrooom! (1999), is a garage in Nagoya featuring a looping strip of road that starts as the driveway, becomes the garage floor and finally folds over to form a roof.

Prada Epicentre

Date **2003**

Place **Tokyo, Japan**

Architect **Herzog & de Meuron**

Built as the Japanese flagship for fashion brand Prada, this six-storey store on Omotesando boulevard marked the start of a new era in retail architecture. With global brands competing to establish their credentials to a global audience, luxury fashion houses, such as Prada, are having to do more than merely provide interesting interior design schemes and instead use cutting-edge architecture to give them a visible presence on the streetscape. Prada had already worked with Rem Koolhaas on its New York Epicenter – which opened in 2001 in a converted building in SoHo. Yet the collaboration with Swiss practice Herzog & de Meuron in Tokyo produced perhaps the most critically acclaimed shop ever designed.

The five-sided, crystal-like form of the building has a sliced-off top, that mimics the ad-hoc style of many of the residential buildings in Tokyo's upmarket Aoyama district. The entire building is framed in a diagonal grid of criss-crossing black steel members and clad in diamond-shaped panels of glass. These windows feature four different types of glass: clear panels, opaque panels (used to shield changing rooms and private areas from view), panels that bulge outwards like bubbles and others that bubble inwards. The result is an extraordinary series of optical effects: the surrounding city shifts like a kaleidoscope when viewed from inside, while pedestrians get a series of distorted glimpses of the interior of the store as they walk past.

In a European-style gesture of civic generosity, Herzog & de Meuron confined the store to a corner of the site, creating a small public piazza, beneath which sits an underground store for Prada Sport that is accessed by a moss-clad stairwell.

Both Herzog and de Meuron were born in Basel, Switzerland, in 1950 and set up their practice together in the town in 1978. Early projects include the 1993 Signal Box Auf dem Wolf in Basel. Located amid railway tracks and industrial land, this exquisite building consisted of a fairly conventional box with windows that had been wrapped in horizontal bands of woven copper to resemble an electrical transformer.

Popstage Mezz

Date: **2003**
Place: **Breda, Netherlands**
Architects: **Erick van Egeraat Associated Architects**

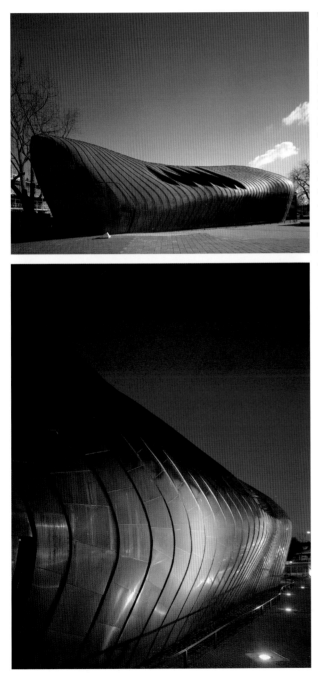

With its windowless, asymmetrical form, clad in unpatinated copper, this concert hall by Erick van Egeraat Associated Architects is another example of turn of the twenty-first century "blob" architecture (also see pages 18 and 70). Here, however, the form is dark and menacing rather than endearing, with the building resembling a giant slug or larvae attached like a parasite to the adjoining building. Erick van Egeraat, born in 1956, co-founded pioneering Dutch architectural firm Mecanoo in 1983. He left in 1995 to form his own practice, which has offices in Rotterdam and Budapest.

The project, completed in 2003, is part of the regeneration of a vast former military barracks at Breda in the Netherlands. It is joined to a former mess building that has been converted into a café and bar while the new structure contains an auditorium for 650 people and which is used for pop concerts.

The building, with the seams of its copper cladding resembling the grid lines on a CAD programme, is an example of the way that computers are increasingly being used to generate architectural forms. On first sight, the building gives no clues to its function: the only markings on the external carapace are a series of slashes that serve as ventilation ducts. The entrance to the centre is at the point where the old and new buildings meet and is revealed when a large section of the cladding swings upwards like the bow door of a ferry. A second sliding door beneath the building's prow provides service access.

The building actually consists of two shells, one inside the other. The outer chrysalis is fabricated in steel with a 100 mm (4 in) skin of poured concrete, on top of which are affixed the ribbed sheets of copper. The inner shell is suspended from the outer layer and is clad internally with timber and lined with acoustic insulation. The void running between the two shells provides access to dressing rooms and backstage areas.

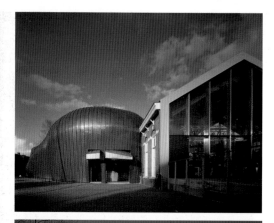

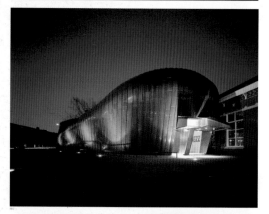

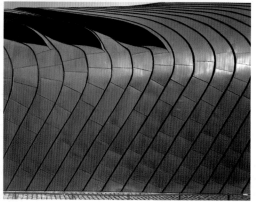

León Auditorium

Date: **2002**

Place: **León, Spain**

Architect: **Mansilla + Tuñón**

Mansilla + Tuñón are part of a new generation of Spanish architects to have emerged since the death of General Franco in 1975, who have established their country as one of the most architecturally progressive in the world. Based in Madrid, Luis Moreno Mansilla (born 1959) and Emilio Tuñón Mansilla (born 1958) worked for leading Spanish architect Rafael Moneo for ten years before starting their own office in 1992. They are best known for two recent cultural buildings in the city of León in northern Spain. The first, the León Auditorium, is a modestly sized concert hall. Located on a public square opposite the historic sixteenth-century monastery of San Marcos, the building is both strikingly contemporary and respectful of Spanish architectural tradition.

The façade consists of a grid of recessed bays, arranged in five horizontal bands in reference to a musical score and which increase in height as they ascend. Each of the 42 concave bays contains an irregularly placed window set back from the façade to resemble gun placements in a fort. These allow shafts of light to penetrate the interior and refer to the way windows are set in the thick walls of Spanish churches. The façade is painted white in reference to both early Modernism and the Iberian whitewashed vernacular, while panels of Travertine marble refer to the town's Roman past. Inside, the 1,128-seater auditorium is lined in dark wood.

Mansilla + Tuñón's second contribution to León is the MUSAC contemporary arts museum. This far larger project, which opened in 2004, contains an extensive arts complex arranged as an irregular cluster of linked, three-storey galleries punctuated by a number of six-storey towers. The building's mass is broken up by numerous courtyards in the manner of historic Spanish palaces and monasteries. The building is mostly clad in narrow vertical glass panels and zinc, but the façade facing onto the adjacent public square is finished in a riot of rainbow-coloured glass bands.

Rubber House

Date: **2003**
Place: **Dungeness, England, UK**
Architect: **Simon Conder Associates**

Small private houses are the mainstay of most young architects and this idiosyncratic project on a shingle beach in southern England is one of the most interesting of recent years. Designed by Simon Conder Associates, it is the antithesis of the slick, computer-generated work favoured by many contemporary architects and instead takes its cue from the shabby seaside vernacular of boat sheds and beach shacks found at Dungeness in Kent – a surreal, flat, treeless landscape of tide-borne shingle dominated by a nearby nuclear power station.

The house blends perfectly with its eerie surroundings and appears to have been built incrementally over many years. Covering 92 sq m (300 sq ft) the project is in fact a conversion of an existing 1930s fisherman's hut, designed for a couple based in London to use as a weekend retreat. It incorporates an old shed formerly used to store fishing tackle, which now serves as the entrance and which is linked to the new structure by a glass corridor. Conder rebuilt and extended the original structure using low-budget timber and plywood and then made the building waterproof by cladding it a black rubber material, similar to that used to make wetsuits, that keeps out the elements while allowing the house to breathe.

The house is officially called Vista but, thanks to its novel exterior finish, it has come to be known as Rubber House. Internally the house is lined entirely in raw plywood. The rear, sea-facing facade features a glass folding door that peels back to open up the entire interior to the elements. A further quirk is provided by the presence of an original 1950s aluminium Airstream caravan which is used as an adjacent guest room. In 2004, Rubber House won the Stephen Lawrence Prize for the best building built on a budget of less than £350,000.

Christian Dior Omotesando

Date: **2003**

Place: **Tokyo, Japan**

Architects: **Kazuyo Sejima & Ryue Nishizawa/SANAA**

This sharp-edged, glass-clad fashion emporium on Tokyo's glamorous Omotesando boulevard takes twentieth-century Modernism's obsession with rationality and transparency and plays games with it.

Designed as a flagship store for Christian Dior, it is one of a cluster of radical retail buildings in a part of Tokyo that is rapidly becoming a playground of avant-garde architecture. Toyo Ito's Tod's building (see page 16) is just a few doors away and Herzog & de Meuron's Prada Epicentre is at the other end of the street. The Dior building is designed by SANAA, the collaborative architectural firm of Kazuyo Sejima and Ryue Nishizawa, which is considered one of the most exciting practices in the world. Until recently they were virtually unknown outside their native Japan, but are now building major projects in both America and Europe. Having formed SANAA in 1995, both of them continue to design under their own names as well. Their largest project to date is the circular Twenty-first Century Museum of Contemporary Art in Kanazawa, Japan, completed in 2004.

This project, like most of their work, is unapologetically Modernist in its materiality; here they have used sheer glass curtain walling relieved externally only by seven horizontal bandings of aluminium extrusions. However, the building is not quite what it seems. Glass façades usually allow people inside the building to see out and vice versa: here, white translucent drapes hung behind the double-skin glass effectively shield views into the store, the interior being only faintly visible through the fabric. At night, the building is lit from within so these drapes glow brightly making the building appear to be a solid block of white.

Externally, there are no visible signs of structure whatsoever: the façade is cantilevered from structural columns hidden behind the drapes. Even the horizontal bandings are illusory: they give the impression that the building is a mini-skyscraper of eight storeys, but in fact it has only five and is just 30 m (100 ft) high.

Yokohama Ferry Terminal

Date: **2002**

Place: **Yokohama, Japan**

Architect: **Foreign Office Architects**

Yokohama Ferry Terminal is a category-defying project that is part architecture, part infrastructure and part landscape. Designed by London-based Foreign Office Architects, it provides a new terminal for ferries and cruise ships at Yokohama, Japan's second city and the major seaport for nearby Tokyo. The 70 by 430 m (230 by 1,411 ft) structure is capable of handling huge numbers of both passengers and vehicles and is topped by an undulating public open space that extends a nearby park out into the harbour.

The husband and wife team of Alejandro Zaera Polo (Spanish, born 1963) and Farshid Moussavi (Iranian, born 1965) who lead FOA were both still in their early 30s when they won the competition to design the $200 million terminal in 1994. This was an extraordinarily young age, given that many architects do not achieve international recognition until much later in their careers. Their highly complex design would not have been possible without sophisticated computer modelling techniques. The architect used them to analyse the routes passengers would take to park their cars and access ferries, and then generated an architectural diagram that allowed this to happen as efficiently as possible. This approach stands in contrast to the computer-generated work of many contemporary architects, who strive first to create a beguiling shape and then use processing power to work out how to build it.

The most striking aspect of the project is the way it plays with notions of exterior and interior spaces, and of landscape and structure. The upper surface undulates and buckles, peeling away in places to allow access roads to disappear into the bowels of the building, while creating a series of timber-clad hills and valleys that serve as public promenades. Built on top of an existing pier, the superstructure is fabricated in sheet steel employing techniques normally used in shipbuilding.

NatWest Media Centre

Date: **1999**

Place: **London, England, UK**

Architect: **Future Systems**

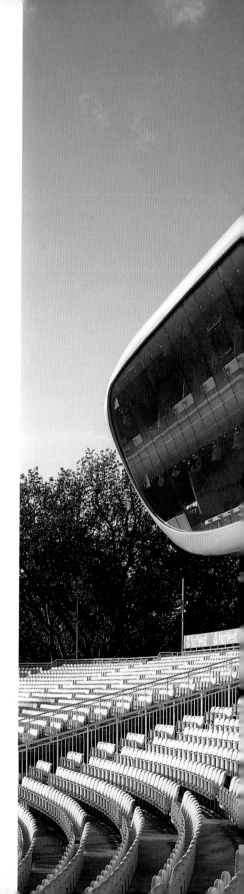

This media facility at Lords Cricket Ground in London was one of the first built examples of what was to become a glut of blob-shaped buildings around the turn of the twenty-first century. With its glossy, white, egg-shaped form raised 15 m (50 ft) above the ground on stilts, the structure invited inevitable comparisons with spaceships and is representative of architects' and designers' brief fascination with retro-futuristic forms that appear derived from science fiction views of what the future might look like.

Richard Rogers' 2000 Millennium Dome in London and Nicholas Grimshaw's bubble-shaped Eden Project (see page 50, and even Jonathan Ive's products for Apple (see page 290) share the NatWest Media Centre's pristine white curves that recall the sets of Stanley Kubrick's 1968 sci-fi film *2001: A Space Odyssey*.

The NatWest Media Centre was the first major project by London architects Future Systems, led by principals Jan Kaplicky and Amanda Levete. Despite its space-age looks, the building is as much a product of traditional craftsmanship as modern technology. It was designed on a computer, which created manufacturing instructions for the curved aluminium panels that make up the semi-monocoque carapace. These were then fabricated by hand by craftsmen at a boat-building yard in Cornwall. The building is designed to give journalists, photographers and TV camera crews an unobstructed view of the pitch. The west-facing glazing is inclined downwards to prevent glare from distracting either the media or the players.

Future Systems' work is inspired by both natural forms and technological imagery. Their biggest project to date is Selfridges department store in Birmingham, England, which opened in 2003. This blob-shaped structure is painted blue and clad in thousands of spun aluminium disks. They have also designed store interiors for fashion chains Comme des Garçons, Marni and New Look, and are currently working on a new metro system for Naples with artist Anish Kapoor.

Caltrans District 7 Headquarters

Date: **2004**

Place: **Los Angeles, California, USA**

Architect: **Thom Mayne/Morphosis**

Built to house the state agency that oversees Southern California's freeway network, the Caltrans District 7 Headquarters is, at first glance, an exuberant celebration of Los Angeles car culture. Yet it is also an attempt to create a pedestrian-friendly, sustainable piece of civic architecture in downtown LA.

Designed by American architect Thom Mayne of Santa Monica-based practice Morphosis, and opened in 2004, the building is part of the US General Services Administration's ongoing Design Excellence programme, which has seen leading architects appointed to design federal buildings across the country and which amounts to one of the most progressive governmental architecture programmes anywhere in the world.

The building is a curious hybrid of Deconstructivism and pop-inspired Postmodernism, combining references to elevated highways (with its exaggerated, exposed structural forms and restlessly articulated façades), rush-hour traffic (with a giant installation of red and white neon and argon strips, evoking slow-moving headlights and tail-lights) and American roadside vernacular. This is expressed in the super-sized graphic "100" – signifying the building's location at 100 South Main Street – that cants 12 m (40 ft) over the sidewalk and recalls motel symbols and the famous Hollywood sign.

Yet the building is also progressive in its consideration both for the public and the environment. Most notably, it features a vast, open-air lobby, shielded by steel and concrete pergolas and providing a democratic civic space open to both employees and non-employees. Internally, Mayne has reversed the usual hierarchical floorplans, placing executive offices at the centre and giving workers in the open-plan sections views out of the windows. The building also features a façade made of perforated aluminium panels that open and close automatically to shade workers from the sun, and another façade clad in photovoltaic panels that generate five per cent of the building's energy needs.

Mayne is one of America's leading avant-garde architects and has until recently been considered something of a radical outsider in his native land. Born in Waterbury, Connecticut, in 1944, he co-founded the influential Southern California Institute of Architecture (SCI-Arc) school after being fired from a previous teaching job. He formed Morphosis in 1972 and won the prestigious Pritzker Prize in 2005.

Interiors

Interior design has become a frenetic area of experimentation in recent years. It has been driven largely by the boom in retailing, hotels, bars and restaurants that has resulted from buoyant economies and the all-encompassing notion of "lifestyle", in which every aspect of consumption, from the shopping environment to the hotel toilets, are now expected to be given the same amount of attention as the service or product itself. Until recently, the trend among upmarket retail brands was to commission architects or designers to roll out global concepts for their stores, so that shoppers could experience similar palettes of materials and spatial arrangements, wherever in the world they happened to be. An example of this is Dolce & Gabbana, who employed David Chipperfield Architects to design their stores worldwide.

However, this trend is rapidly being replaced among avant-garde retailers by a more ambitious strategy that encourages local diversity and idiosyncrasy. Prada has recently opened a handful of spectacular "Epicentre" stores in Tokyo, New York and Los Angeles designed by cutting-edge architects Herzog & de Meuron (see Architecture, page 60) and Rem Koolhaas, each of which is completely different. Comme des Garçons has adopted a similar policy, with its "guerrilla" stores and the anti-design vibe of its Dover Street Market in London. Dover Street Market is a pivotal project as it subverts the exclusivity of the product by displaying it in a raw, salvaged environment. The concept in operation here is that as luxury becomes ubiquitous, so sophisticated consumers are happy to forfeit ostentatious retail trappings in order to seek

out genuinely unique purchases. Here the fashion chain is borrowing the aesthetic of the flea market or the cult boutique, known only to fashion insiders.

The backlash against the slick corporatism of global brands can also be seen in hotels, such as Soho House in New York, which is a charming juxtaposition of found objects, design classics and raw industrial interiors, and Hotel Fox in Copenhagen, a former low-life hostel where every room has been decorated by underground artists and illustrators (and which, tellingly, was commissioned by car brand Volkswagen as a piece of guerrilla marketing). The ubiquitous calm minimalism of 1990s interiors has been swept away by a new mood of colourful eclecticism and decorative eccentricity, a mood expressed by interiors such as Camper's FoodBall

concept restaurant in Barcelona, with its quirky murals and terraced seating, and Marcel Wanders' delightfully cluttered Lute Suites in Amsterdam.

In the office, the predicted rise of buzzy technology-driven concepts such as tele-cottaging (working from home) and hot-desking (not giving workers a dedicated workspace) have failed to catch on and designers' experiments in this area have largely been ripped out and replaced with more traditional office set-ups. Some of the most innovative interiors these days are being commissioned by airlines keen to entice travellers into their business class lounges, which are increasingly coming to resemble sophisticated members' clubs. Virgin Atlantic's Upper Class lounge is such an example.

Una Hotel Vittorio

Date **2003**

Place **Florence, Italy**

Designer **Fabio Novembre**

In recent years, Italy's talent pool of exciting young designers seems to have dried up, but Fabio Novembre is a glorious exception. He has developed an unmistakeable signature style that features swirling forms, Baroque patterns and mosaics. Completed in 2003, this 84-room hotel in the San Frediano district of Florence typifies his exuberant approach. Local planners would not allow Novembre to alter the exterior of the building, a former warehouse. Novembre has made up for this with the interior, notably the reception area, where a floral mosaic swirls across the floor, walls and ceiling, leading guests from the entrance to the front desk. The lobby is furnished with Novembre's equally swirly, spiral-shaped And sofa, which he designed for Cappellini in 2002. In the dining room, Novembre commissioned cult Dutch artist/designer Joep van Lieshout to create a snaking refectory table that is lit by a sinuous stained glass ceiling light.

Born in Lecce in southern Italy in 1966, Novembre studied architecture in Milan. He then embarked on a film studies' course in New York and it was during his time there that he met fashion designer Anna Molinari, who asked him to design her Hong Kong store for her. There followed a string of boutique, bar and nightclub commissions in which Novembre perfected a style that has been described as "narcissistic neo-baroque". These featured materials such as fake crocodile skin, gold and particularly mosaics – Novembre was creative director of Italian mosaic brand Bisazza from 2000–03, during which time he transformed the company's image through projects such as Hotel Vittorio.

Novembre claims the female body is his greatest inspiration and super-scale representations dominate several of this projects: the L'Origine du Monde nightclub in Milan features huge pornographic mosaic murals, a pair of legs straddles the entrance to his Anna Molinari store in London and the ceiling of his Shu Café in Milan is held up by a pair of oversized arms.

Dover Street Market

Date **2004**
Place **London, England, UK**
Designer **Rei Kawakubo**

This fashion store is the antithesis of the luxury emporium. Opened in Mayfair, London, in 2004, it is the latest avant-garde retail experiment by Comme des Garçons' founder and designer, Rei Kawakubo. The store is located in a four-storey Georgian-fronted building on a street close to the glamorous fashion stores of Old Bond Street, yet inside it could not be more different from them. The interior is a raw, concrete shell devoid of any architectural niceties – in fact, Kawakubo did not employ an architect at all, instead calling on theatre and film designers to address the various parts of the rambling floorplan.

Kawakubo took her cue from the famous Kensington Market in London – a scruffy indoor bazaar that showcased the work of upcoming fashion designers and which closed in 2003. The look is very much anti-design: changing rooms are in shacks and Portakabins, display stands are constructed of salvaged materials

and furniture is all second-hand. Floor space is given over to cult designers such as Raf Simons, Alber Elbaz and Junya Watanabe, as well as Comme des Garçons.

Kawakubo has proven one of the world's most influential fashion retailers over the years. She started the trend for using cutting-edge architects to design boutiques when she hired Future Systems for her outlet in New York's Meatpacking District in 1998. More recently she has moved away from high-octane design to a more underground approach to retailing. In 2004, she pioneered the "guerilla store" concept, opening a temporary outlet in a former bookshop in East Berlin's upcoming Mitte district. The dilapidated building was not altered and the store was not even advertised, instead relying on word of mouth. It was shut down after exactly one year, followed by similar ventures in other cities.

Soho House

Date **2003**
Place **New York, New York, USA**
Designer **Ilse Crawford**

This hotel in New York's Meatpacking District helped define a new approach to luxury hotel design when it opened in May 2003. A reaction against the over-styled and hard-edged "designer" hotels that were so popular in the 1990s, Soho House is informal, bohemian and slightly rough around the edges. It has become a firm favourite with the arts and media crowd, eclipsing establishments such as Philippe Starck's Royalton as the most fashionable hotel in town, and reflecting the current popularity of the mix-and-match approach to interior decoration over the rigid adherence to a particular style.

Located over six floors of a converted warehouse, the hotel's 24 rooms were styled by British creative director Ilse Crawford. No two rooms are the same, and each contains an eclectic mix of antiques, classic modern pieces and junk-shop finds. Luxurious items such as chandeliers and goat-skin rugs are juxtaposed with the raw surfaces of the building, which has been altered as little as possible. The most popular bedroom features unfinished brick walls that retain paint splodges from Crawford's colour tryouts and graffiti from the building's warehouse days. The large, open-plan rooms feel like loft apartments and feature free-standing bathtubs located in the bedrooms.

Crawford intended the hotel as a comfortable yet erotic home-from-home and her styling is more about creating the right kind of emotion than trying to achieve a particular look. When she presented her ideas to Soho House owner Nick Jones, she famously played Serge Gainsbourg's highly suggestive track "69 Année Erotique" to get across the mood she intended for the hotel. The New York venture was the first overseas outpost of Jones' London members club Soho House. Crawford had previously worked with Jones on Babington House near Bath, a Georgian building converted into a retreat modelled on a playboy mansion. In 2005 she was appointed creative director of Soho House Ltd and is working on hotels for other locations, starting with Miami.

Crawford began her career as a journalist, launching the UK edition of interiors magazine *Elle Deco* in 1989 and writing the influential book *Sensual Home: Liberate Your Senses and Change Your Life* in 1999, in which she set out her philosophy of creating interiors that served people's emotional needs rather than purely functional ones. Crawford is head of the Man and Wellbeing department at Design Academy Eindhoven.

Shoebaloo

Date **2004**
Place **Amsterdam, Netherlands**
Designer **Meyer en Van Schooten**

This shoe store in Amsterdam makes unashamed references to science fiction films and is an over-the-top parody of mid-twentieth-century guesses about how the future might look.

Designed by Amsterdam-based architects Meyer en Van Schooten for small, upmarket Dutch shoe chain Shoebaloo, the long, narrow store opened on fashionable PC Hoofstraat in 2004. The dramatic interior is almost invisible from the street, as the storefront is constructed of one-way mirror glass and is unlit, except for spotlights shining on shoes, which are the only things that can be seen through the glass from the outside.

Approaching the storefront, however, causes the sliding glass door to open and the spaceship-styled store reveals itself as a luminous tunnel. The walls are lined with curved, translucent polyacrylic panels containing niches used to display shoes and resembling a cryogenic laboratory. The ceiling is clad in similar flat panels, as is the area beneath the glass floor. The store is lit by 540 florescent tubes

concealed behind the cladding panels. These can be programmed to alter the colour in different parts of the store or to animate the whole space with constantly shifting patterns of coloured light in pink, blue, red or green hues.

Three glossy white, organically shaped pieces of furniture resembling stylized clouds float in the central aisle of the store; two are benches while the third is a display unit for accessories. The cash desk at the far end of the shop resembles a giant, illuminated eye glaring out from the back wall.

Meyer en Van Schooten more usually design large-scale architectural projects, particularly housing, municipal and commercial buildings. Their best-known work to date is the 2002 ING Group Headquarters in Amsterdam. Resembling the front part of a giant bullet train raised up on stilts, this corporate headquarters for the banking and insurance giant was designed to give the impression of speed and power.

Hotel Puerta de America

Date **2005**
Place **Madrid, Spain**
Designer **Various**

Hotels – even designer hotels – tend to play it fairly safe when it comes to interior design, but this project pulls out all the stops. Located close to the airport on the outskirts of Madrid, Hotel Puerta de America showcases the work of 23 international architects and designers, including some of the biggest names in the world, such as Zaha Hadid, Norman Foster and Ron Arad. All were encouraged to let their imaginations run riot, and the results are some of the most radical hotel interiors ever seen.

The 194-room hotel, built by Spanish chain Hoteles Silken and opened in summer 2005, has 12 floors of rooms, each of which was assigned to a different designer. The designers were also asked to design the corridors and lift lobby on their floor. Hence, each level is completely different, with Zaha Hadid's floor one featuring rooms resembling ice caverns and David Chipperfield's floor three containing luxuriously monastic cells with black terracotta-tiled floors. Floor four, by young London-based architectural practice Plasma Studio, has

walls of folded stainless steel and glass panels around the bathrooms that look as if they are exploding. Other highlights include Ron Arad's circular beds facing window blinds that double as screens for digitally projected TV and internet, and Kathryn Findlay's all-white space-age suites based on love hotels in Tokyo.

Several designers were employed to work on the ground floor, including Marc Newson, whose bar contains a solid marble bar that measures 9 m (29.5 ft) and weighs around 6 tonnes, and a serene lobby in natural stone and wood by John Pawson.

Jean Nouvel was given the penthouse suites – which, instead of walls, contain sliding glass screens printed with the erotic photographs of Japanese artist Araki – and the rooftop health club, notable for its black swimming pool. Nouvel also worked on transforming the mundane façade of the building, originally planned as a standard business hotel, by covering it in yellow and red PVC awnings printed with the words of Paul Éluard's poem "Freedom".

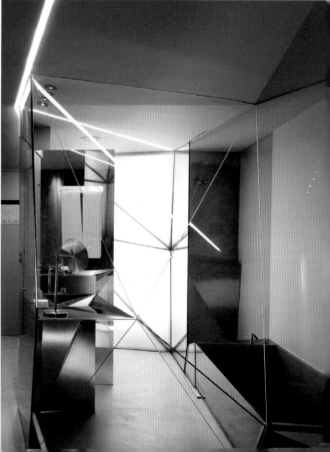

Lute Suites

Date **2005**
Place **Amsterdam, Netherlands**
Designer **Marcel Wanders**

A row of eighteenth-century workers' cottages beside the Amstel River is the location for Marcel Wanders' first major interiors project. The Dutch designer created seven 70 sq m (753 sq ft) guest suites, as well as a reception area and meeting rooms, in the brick terrace located in the village of Ouderkerk on the outskirts of Amsterdam.

The project is the brainchild of Dutch chef Peter Lute, who opened a restaurant in the historic complex in 2003. Following the restaurant's success, Lute teamed up with Wanders to develop a new type of guest accommodation that is a cross between a hotel and holiday cottages. The suites, which are the size of small apartments and which contain a living room with kitchenette, a mezzanine level bedroom and a bathroom, can be rented for short or long periods of time. Lute and Wanders plan to open more suites in various locations around Amsterdam in the coming years. Each suite has its own front door and views over the river. Inside, each is different in terms of layout and decor, although most are furnished with items designed by Wanders over the years, making them showcases for the designer's prolific output. The eclectic mixture of furniture styles recalls the approach adopted by Ilse Crawford at Soho House, New York (see page 83) but the difference here is that almost everything has been created by the same designer. However, Wanders has also included products by fellow Dutch designers, including Bertjan Pot's Random light (see page 210), Jurgen Bey's Light Shade Shade (see page 204) and Maarten Baas' blowtorched Smoke furniture (see page 150).

Most spectacular are Wanders' huge Corian Soap bathtubs, which are situated in several of the suites and which resemble enormous, hollowed-out bars of soap.

FoodBall

Date **2004**
Place **Barcelona, Spain**
Designer **Martí Guixé**

This take-away outlet in Barcelona attempts to redefine the concept of fast food as well as turning restaurant design on its head. Designed by self-declared "ex-designer" Martí Guixé, it sells organic snacks prepared on the premises with locally grown ingredients and served in biodegradeable packing. It is owned by Spanish shoe brand Camper, which wanted to extend its rural, sustainable brand values into the restaurant trade. Guixé's interior has no chairs or tables: instead, it features a series of wide steps similar to a grandstand, upon which people can sit to eat their food. The idea is to recreate the sense of being in the street rather than in a restaurant, thereby encouraging more informal behaviour.

The walls are covered with a mural created by Guixé depicting figures in a naively painted pastoral landscape, reinforcing the provenance of the food. Guixé also designed the cartoonish menus, which are painted on the wall above the counter. The food is every bit as novel as the interior design. The staple product on sale is the foodball – a new type of food developed specially for the outlet that features a variety of sweet and savoury fillings contained within a hollow ball of rice.

Martí Guixé is one of Spain's most interesting young designers, and has a low-fi, subversive style. He is best known for the shoe stores he has designed for Camper, but he has also worked on a string of conceptual interiors projects that often involve food. His proposed Pharmabar was a restaurant in which diners inhaled food dust rather than eating, while his somewhat more practical Food Facility involved creating a temporary restaurant in a disused space that did not have a kitchen; instead, diners selected and ordered from a range of menus from local take-away restaurants, who then delivered to Food Facility. A prototype Food Facility opened for a month in Amsterdam in November 2005.

Palais de Tokyo

Date **2002**
Place **Paris, France**
Designer **Lacaton & Vassal Architects**

French architects Anne Lacaton and Jean-Philippe Vassal's philosophy of achieving maximum impact with minimal cost is exemplified by this arts centre in the heart of Paris. A conversion of the disused Palais de Tokyo into a gallery and artists' workspace, it is as much a work of appropriation and cannibalization.

The Palais de Tokyo, located close to the Seine opposite the Eiffel Tower, was originally built in 1937 to house the French national modern art collection – one of a number of new cultural buildings constructed in preparation for the International Exposition held in Paris the following year. It was abandoned and fell into disrepair when the collection was transferred to the then-new Pompidou Centre in 1976. Lacaton & Vassal were commissioned to bring the building back into use as a cultural centre on an extremely limited budget, and it reopened as a "site of contemporary creation" in January 2002. Vassal, who was born in Casablanca, Morocco, and who spent several years working as a planner in Niger, takes much of his inspiration from the creative recycling of objects he witnessed in Africa.

The conversion achieved instant notoriety for breaking almost all the rules of traditional gallery design: rather than fully restoring the Art Deco building, they had merely patched it up, filling gaps in the stone flooring with concrete and leaving columns and staircases chipped and cracked. Rather than a signage system, the public are guided through the building by black and yellow plastic tape, and the marble desks in the entrance have been customized by spray-painted stencils. Further interventions include a bookshop surrounded by construction site fencing and a ticket office housed in a caravan that was formerly used as a hotdog stand. The project was also intended to mix up the activities of creating and viewing art, with resident artists living and working in the building – an idea inspired by the famous Djemaa El-Fnaa square in Marrakech, Morocco, where vendors, performers and the public mingle in an ever-shifting melee. The project has proven extremely influential and is the forerunner of projects such as Comme des Garçons' Dover Street Market (see page 81), which has a similar anti-design aesthetic and relies on found objects, graffiti and construction detritus.

Dr James Chang's Plastic and Cosmetic Surgery

Date **2005**

Place **Taipei, Taiwan**

Designer **Michael Young and Katrin Pétursdottir Young**

This is an exclusive cosmetic surgery clinic in Taipei, Taiwan, also known as the Lucy Clinic. Designed by British designer Michael Young and his wife, Icelandic designer-artist Katrin Pétursdottir Young, it is a radical project both aesthetically and technologically. The duo were invited to work on the project by Dr James, one of Taiwan's leading cosmetic surgeons, who already owned a string of beauty salons in the capital but wanted his latest venture to set him apart from his rivals.

The 300 m sq (3,229 sq ft) surgery makes extensive use of Corian, a relatively new and highly versatile composite material made of natural minerals and acrylic and manufactured by DuPont. Young and Pétursdottir created highly decorative wall panels made of Corian sheets cut with a geometric pattern using CNC (computer-numeric-controlled) milling techniques. The pattern is derived from a diamond, signifying purity and precision in reference to the diamond-tipped scalpels used by cosmetic surgeons. These panels glow thanks to lights concealed within the walls.

The floor is constructed from advanced laminated safety glass panels. Each of these measures 1.5 by 1.5 m (5 by 5 ft), and features a blue floral pattern printed on the underside of the panels. The panels provide an element to link the rooms by flowing continually throughout the surgery's 14 treatment rooms. The floor reflects the illuminated wall panels to ethereal effect. The surgery's reception and circulation areas are furnished by pieces designed by Young over the years for a variety of companies including Cappellini, Poltrona Frau and Eurolounge.

Young, born in 1966, is a highly accomplished designer who made his name in the 1990s designing furniture for European and Japanese brands. Classic pieces include his Sticklight for Eurolounge (1997), Magazine sofa and table for E&Y (1994) and the cartoonish Dog House for Magis (2001). He is now based in Hong Kong, where he increasingly works with Far Eastern manufacturers such as Kuro, for whom he designed an MP3 player in 2005.

Restaurant Georges

Date **2000**

Place **Pompidou Centre, Paris, France**

Designer/Architect **Jakob + MacFarlane**

Twenty-first century blobs meet 1970s high-tech in this restaurant on the top floor of the Pompidou Centre in Paris. One of the most important buildings of the twentieth century, the Pompidou Centre was designed by Richard Rogers and Renzo Piano and opened in 1977, introducing a new architectural style to the world with its visible steel structure and externally expressed air ducts and pipework.

But by the end of the century the building was in great need of refurbishment. As part of the improvements, Paris-based architects Dominique Jakob and Brendan MacFarlane were selected to design a new restaurant, called Georges, on the building's sixth floor. Jakob, a French national, and MacFarlane, from New Zealand, met when they both worked at Morphosis architects in California.

The high-ceilinged, open-plan space beneath a forest of colourfully painted pipes and ducts lacked atmosphere, but the all-glass walls offered unparalleled views over Paris on three sides. To solve the former without sacrificing the latter, Jakob and MacFarlane proposed inserting a number of intimate, organic volumes similar to grottoes, housing the bar, kitchen, bathrooms and a private dining room. These curious forms, which are clad in brushed aluminium and owe a debt to the architecture of Frank Gehry (see page 44), are conceived as bubbles that have bulged up from the aluminium floor. Between these are arranged tables that can seat 100 people, with a further 150 on the outdoor terrace.

Each blob-like volume functions like a parasite existing within the Pompidou Centre, with services such as water, electricity and air fed in pipes and cables from the ceiling above. The interior of each type of pod is colour coded with a yellow (bar), red (VIP room), green (lavatories) or grey (kitchen) rubber lining, in reference to the bold colour scheme that colour-codes the Pompidou itself. The overall effect is to create a dialogue between indoors and outdoors, with the shiny exteriors of the pods merging with the sky and city beyond, while their richly hued interiors cocoon diners and staff.

Semiramis Hotel

Date **2004**

Place **Athens, Greece**

Designer **Karim Rashid**

The Semiramis Hotel opened in Athens in 2004 and saw New York-based Karim Rashid's distinctive interior style exported to Europe for the first time. The 52-room hotel, a conversion of a 1919 hotel of the same name, is located in the wealthy northern suburb of Kifissia and is the brainchild of Dakis Joannou, a Greek industrialist and art collector, who displays many of his contemporary works on art in the public areas.

The project is a showcase for Rashid's "sensual minimalism" design language, which features soft, organic curves on everything from the swimming pool to the furniture. Bright colours are applied throughout, from the citrus yellow of the balconies to the apricot and primrose carpets and the furniture in ruby red and Rashid's trademark cotton candy pink. Most of the items of furniture are Rashid's own designs and instead of numbers, each room is identified by a symbol, or "Karimagologo". These shapes, which include hieroglyphic-style variations on crosses, stars and amoeba forms, are from a catalogue of such symbols Rashid has been developing for many years. Instead of signing for items, guests are given a sheet of stickers of their room's symbol, which adhere to bar bills and invoices.

Rashid is America's best-known designer. His prolific output includes more than 2,000 manufactured products, including his 1996 polypropylene Garbo wastepaper basket, which, with over two million sold, is one of the best-selling designer objects of all time. He has designed countless products and items of furniture, working with clients including Prada – for whom he designed packaging for skincare products – and Magis.

Recently he has branched into interior design, with the 2002 Morimoto restaurant in Philadelphia among his best-known works. Half Egyptian and half English, Rashid was born in Cairo in 1960 and lived briefly in London before being raised in Canada. He is known throughout the design community for his penchant for always wearing white suits – a practice he initiated in 2000, when he gave his previous all-black wardrobe to charity. His brother, Hani Rashid, is a partner at avant-garde American architecture practice Asymptote.

Interpolis

Date **2003**
Place **Tilburg, Netherlands**
Designer **Various**

This experimental new wing at the headquarters of Dutch insurance company Interpolis in the town of Tilburg features the work of no less than eight different Dutch designers and artists, including world-renowned figures such as Jurgen Bey, Marcel Wanders and Joep van Lieshout. It marks an attempt by Interpolis to create an office environment more in tune with the needs of its employees, many of whom are increasingly working from home one or two days a week but who still need to come into the office for a variety of reasons. Called Project Tivoli, the 7,000 sq m (23,000 sq ft) floor is conceived as an indoor town, offering staff places to eat, relax, have meetings or work alone.

Amsterdam design firm Kho Liang Ie selected the eight designers – Piet Hein Eek, Irene Fortuyn, Ellen Sander, Bas van Tol and Marc Warning as well as Bey, Wanders and van Lieshout – and briefed each of them to create a "club house" that would provide flexibility while also making employees feel they were valued members of a team rather than disenfranchised individuals. The result is eight very different areas that reflect the personalities of their designers and offer employees the choice of a variety of environments depending on the nature of their work or their mood. Wanders' Stone House, for example, features giant, hollow polyester "boulders" decorated with floral patterns and containing workspaces and meeting facilities.

Warning's Light House resembles a workshop and contains a single concrete bench clad in red rubber and running the length of the space. This is furnished with mismatched chairs while an assortment of lamps and power sources are suspended overhead. Piet Hein Eek's House in the Wood features computer stations resembling lecterns made of recycled wood while Bas van Tol's Weave House is decorated with motifs from tapestries and delineated by dividers made of suspended yellow ropes. Jurgen Bey's Living Room, meanwhile, refers to Interpolis' roots in Dutch agriculture and farming, featuring furniture and fittings based on exaggerated traditional forms such as the "ear chairs" with oversized wings that create a comfortable and private environment.

Hotel Fox

Date **2005**

Place **Copenhagen, Denmark**

Designer **Various**

With its 61 rooms each individually customized by a total of 21 artists and graphic designers, Hotel Fox has become one of the most popular hotels in Copenhagen since it opened. Yet equally interesting is the manner in which the project came about. When German marketing company Event Lab was asked to handle the launch of Volkswagen's new compact car, the Fox, it discovered there was a shortage of suitable hotel space in Copenhagen in which to accommodate journalists. The decision was made to customize an existing three-star hotel in the city centre, creating a hip, urban hangout that would express the car's brand values without resorting to heavy-handed marketing. After a string of launch events over the course of a month, the hotel was handed back to its owners and subsequently reopened to the public in the summer.

Young designers and collectives from around the world were invited to design rooms, the only standard elements being the bathroom and the bed. Participants include Norwegian graphic designer and musician Kim Hiorthøy, illustrators Neasden Control Centre from England and Brazilian graffiti artist Speto. Many of the rooms reflect the recent revival of hand-drawn illustration and feature intricate murals that are painted onto the walls and fixtures. One, by Australian collective Pandarosa in rooms 314 and 405, is called Supernova and Lifelines and features all white walls, floors and furniture decorated with black patterns inspired by the way projections distort as they curve around corners.

The English interiors outfit Container produced four rooms themed around the four suits in a pack of cards. Hearts – The Secret Palace, for example, is painted deep red and features flowing illustrations of princesses and masqueraders. Not all the rooms feature cutting-edge illustrations, however: Benjamin Güdel's Heidi room is a kitsch folkloric evocation of an Alpine cabin, with murals depicting pastoral, alpine scenes of goatherds and mountains and fake wood panels decorated with antlers.

Brick House

Date **2005**
Place **London, England, UK**
Designer **Caruso St John Architects**

Built on an odd-shaped infill site between Georgian terraces in West London, this two-storey private house takes a construction material most commonly associated with exteriors – bricks – and employs it as an interior finish. It is almost as if the house, which has no street façade, has been turned inside out. The raw, monastic texture of the brickwork – set in traditional lime mortar – is offset by the highly sophisticated way the architects have configured the interior: the dimensions of the standard brick have been used to generate the house's proportions, so that walls are a certain number of bricks high and doors a certain number wide. Likewise, electricity sockets and even taps (faucets) in the bathroom are carefully set within the pattern of the brick. Thus, an everyday material has been treated with the respect usually accorded to a luxury substance. The only other significant material in the house is raw cast concrete, which forms the floors and stairs and also the complex, angular roof, which is set with irregular-shaped skylights.

The two-storey house is approached from the street via a rising ramp, taking visitors to the upper level, which features a large open-plan living area. The semi-subterranean lower level contains four modestly sized bedrooms, all of which have windows overlooking small courtyards.

Young East London architectural practice Caruso St John is led by Adam Caruso and Peter St John. They have developed a reputation for producing rigorously intelligent buildings that manage to be both austere and sensual. Their best-known work is the exquisite New Art Gallery in Walsall, England, which was completed in 2000. They also redesigned Stortorget square in Kalmar, Sweden (see page 446).

Lever House Restaurant

Date **2003**
Place **New York, New York, USA**
Designer **Marc Newson**

Marc Newson is best known for his industrial and furniture designs but this New York restaurant gave him a chance to apply his distinctive retro-futuristic styling to a large interior space. Lever House is one of the city's most important architectural landmarks. Designed by Pritzker Prize-winner Gordon Bunschaft of Skidmore, Owings and Merrill, the 1952 slab and pedestal corporate headquarters is considered a key work of the International Style.

Newson's restaurant is located inside the Park Avenue skyscraper. But rather than be intimidated by the austere Modernism of the host building, Newson chose to ignore it. His design offers an alternative version of 1950s America, with echoes of movie theatres, diners and space-age TV cartoon family, The Jetsons. Hexagons feature prominently in the windowless 130-seat restaurant. It is entered via a descending white tunnel that is a squashed hexagon in section and which features honeycomb patterns on the carpet, ceiling and bar. A series of alcoves are cut into the inclined, American-oak-lined walls along both lengths of the restaurant, at the far end of which an

elevated private dining arena is screened by a huge window in the shape of a rear-view mirror.

Australian-born Newson came to prominence in 1986 when he exhibited his Lockheed Lounge – a chaise longue made of riveted aluminium panels that resembled a blob of mercury on legs. In 1989, Japanese entrepreneur Teruo Kurosaki put several of Newson's furniture designs into production. When the collection was exhibited in Milan, Newson was approached by major Italian brands Cappellini and Flos, and he moved to Europe in 1992. Working out of Paris and London, he designed his first restaurant, Coast, in London in 1995, and styled the interior and livery of a Falcon 900B long-range jet in 1997. He has since focused increasingly on a range of consumer product designs, designing the hit Tably phone for KDDI (see page 296), reclining business class seats for Qantas in 2002 and cookware for Tefal in 2003. More recently, he designed the limited edition Zvezdochka training shoe for Nike in 2004 (see page 360) and a range of clothing for G-Star.

Sketch

Date **2003**
Place **London, England, UK**
Designer **Noé Duchaufour-Lawrance**

This eclectic, rambling and somewhat kitsch dining and drinking establishment in central London quickly become one of the city's most talked-about eateries when it opened in 2003. Featuring interior designs, furniture and artworks by a host of famous and not-so-famous names, Sketch marks a move away from the single-signature "designer" establishment towards a less uniform, more idiosyncratic approach that happily juxtaposes the ornate stucco-work, mosaic floors and other restored features of the elegant Georgian townhouse with avant-garde insertions, some deliberately raw and scruffy elements and numerous whimsical touches. This magpie approach to design is reflected in the building's contents, which include two restaurants – one doubling as an art gallery – plus two bars and a patisserie.

Sketch is the brainchild of Algerian-born restaurateur Mourad "Momo" Mazouz, well known in London for his eponymous Moroccan-themed restaurant, Momo. The conversion of the Grade-II listed property, designed in 1779 by James Wyatt but which was falling into disrepair, was overseen by young French interior designer Noé Duchaufour-Lawrance, with structural work and some of the spatial design by Manser Practice Architects.

The names of the rooms in the Conduit Street building recall their former uses: the ground floor Parlour hosts a patisserie and tea room while the upper floors feature a Gallery and a Library. A sculptural steel reception desk and chair by Ron Arad graces the lobby and the stone stairs have been splashed with liquid resin that resembles spilled paint, while the parlour is furnished in custom-made pieces by Jurgen Bey, including a variety of chairs upholstered in damask and a batch of his iconic Light Shade Shades (see page 204). Beyond this are toilets by jewellery designer Mehbs Yaqub, clad entirely in laser-etched, antique-style glass and featuring toilet roll holders made of chains of crystals. At the back of the building are a number of more contemporary spaces, including the white, ovoid plaster Egg Bar flanked by two curving staircases that lead up to a mezzanine containing a dozen opalescent fibreglass pods shaped like giant grains of rice, which contain toilets. Upstairs is the opulent main dining area, designed by Gabhan O'Keeffe and featuring padded walls.

Hotel du Petit Moulin

Date **2005**

Place **Paris, France**

Designer **Christian Lacroix**

Designed by Parisian couturier Christian Lacroix, this hotel in the Marais district of the French capital represents, like Soho House in New York, a new spirit in interior design that is more about atmospheric assemblage than obsessive formal innovation.

Lacroix has "dressed" rather than designed the hotel's 17 rooms using a combination of market finds, off-the-peg furniture and bespoke objects of his own creation. Walls and soft furnishings are finished in an operatic mix of leather, brocade, fur and damask, as well as an almost psychedelic range of colours. The approach has more in common with the way a costume designer creates a range of distinctive outfits for the cast of a theatre production than the standard approach to a "designer" boutique hotel, where everything from the choice of furnishings to the colour palette is ruthlessly co-ordinated.

The project came about following a chance meeting between the hotel's owners, Nadia Murano and Denis Nourry, and Lacroix, who was immediately charmed by the seventeenth-century building's rambling, maze-like interior. The hotel occupies both this four-storey building – which was formerly a bakery and which sits behind a relatively austere 1900 façade – and the neighbouring three-storey structure that was previously a boarding house. In order to link the floors in these two mismatching buildings, Lacroix worked with local architect Cabinet Vincent Bastie to strip the ramshackle buildings back to their frames, retaining characterful elements such as a seventeenth-century timber staircase, some gilded and painted glass panelling and shopfittings, and the external sign from the boulangerie that previously occupied the ground floor and which now serves as the hotel's reception.

Rooms are decorated according to whimsical themes, often reflecting Lacroix's personal tastes or childhood memories. One is entirely decked out in fabrics by Finnish brand Marimekko while another contains eighteenth-century furnishings and is inspired by Josephine de Beauharnais, who was Napoleon's first wife and one-time Empress of France.

Dolce & Gabbana

Date **2001**
Place **Beverly Hills, California, USA**
Designer **David Chipperfield Architects**

The clothes designed by Italian fashion duo Domenico Dolce and Stefano Gabbana are famously theatrical but the duo opted for sobriety and calm when it came to choosing an architect for their stores. Unlike the radical approach adopted by brands such as Comme des Garçons (see page 81) and Prada (see page 60) – who use experimental architecture and interior design to express their cutting-edge brand values – Dolce & Gabbana instead wanted a simple yet luxurious look that they could roll out in their outlets around the world.

In 1999, Dolce & Gabbana commissioned London-based David Chipperfield Architects to oversee the upgrade of their international stores. Chipperfield is known for his highly controlled, rational, almost minimalist approach and his designs for Dolce & Gabbana are designed to allow the clothes to take centre stage. The concept is to combine darkness and light, antiquity and modernity, and the same palette of materials is used in every store. The floors are of dark grey basalt while the walls and ceiling are pristine white, and laminated glass screens are used to break up the floor areas. Store-fronts are all of black-painted aluminium and light fixtures are invisible, concealed behind polycarbonate strips on the ceiling or within floor-to-ceiling wall panels. A hint of playfulness is provided by the burgundy velvet curtains used to screen the changing rooms. Chipperfield also designed the display systems, which consist of moveable, freestanding teak racks and black-stained oak shelving, all of which are manufactured by Italian furniture brand B&B Italia.

Against this sober backdrop, however, Dolce & Gabbana have dressed each store with a selection of furnishings, rugs and objects that reflect their opulent tastes. These include baroque chairs, antique gilt mirrors, zebra skins and Mediterranean plants in huge Sicilian urns. These are distributed sparsely enough to avoid appearing kitsch and to prevent their extravagance upstaging Chipperfield's restrained interior design. Chipperfield's first Dolce & Gabbana store opened in Milan in 2000 and was followed by outlets in locations including Osaka, Moscow and London.

Hi Hotel

Date **2003**
Place **Nice, France**
Designer **Matali Crasset**

French designer Matali Crasset created almost every element of this 38-room hotel herself, designing the interior spaces, furniture and fittings and even the graphics and service concept. Located about 200 m (656 ft) from the sea in Nice on the French Riviera, the four-star Hi Hotel is located in a converted 1930s boarding house and is conceived as a place where guests can experience new ways of living during their short stays. It is representative of a breed of boutique hotels that eschew conventional luxury as expressed by opulent decor and obsequious service in favour of creating a stylish backdrop that gives guests the freedom to express themselves.

Crasset herself believes that comfort derives not from luxury but from freedom, and has designed the hotel to maximize the sense of having a degree of control over the environment. Yet Crasset, in common with fellow French designers the Bouroullec Brothers (see pages 139 and 266), is interested in challenging existing design typologies. Thus the lounge features a range of furniture called Interface designed specifically for the hotel, which consists of chairs, stools and tables that fit together in varying combinations. This allows guests to customize the space according to their needs. A palette of raspberry, pistachio, vanilla and chartreuse is used both here and in the reception. The heart of the hotel is the double-height Happy Bar, at the back of which is a large, cocooning birch plywood structure containing U-shaped bank seating and called La Nacelle after the French word for the wicker basket suspended beneath hot air balloons.

Crasset's notions of freedom extend to breakfast, which guests make themselves, and dinner, which is self-service: guests select their meals from a counter and are served in rubber-sealed glass jars. Crasset created nine different room concepts for the hotel, all of which attempt to provide guests with a different range of living experiences. "Strates", for example, features a stratified colour scheme that signifies how different levels might be used for different functions. Storage is at ground level and is picked out in white, while bathroom functions are elevated on plinths, flagged in yellow and purple and located in the bedroom. The result is a raised shower cubicle and toilet that turn private activities into performances.

One of France's leading designers, Crasset was born into a rural French farming family in 1965 and, after briefly studying marketing, switched to design. In 1993 she began a five-year stint with Philippe Starck in Paris where she worked on a range of products for electronics group Thomson before setting up her own studio.

Her output includes interiors, industrial products and furniture. One of her best-known designs is Digestion, a pouf made from cheap checked plastic laundry bags stuffed with foam. First shown in 1998, this was later put into production by Edra.

Bapexclusive

Date **2005**

Place **Aoyama, Tokyo**

Designer **WonderWall**

Opened in July 2005, this store for cult Japanese streetwear brand A Bathing Ape in the chic district of Aoyama in Tokyo was designed by Masamichi Katayama, the head of Tokyo interior design firm WonderWall. One of Japan's leading interior designers, Katayama works extensively for restaurant and retail clients in Tokyo and other major cities. Previous projects include another store built for A Bathing Ape sub-brand, Bape, in Aoyama in 2002, in which the entire three-storey building was conceived as a bathroom, complete with mosaic tiled floors and mirrored walls, with bathtubs, showers and basins plumbed in on the sales floors.

Bapexclusive is even more radical. The two-storey building is a simple box on the outside but the interior is full of confusing surprises. The ground floor showroom is clad in sanitorium-white tiles and harshly lit, recalling municipal changing rooms. The ceiling – which is covered in a camouflage pattern based on the brand's ape-head logo – contains a pill-shaped void that reveals views of trainers revolving on an upside-down conveyor belt on a ceiling high above. It is an illusion: the upper-floor ceiling is mirrored to reflect a sushi-restaurant-style conveyor that runs around the ceiling void. On climbing the stairs, confusion heightens: you find yourself in a confined lobby with seemingly no escape. Only by pushing on the mirrored panels can you eventually locate the doors to the upper sales floor. Here, you discover that the conveyor belt is encased in glass. This is a deliberately disorientating interior that replicates the apparent chaos, idiosyncrasy and discordant variety of Tokyo itself.

Katayama was born in Okayama in 1966 and worked in various Tokyo design offices until going it alone in 1990. He set up WonderWall in 2000. He has recently completed his first overseas projects, including designing the interior of Busy Work Shop, a shoe store in New York, in 2004.

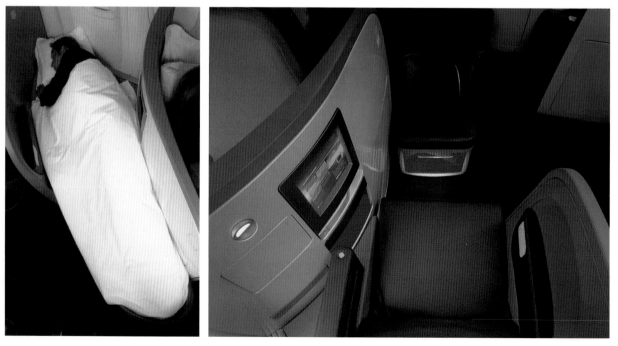

Virgin Atlantic's Upper Class Cabin

Date **2003**

Place **Virgin Atlantic's Boeing 747-400 and Airbus A340-600**

Designer **Pearson Lloyd, Softroom and Design Q**

Long-haul airlines are involved in increasingly cut-throat competition with one another over the lucrative first- and business-class market, with cabins offering an ever-increasing array of luxurious services and facilities. Virgin Atlantic, however, opted for a more holistic, design-led re-examination of its first-class cabin, assembling a team consisting of architects Softroom, industrial designers Pearson Lloyd and transport design consultant Design Q, as well as its own in-house design team. The result, which went into service in 2003 on Virgin's Boeing 747-400s and Airbus A340-600s, is the Upper Class Suite, which features Pearson Lloyd's ground-breaking seat – an innovative concept that has won a string of design awards.

Rather than extending into a bed, as in other first-class cabins, Pearson Lloyd's design features a leather armchair with a seat-back that folds forward to create a completely flat bed with a mattress. At 200 cm (79 $\frac{1}{5}$ in) long and 84 cm (33 in) wide at the shoulder, it is the largest bed on any airline. The cabin layout is also innovative, with seats set at angles to the direction of travel so they face those of other travellers, while a small ottoman at the foot of each one encourages sociability. The seats are screened by side panels containing fold-out TV screens and tables.

Softroom created the overall concept for the cabin – it aims to create an atmosphere of natural, effortless glamour and relaxed sociability rather than cocooning and obsequious pampering, and which is modelled on the idea of recliners ranged around a hotel swimming pool. The largely neutral materials are selected for the way they reflect light, while avoiding the standard aircraft interior palette of plastics and metals. Touches of drama are added with the sparing use of crystal sculptural forms and even a chandelier. The highlight is the glamorous self-service bar with its illuminated bottle racks. The bar is located at the bulkhead where passengers enter the aeroplane, thereby inducing feelings of envy in economy passengers who are not allowed to make use of the facility.

Yotel

Date **2006**
Place **London, England, UK**
Designer **Priestman Goode**

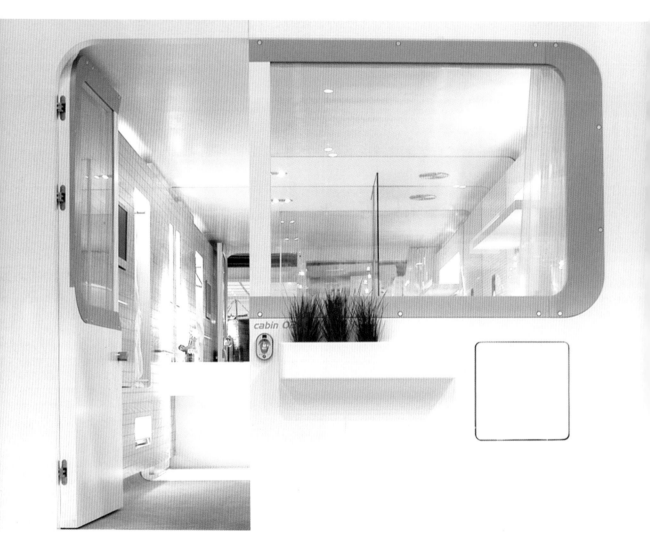

Inspired by Business Class airline cabins and Japanese capsule hotels, Yotel is a concept for a new chain of affordable city-centre hotels featuring compact, prefabricated rooms with high-tech fixtures and fittings. Yotel – the first of which is due to open in London in 2006 – is one of a number of proposals for micro-hotels designed in response to the high prices and poor service experienced in traditional hotels. Yotel is the brainchild of Simon Woodroffe, an entrepreneur who introduced conveyor-belt sushi restaurants to the UK with his Yo! Sushi chain.

Designed by London-based industrial design firm Priestman Goode, the Yotel's 10 sq m (108 sq ft) rooms feature inward-facing windows that overlook the corridor rather than the surrounding city. This means the capsules can be placed inside larger structures such as airports, railway stations or even underground. Rooms feature double beds that rotate into a padded alcove to double as sofas, and recessed storage in the walls instead of wardrobes. A glass screen divides the living quarters from a wet-room with a toilet, washbasin and ceiling-mounted rain shower.

Priestman Goode have worked extensively on aircraft interiors – including the cabin designs for the new Airbus A380 super-jumbo – and Yotel is directly inspired by air travel. Cabins come in Premium and Economy versions and airline-style features include tip-down tables, mood lighting concealed in wall and ceiling panels, pull-down shelves resembling overhead storage bins and an in-room entertainment system featuring downloadable movies and CDs. As with Japanese capsule hotels, guests will be able to book for blocks of four hours instead of the standard 24 hours. The rooms' practical wipe-down surfaces are a convenient bonus as they can be cleaned in just seven minutes, instead of the standard 45.

Marni

Date **2003**
Place **London, England, UK**
Designer **Sybarite**

With its liquid surfaces and sinuous curves, this London store for Italian fashion brand Marni reflects the recent vogue for retro-futuristic styling as witnessed in the blobby work of Karim Rashid (see page 100), Marc Newson (see pages 88 and 108) and Ross Lovegrove. Indeed, its designers, Torquil McIntosh and Simon Mitchell of London architects Sybarite, worked for Future Systems (see page 70) before setting up their company in 2002, and their work for Marni strongly resembles the organic aesthetic pioneered by their former employer – albeit with a more aggressive colour scheme and more masculine forms.

The two levels of the Sloane Street store are linked by a steel ramp coated in glossy white resin, designed to look as if the two floors flow into one. A chute-like staircase with red resin walls has been cut out of the snowdrift-like surface, while a continuous loop of chromed steel tubing serves as a handrail. Display racks are similarly fabricated from seamlessly welded polished stainless steel, with rails leaping between floors and fusing into mirror-finished pedestals in arrangements that resemble grotesquely distorted cutlery. A white lighting pod is suspended from the emergency red ceiling, while curved banks of white upholstered seating blend into the fluid topography of the store.

The London store was opened in 2003 and has since been joined by matching boutiques designed by Sybarite in Tokyo, Rome and Milan. The practice has produced work for a number of retail clients, including West London children's clothing store Guys & Dolls and jewellery company Cox & Power of Marylebone in Central London. Their store for the latter, which opened in 2004, is based on the solar system and features a circular retail space with walls finished in milky blue lacquer into which are set irregularly placed, hemispherical Perspex display cases intended to evoke planets in orbit.

Within Reach

Date **2003**
Place **British Pavilion, Venice Art Biennale, Italy**
Designer **David Adjaye and Chris Ofili**

This temporary interior was the highlight of the Venice Art Biennale in 2003, with art and architecture merging seamlessly to create an overwhelmingly sensorial experience. Architect David Adjaye and artist Chris Ofili collaborated to create the show, held within the neo-classical British Pavilion in the Biennale gardens. Called Within Reach, the exhibition featured a series of Ofili's canvases that tell the story of a pair of lovers and are painted in the artist's trademark saturated colours and set with reflective and gold glitter. Adjaye's interior scheme took the colours and themes from the paintings and applied them to the entire pavilion, colouring the three rooms respectively black, red and green by rubbing the walls with pure pigment. Floors and ceilings were similarly covered in colour and skylights were blacked out with matching fabric. The centrepiece was an installation of steel and glass fragments suspended in the central dome of the pavilion and called Afro Kaleidoscope. Resembling a giant fractured chandelier, the installation represents the star-like celestial body that is a recurring motif in Ofili's work.

Adjaye, Britain's leading black architect, made his reputation with a series of striking houses for artists in London – including Ofili – but is now working on a number of large-scale projects around the world. These include the Nobel Peace Centre in Oslo, completed in 2005, and the Museum of Contemporary Art in Denver, Colorado, which is due for completion in 2006. Adjaye's work often strives to create intense emotional experience in spaces through the use of light, colour and materials rather than dramatic formal gestures, as is the fashion in much contemporary architecture. He regularly collaborates with artists and in 2005 created a second pavilion at the Venice Biennale, this time with Olafur Eliasson.

Aoba-Tei

Date **2005**
Place **Sendai, Japan**
Designer **Hitoshi Abe**

Aoba-Tei is Japanese for "leafy place" but it took shipbuilding techniques to create the shady, forest-like ambience of this gourmet French restaurant in Sendai, 400 km (250 miles) north-east of Tokyo. Designed by Sendai-based architect Hitoshi Abe, it was completed in 2005 and occupies the lower two floors of a seven-storey office block beside a busy avenue in the city centre. Abe has taken his visual cue from the majestic zelkova trees – the symbol of Sendai – that line the street, creating the illusion of dappled light by shining spotlights through a pattern of dots resembling leaves and branches that are punched into the steel floor and ceiling. This cocoons diners from the busy street outside while still retaining a filtered visual connection with the world beyond.

The restaurant's internal envelope is constructed of a continuous sheet of 22 mm (³/₄ in) thick steel folded in a giant S-shape that first forms a ground floor wall, then bends 90 degrees to create the ceiling, a second floor wall and finally the upper ceiling. The seamless steel monocoque sits inside the glass curtain walling and concrete frame of the original building (Japanese landlords often forbid any tampering with buildings' structures). It was created using a folding

method developed by the shipbuilding industry that involves heating certain parts of the steel while chilling others. The restaurant was commissioned by a local businessman who made a fortune producing beef tongue, a local delicacy. The upper floor contains a 30-seat, invitation-only dining club reached by a twisting staircase rising through a hole punched in the steel. A massive walnut wood counter zigzags through the room, while the tables and chairs are each made of a single sheet of black-painted plywood that is cut and formed in a manner that recalls the surrounding steelwork.

Born in 1962, Abe studied architecture in Tokyo and then at SCIARC in Southern California. He worked with Coop Himmelblau, in Austria before returning to Japan to set up his own practice in 1992, the year he won the stadium project. Relatively unknown abroad, Abe is well-known in Japan for his architectural projects, notably the Miyagi Stadium in Sendai, which was built for the 2002 football World Cup. This graceful yet brutal concrete structure features two grandstands in the shape of giant scythes facing each other across the pitch and supported by elephantine concrete columns.

De Lairesse Apotheek

Date **2002**
Place **Amsterdam, Netherlands**
Designer **Concrete Architectural Associates**

A harmonious balance between the natural and the artificial is the theme underpinning this Amsterdam apothecary by architects and interior designers Concrete Architectural Associates. Based in Amsterdam, the firm is best known for its interior projects, notably bars and nightclubs.

Opened in 2002 in a former bank building on De Lairesse Street in a quiet residential district, the store creates a radical departure in the way medicines are sold. The client briefed the designers to overturn the Dutch custom of displaying conventional and natural remedies separately – the former are always stocked behind the counter while the latter are stored at the other end of the pharmacy. The aim was to express the notion that good health is the result of a combination of both types of medicine. Concrete responded by conceiving the main retail space as a circle – a traditional symbol of harmony – and using a mixed palette of natural and artificial materials and colours. Standing slightly off-centre of this circle is a tree trunk, a somewhat surreal feature that represents the tree of life and also plays the pragmatic role of concealing a structural steel column. The floor is covered in a pattern of green gingko leaves – the extract of which is traditionally used to improve circulation – printed onto sheets of paper and then covered with synthetic epoxy resin.

The natural/artificial duality extends to the furniture: the tree trunk supports a horseshoe-shaped, cantilevered steel and white concrete serving counter, while opposite is a curving bench for customers that is made of wood and upholstered in leather. Circumnavigating the entire space is a dramatic circular wall of plywood cabinets, broken only by entrance voids and divided into 36 segments holding a total of 522 drawers made of translucent green Plexiglas and lit from within by 72 fluorescent tubes.

These drawers hold both pharmaceuticals and herbal remedies. The overall effect of the store is a combination of a forest glade and a high-tech laboratory.

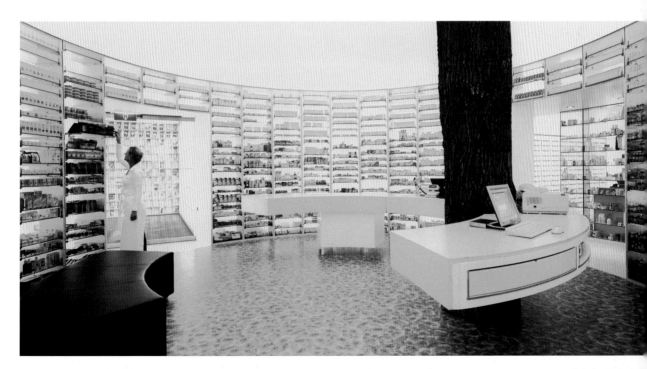

Furniture

Furniture design has emerged in recent years as one of the most dynamic all the design disciplines. A surge of consumer interest in contemporary domestic furniture has revitalized the industry, as manufacturers hire designers to give their products the edge over rivals. With more disposable income and a greater interest in home decorating, consumers are now willing to be more adventurous and fashion-oriented in their purchases.

The phenomenal success of Swedish giant IKEA, which sells contemporary furniture at extremely low prices, has raised the stakes and forced more traditional brands to constantly innovate to stay ahead. There are clear parallels here with the fashion industry, where luxury brands strive to stay a step ahead of high street brands that are able to produce far cheaper versions of catwalk styles. The fashion comparison extends to the way the contemporary furniture industry works, with new trends coming and going with frightening speed. The focus of the industry is the Salone Internazionale del Mobile – the international furniture fair held in Milan each April. Here, leading brands display endless numbers of prototypes designed by a roster of international designers. Those that generate most interest from buyers and the press go into production. Alongside the Salone, in venues around the city of Milan, young designers hoping to catch the attention of the big companies display their own ideas. These off-site shows often throw up the stars and trends of the future as brands hungry for new designers and ideas voraciously track down promising talent.

Contemporary furniture design has long been dominated by Italian brands and designers but in the last few years

the most exciting designers have emerged from countries such as the UK, France, Sweden and, most importantly, the Netherlands. Inspired by Dutch conceptual designers of the 1990s, such as Marcel Wanders, Jurgen Bey and other members of the Droog collective, a new generation of Dutch designers is producing work that straddles the boundaries between art and design. Dutch design is often characterized by a strong narrative content – that is, the pieces have a story to them – and a penchant for using traditional materials or techniques, or referring to past furniture styles. Maarten Baas, for example, made a name for himself within months of graduating from design school with Smoke, a project that involved singeing reproduction antique furniture with a blowtorch to create strangely beautiful pieces that now sell in art galleries and subvert the notion of luxury.

The Dutch pioneers have now been joined by a host of young designers from other parts of Europe and beyond, who reject the slick, minimalist look of much late twentieth-century furniture – which, in any case, is now produced far more cheaply by IKEA – in favour of pieces that display character and idiosyncratic touches and involve innovative, but often craft-based, manufacturing techniques. The Sponge chair by London-based designer Peter Traag, for example, involves pouring polyurethane foam into an oversized fabric chair cover. The resulting wrinkles and indentations ensure that each chair is unique and appears to have been in use for years.

New Antiques

Date **2004**
Designer **Marcel Wanders**
Material **Wood, leather and glass**
Manufacturer **Cappellini, Italy**

Marcel Wanders' 2005 New Antiques range of furniture for Cappellini is based on traditional Italian turned-wood furniture. It features lacquered wood smoking chairs with leather seats tooled with decorative patterns, and occasional tables with spindly turned legs and smoked glass tops. Available in both black and white, Wanders sees the range as a deliberate provocation against the minimal simplicity of much contemporary furniture.

In the last few years, Marcel Wanders has emerged as one of the most prolific and imaginative furniture designer of our time. He has recently become a one-man industry involved in interiors, such as his Lute Suites hotel (see page 92), and industrial design, such as his range of home electronics products for HE (see page 314) and his bathroom fittings for Boffi. He is also employed as creative director by Italian mosaic tile company Bisazza, for whom he designed a car entirely clad in floral mosaics.

Born in Boxtel near Amsterdam in 1963, Wanders studied design at the Hogeschool voor de Kunsten in Arnhem (this makes him one of the few prominent Dutch designers not to study at Design Academy Eindhoven). He came to prominence in the 1990s working with Droog, the hugely influential Amsterdam-based brand that launched the careers of numerous Dutch designers including Hella Jongerius and Jurgen Bey and was instrumental in putting the new school of conceptual Dutch design on the world map.

An exuberant showman, the 193 cm (6 ft 4 in) Dutchman is the most media-friendly designer since Philippe Starck – his website features a photo of him wearing a gold clown nose – and at the Milan Furniture Fair in 2005, he organized a spectacle that saw his girlfriend hanging upside-down from a rotating chandelier dispensing champagne and feeding him grapes. Wanders represents the new spirit of playfulness and romance in contemporary design and his work often employs vibrant colour, delicate pattern and jokey forms. He cites junkshop kitsch as his greatest inspiration and claims to be interested more in beauty than functionality. Wanders shares with Starck the ability to take archetypal ideas from the past and breathe new life into them. He is now at the forefront of a movement that is exploring furniture designs from the past.

Crochet Table

Date **2001**
Designer **Marcel Wanders**
Material **Epoxy-coated cotton**
Manufacturer **Moooi, Netherlands**

The Crochet table epitomizes one strand of Marcel Wanders' work that is typically Dutch: the reinterpretation of a traditional technique by combining it with new materials and giving it a new function. The table is made of crochet cotton stretched over a mould and coated in epoxy resin to make it solid. Designed in 2001 for Dutch manufacturer Moooi, it comes in two sizes – a cube-shaped version and a rectangular version – and is reminiscent in its method of manufacture of his iconic 1995–96 Knotted Chair for Droog, which was made of hand-knotted, epoxy-coated string. This chair made his international reputation and remains one of Droog's most iconic products (it later went into production with Cappellini).

Wanders set up his own studio in 1996, when he began producing an ongoing series of mostly smaller-scale, idiosyncratic objects such as vases and sculptures, called Wanders Wonders. Another project is Can of Gold, in which he plates used food tins in 24-carat gold and sells them in aid of a homeless charity. In 2001, frustrated by what he saw as Dutch design's preference for conceptual one-offs rather than commercially viable pieces, he became art director of Moooi, set up to give talented young designers the chance to get their ideas into mass production. Maarten Baas, Bertjan Pot and Studio Job are among the designers Wanders has taken under his wing. Despite still living and working in Amsterdam, he has managed to break away from the somewhat incestuous Dutch scene, working extensively for leading Italian brands such as Moroso, B&B Italia and Flos.

Cloud

Date **2002**
Designer **Ronan and Erwan Bouroullec**
Material **Polyethylene**
Manufacturer **Cappellini, Italy**

The contemporary furniture scene is often an incessant production line, with leading brands hiring a stream of big-name designers each year to churn out pieces in their signature styles. With designers working at high speed for multiple clients, they tend to stick to producing variants on tried-and-tested typologies, such as sofas, dining chairs and coffee tables. Not so French brothers Ronan and Erwan Bouroullec. Ronan and Erwan were born in Quimper, Brittany, in 1971 and 1976 respectively. Ronan studied at the École Nationale Supérieure des Arts Décoratifs and set himself up as a designer on graduation. In 1999, Erwan, who studied at the École des Beaux-Arts at Cergy-Pontoise, joined his brother in Paris.

Shy and quiet in person, the brothers take their time over their designing and invest it with a rare depth of thought. The result is a body of work that consistently challenges existing preconceptions of what furniture could be. Rather than dictating how people should use furniture – as designers tended to in the past – the Bouroullecs often produce pieces that do not have a defined function but which serve as building blocks to be customized and adapted. Their 2002 Cloud system consists of large lightweight modules, measuring 105 by 187 by 40 cm (41 by 74 by 16 in) that resemble cloud weather symbols pierced with large circular holes.

The units can be stacked in a variety of configurations, much like the elements of children's building blocks, to make shelves, room dividers or, by using more modules, vast, ethereal interior landscapes. Originally made from blocks of expanded polystyrene cut with a hot wire, they could theoretically be manufactured to the Bouroullec's specifications anywhere in the world, thereby suggesting an alternative to traditional systems of manufacture and distribution. The Bouroullecs describe this kind of product as micro-architecture, because the multiplication of a single element leads to forms that define interior spaces rather than simply furnishing them. The Cloud system was re-engineered in heavier (but more durable) moulded white polyethylene and put into production by Cappellini in 2003.

IKEA PS Collection

Date **2004**
Designer **Various**
Material **Various**
Manufacturer **IKEA, Sweden**

Swedish discount furniture brand IKEA is a global phenomenon, with over 200 stores in 31 countries. Its founder, Ingvar Kamprad, is one of the richest people in the world. The chain, famous for its cheap, flat-pack, self-assembly furniture and warehouse-like stores, has nonetheless had a huge cultural impact, making contemporary furniture affordable to the masses and – especially in conservative markets such as the United Kingdom – helping to shift popular taste away from traditional styles to a cleaner, bolder modern look.

In 2005, IKEA introduced its own "designer" range of goods called IKEA PS in an attempt to overcome its reputation for mediocre design. It invited 28 designers – mostly unknown, but including legendary homeware designer Hella Jongerius – to produce 40 items that were imaginative, quirky and fashion-oriented but also affordable. Many of the items are made of recycled materials.

Highlights include the PS Ellan chair, by Chris Martin (opposite). Made of wood fibre composite wood chips mixed with plastic,
the budget-priced flat-pack chair simply snaps together and has removable runners, allowing it to be used as a rocking chair. The idea was inspired by Martin's memories of being told not to rock back on his chair at school. The PS Eden table by Jon Karlsson (below left) is made of core birch – the wood from the centre of the tree that is usually thrown away. The tabletop is in two parts with a gap down the centre, reducing tension if the low-grade wood warps. It also features a three-tier cake rack.

Maria Vinka's Bolso occasional table (below right) has a top that is made of recycled plastic drinks bottles. The hollow legs are also plastic and transparent. They can be filled with objects of the owners' choice before being screwed onto the tabletop.

Kamprad founded IKEA in 1943 when he was just 17, delivering household goods that he bought in bulk to neighbours. He named the company after his own initials and those of Elmtaryd and Agunnaryd, the farm and village where he grew up.

Favela Chair

Date **2003**
Designer **Fernando and Humberto Campana**
Material **Wood**
 Manufacturer **Edra, Italy**

Based in São Paolo, Brazil, the Campana Brothers are one of the most refreshing new furniture design talents to emerge in the last few years. Their work is emphatically a product of their homeland, with the Brazilian landscape and the street culture of their home city being the most prominent influences.

Humberto was born in 1953 and trained as a lawyer, but gave up his profession to study jewellery and sculpture. Fernando was born in 1961 and studied architecture, joining his older brother in his workshop in 1984.

Inspired by the resourcefulness of São Paolo's street vendors and slum dwellers, the brothers took off-the-peg materials such as hose pipes, rope and even children's cuddly toys and fashioned them into strikingly original furniture. They met with little success in their home market where wealthy individuals prefer the cachet of European products, but were spotted by Massimo Morrozi of upmarket Italian furniture brand Edra, who started to put their pieces into production. The first of these was the 1998 Vermelha chair: a steel framework upholstered by a single, 150 m (59 in) long piece of red cotton rope. The brothers famously produced no drawings or instructions for the piece, instead explaining to Edra's craftsmen the complex manner in which the rope was to be woven via a video demonstration.

The Favela chair, originally designed in 1991, quickly became their most famous piece after Edra unveiled it the Milan Furniture Fair in 2003. Favela is the Brazilian word for slum, and the chair is inspired by the "spontaneous architecture" that is characteristic of these districts. Seemingly constructed of hundreds of timber offcuts randomly nailed together in an approximation of a favela shack, it is in fact produced by highly skilled craftsmen who apply precision-cut slivers of Brazilian Pinus wood to a plywood frame according to a precise set of instructions – although inevitably, each chair has its own unique quirks. Despite borrowing the aesthetic of Brazilian street culture, the Campana's work does not make any kind of political statement – instead they are a luxury brand selling expensive, limited edition, hand-crafted pieces to a wealthy elite.

Their 2002 Banquete sofa is upholstered in soft toys similar to those sold in São Paolo street markets, and squeaks when the cuddly animals are sat on, while their 2000 Anemone chair features a steel frame upholstered in clear plastic hosepipe. Their 2002 Sushi chair consists of offcuts of various materials, including carpet and rubber, arranged in layers around a doughnut-shaped stool to resemble the petals of a flower.

After years of European styles dominating the upper eschelons of furniture design, the rise of the Campana Brothers coincides with a renewed interest in the idea of *genius loci*: pieces that are rooted in local culture yet have global appeal and resist the urge to be folkloric or touristic. Ironically, since being adopted by European manufacturers, their work has become highly desirable in Brazil and the brothers have now started to earn commissions from local companies, the most notable example being their plastic, high-heeled jelly shoes and shopping bag for Brazilian fashion brand Melissa (see page 365).

Joyn

Date **2002**
Designer **Ronan and Erwan Bouroullec**
Material **Melamine and aluminium**
Manufacturer **Vitra, Germany**

The kitchen table in the farmhouse where the Bouroullecs' grandparents lived – where people congregated to eat, talk, work and relax – was the inspiration for this office system, designed for Swiss furniture brand Vitra. Based around a vast, trestle-type desk, the system is designed to be spacious enough for each worker to have enough room for themselves but still create a feeling of community. The system is conceived more as a landscape than furniture; it is intended to give workers an endless spectrum of possible uses rather than to respond to specific tasks. To facilitate this, accessories have been designed to compliment the table, allowing workers to customize their own spaces with shelving, lighting and storage, and to vary the degree of privacy by adding partitions that slot onto the tabletop.

Joyn was the Bouroullec Brothers' first attempt at designing office furniture and they deliberately discarded conventional solutions to office design in order to come up with a new typology for Vitra. Whereas the table itself is plain and simple, the wide variety of accessories is brightly coloured and is available in a variety of scales and materials – the partitions are upholstered in fabrics, for example – thereby deformalizing the office environment and reflecting the way that people assemble a landscape of comfortable, useful and often mismatching items around them in their homes.

There is no prescribed way the accessories can be assembled, but rather employees are encouraged to customize their spaces according to their tastes and habits. The brothers also designed a hut-like structure made of clear plastic cladding over timber and metal struts, which can be placed over part of the desk to create a more intimate and sheltered work environment.

Design by Pressure

Date **2003**
Designer **Front**
Material **Wood**

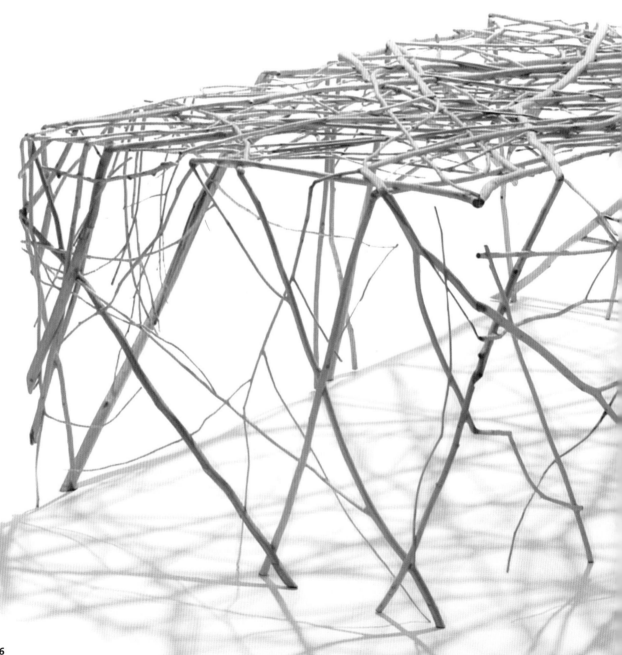

All-female Stockholm collective Front are at the vanguard of a new breed of young Swedish designers that are overturning their nation's tradition for producing coolly functional furniture with a more subversive yet folksy approach. Front, consisting of Sofia Lagerkvist, Charlotte von der Lancken, Anna Lindgren and Katja Sävström, formed in 2002 while all four were still post-graduates studying industrial design at Konstfack School of Arts in Stockholm. Their work is highly conceptual and treats the design process as an event that is expected to produce unpredictable results. Their Animals series, for example, included a ceramic coat-peg deformed by coiling a snake around the still-wet clay, and a wooden table adorned with an abstract relief derived by scanning insect holes bored in a found piece of timber. As with much of their work, an awareness of the design process is essential to understanding these pieces.

Front's Design by Pressure table is part of the "Design by…" series of objects, which explores how natural forces – in this case pressure – can be harnessed to create items of furniture out of unlikely materials and situations. The table is constructed of spindly twigs laid in a criss-cross pattern and subjected to intense pressure in a compacting machine, which bonds the twigs together and flattens them to create a beautiful, if none-too-sturdy, item of furniture. Other pieces in this series include the Design by Explosion chair, which is cast from a mould of the hole created by a small controlled explosion, and their Design by Sunlight wallpaper, which contains a UV-sensitive chemical that darkens on exposure to light, creating a pattern that is the negative of the shadows falling on the wall.

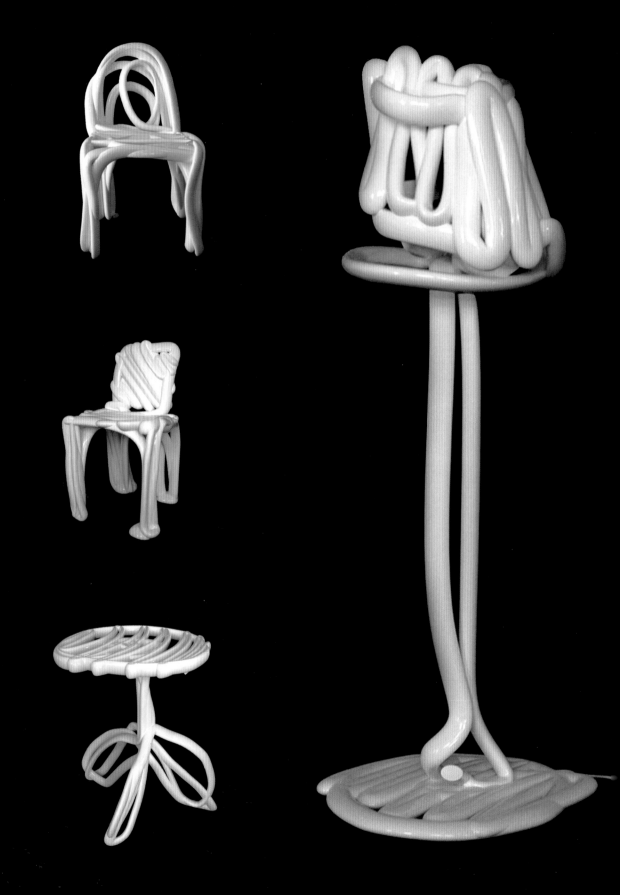

Sketch

Date **2005**
Designer **Front**
Material **Liquid plastic**

This conceptual range of furniture by Swedish design team Front explores how technology can enable designers to cut out the traditional stages of product development. Instead, the designers' initial sketches are directly used to manufacture the items, thanks to "motion capture" technology. Motion capture is a technique used in computer animation and video games to record movement. The digital files created by capturing complex movements such as walking or dancing are then used to produce convincing animations of computer-generated characters. Swedish design team Front have adapted this technology to produce a range of one-off furniture pieces. Using a motion-capture pen, they sketch the three-dimensional form of a chair, table or standard lamp in the air, while a computer captures the data and creates a digital representation of the drawing. The process is akin to the way one uses a long camera exposure to record a "sketch" produced by waving a torch around in the darkness. The data is then sent to a selective laser sintering (SLS) machine – a type of rapid prototyping machine that "prints" three dimensional objects directly from digital files (see also pages 180, 184 and 197). The result is a full-size realization of the original sketch.

The Sketch project allows the first tentative sketch to become the final product, cutting out all the interim stages of the usual design process. It also means that the members of Front can create an infinite number of unique pieces: each sketch is only used to create a single item of furniture. By using advanced computer technology and state-of-the-art manufacturing techniques to produce somewhat crude, childish objects drawn by the human hand, the project is another example of the way the boundaries between industrial design, craft and art are dissolving.

Smoke

Date **2002**
Designer **Maarten Baas**
Material **Wood**

Young Dutch designer Maarten Baas is one of a new breed of designers whose work involves customizing existing items of furniture rather than creating them from scratch. Baas appropriates and metamorphoses found wooden objects, making them his own with a signature technique that involves singeing them with a blowtorch. Along with fellow Dutch designers Piet Hein Eek (see page 188) and Jurgen Bey (see page 162), and Hella Jongerius (see pages 247 and 248), Baas subverts existing notions of beauty, believing that objects that have a history, a patina of use or a degree of unique human intervention are more interesting than flawless, identical objects from a production line. It is interesting to note that the work of all four designers is now highly collectable, with pieces selling for large sums through galleries rather than the traditional design retailers.

Baas developed his Smoke furniture for his graduation show at Design Academy Eindhoven in 2002. He was interested in the way that the wear and damaged suffered by well-used pieces of furniture gave them new – and to him, more interesting – qualities. To replicate this effect, he tried soaking, scratching and throwing chairs off tall buildings before discovering that he could give them an entirely new character by burning them. The wood chars in unpredictable ways, giving even the plainest object a random but highly decorative patina. Baas preserves the fragile charcoal surfaces by applying multiple layers of epoxy resin, which lends them a luxuriant sheen akin to lacquer. For his degree show, Baas burned a series of second-hand, Baroque-style pieces that he bought via Internet auction sites, and a range of cheap IKEA chairs and tables. His work was immediately spotted by innovative Dutch manufacturer Moooi, which put several of his chairs and a chandelier into production. These are now produced in Indonesia, where craftsmen first reproduce the original item and then burn them. Baas also creates one-off pieces by burning design classics or antiques, as shown here.

Air Chair

Date **1999 and 2001**
Designer **Jasper Morrison**
Material **Polypropylene**
Manufacturer **Magis, Italy**

Jasper Morrison's Air series for Italian manufacturer Magis takes an everyday typology – the cheap, moulded plastic tables and chairs used in gardens and cafés – and reinvents it as a stylish, durable, simple yet technologically advanced product. The range exploits a relatively new manufacturing process called gas-injection moulding, in which inert gas is pumped into the hollow centres of still-molten plastic inside the mould, creating enough pressure to ensure the plastic does not shrink away from the mould's surface. This technique means that more complex and aesthetically pleasing forms are possible, requires less material and takes less time to mould. As a result, Morrison's chairs and tables are considerably less expensive than most "designer" furniture. Leading designers have long been criticized for producing expensive items affordable only to wealthy consumers – a situation that has been immensely frustrating to figures such as Morrison, who strongly believe in bringing good design to the masses. Advanced techniques such as gas-injection moulding are finally helping designers produce more affordable goods.

The first Air Chair, moulded in a single piece of hollow polypropylene, was designed in 1999; a folding version that consists of just three pieces that joined by pivoting pins followed in 2001.

Jasper Morrison is widely regarded as one of the greatest living designers, working not just in furniture but also in industrial design. A disciple of the simple, elegantly functional approach of twentieth-century pioneers such as Dieter Rams, Morrison pares down his designs to the minimum, yet consistently manages to produce timeless, iconic forms. Morrison was born in London in 1959 and set up his studio in London in 1984 after studying at the Royal College of Art. He has won numerous awards and produced countless designs, including his iconic 1999 High Pad and Low Pad chairs for Cappellini and his 2003 ATM desk system for Vitra.

Chair One

Date **2002**
Designer **Konstantin Grcic**
Material **Aluminium**
Manufacturer **Magis, Italy**

During the 1990s, German industrial designer Konstantin Grcic became renowned for his rational, pared-down approach to product and lighting design and his honest use of materials. However, as minimalism became ubiquitous to the point of cliché in the later years of the twentieth century, Grcic began to explore different ways of making more complex, strange-looking forms through experimentation with new materials and various manufacturing processes. Chair One and the Miura stool (see page 170) are two of the most striking outcomes of his search for a new design language.

Chair One came about in 2002 when Eugenio Perazza, founder of Italian furniture brand Magis, invited Grcic to design a new chair in die-cast aluminium – a process that had only rarely been used in furniture manufacture before. Die-casting lends itself to thin sections and the spindly web-like form of the chair's skeletal, one-piece seat and back exploits the way molten aluminium runs along channels in the mould during the casting process. Grcic compares the chair's structure to the way a football is constructed from numerous flat components that, when joined edge-to-edge, produce a faceted form. While the stealth-bomber aesthetic suggests a high degree of computerized design, Grcic largely developed the chair intuitively, building dozens of models from flat sheets of cardboard that he cut and folded into three dimensions, minutely adjusting the proportions and angles until he was satisfied with the form. The result is a radical new aesthetic that is highly industrial in appearance and in which form and structure is completely integrated. Chair One was immediately acclaimed as a design classic and has been extremely successful both as an indoor and outdoor chair. It comes in a four-legged café version with extruded aluminium legs inserted directly into the die-cast frame, and a stool version that features a seat mounted on a conical concrete base.

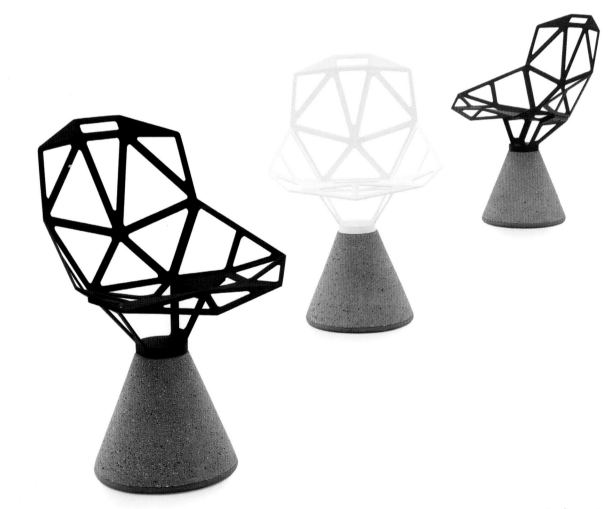

Carbon Chair

Date **2004**
Designer **Bertjan Pot**
Material **Epoxy-coated carbon fibre**
Manufacturer **Moooi, Netherlands**

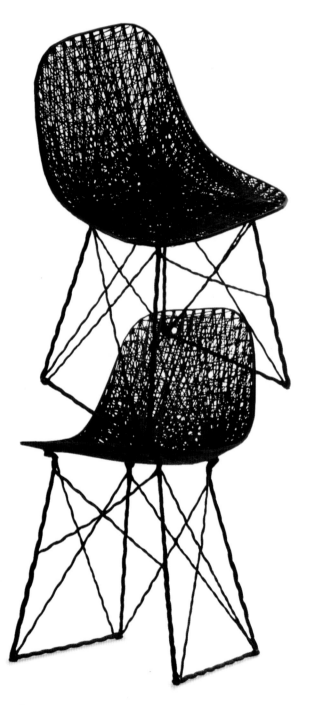

This extremely lightweight product is based on the classic plastic dining chair designed by Charles Eames in the 1950s, but updated with contemporary materials. Designed by young Dutch designer Bertjan Pot, it is made entirely of hand-wrapped carbon fibre soaked in epoxy resin. The fibres that make up the seat appear to be arranged in a random pattern but actually connect every point around the edge of the seat to each of the four points on the base that connect to the legs, ensuring maximum strength. The legs, too, are made in the same manner, with a space-frame construction for stability.

The Carbon chair is a refinement of an earlier chair called Carbon Copy that Pot designed in 2003 and which was derived from a sketch he made of Eames' iconic chair on carbon copy paper. The resulting random, diagonal black lines visible in the drawing were the inspiration for the chair's criss-cross form. The chair caught the eye of designer Marcel Wanders, who is also creative director of Dutch furniture brand Moooi. Wanders worked with Pot to simplify the design, changing the single-piece construction of the Carbon Copy into the two-piece Carbon chair, which has removable legs for ease of manufacture and shipment. The chair was then put into production by Moooi and became an instant classic.

Pot also employed his wrapped carbon fibre technique on his 2003 Random chair – a hollow, web-like easy chair formed on a mould. More recently, he has been experimenting with large-scale carbon fibre structures such as his Carbon Cloud – an ultra-lightweight sleeping chamber exhibited at the Milan Furniture Fair in 2005.

Other recent furniture designs by Pot have experimented with unusual surface treatments. These include 2005's Seamless chair – a steel-framed armchair upholstered in a seamless skin of felt – and Slim table, designed for Arco and featuring an aluminium table with slender, square-section legs and an ultra-thin top covered in timber veneer, so that the wood is used as upholstery rather than structure.

Fjord Relax Chair

Date **2002**
Designer **Patricia Urquiola**
Material **Steel and fabric/leather**
Manufacturer **Moroso, Italy**

Patricia Urquiola is one of the few women to have succeeded in the male-dominated world of Italian furniture design. She is a prolific designer, producing pieces for a host of Italian brands but most famously for B&B Italia and Moroso. She eschews the fashion-driven approach of many of her contemporaries, instead designing pieces that are intended to be comfortable and encourage sociability, rather than serving as status symbols. They are often reinterpretations of existing typologies, such as her Fjord Relax swivel armchair, launched by Moroso as part of her extensive range of Fjord products in 2002. This is perhaps her best-known design and the one that first drew international attention to her. The lopsided design was inspired by Danish designer Arne Jacobsen's classic Swan chair, which she cut in half so that only one arm remained, giving it the appearance of a baseball glove. Mounted on a base of varnished steel, the piece consists of a steel frame covered in injected foam and upholstered in a patchwork of fabric or leather. Along with the other items in the Fjord range, it features a slit in its back from which it derives its name.

Born in Oviedo, Spain, in 1961, Urquiola began studying architecture in Madrid before moving to Milan, where she completed her architectural studies in 1989 under the guidance of the great Italian designer and architect Achille Castiglioni. She worked for a number of Milanese architects and designers including Piero Lissoni, heading his Lissoni Associati design group, before setting up her own studio in 2002. Within two years, she had displayed dozens of pieces for a variety of brands. Urquiola has an eye for unusual materials: other well-known designs include her Flo range of café-style chairs and tables produced for Driade, which are constructed of woven, dyed straw over steel frames, and her Bague lamp for Foscarini, which is made of industrial steel mesh dipped in silicone.

Honey Pop Chair

Date **2001**
Designer **Tokujin Yoshioka**
Material **Glassine paper**

Resembling paper Christmas decorations in its construction, Tokujin Yoshioka's Honey Pop chair is made of a 1 cm ($^1/_2$ in) thick stack of glassine paper – an ultra-thin material used to separate leaves in photo albums and art books. The 120 sheets of paper are joined in thin, alternately set lines of glue and cut into shape while flat. When the sheets are pulled apart, the chair expands like a lightweight concertina, creating a honeycomb structure that is remarkably strong. When sat upon, it moulds itself to the shape of the sitter's body, so the user plays a role in determining the final shape of the product.

Launched in 2001, this chair established Yoshioka's international reputation and led Italian manufacturer Driade to ask him to design a solid, mass-produceable version. This led to his equally well-received Tokyo Pop chair, an organic, one-piece design constructed of a polyethylene shell upholstered in cotton-padded fabric or leather.

Since then, Yoshioka has designed further pieces in a similar vein for Driade, including the Tokyo Pop tables and stools which resemble crushed cans and are cast in hollow polyethylene. He has also produced lights for Yamagiwa – his ToFU lamp consists of a light source embedded in a block of clear acrylic that is moulded in a process similar to the way tofu is made – a chandelier for Swarovski consisting of a cube of 20,000 crystals that acts as a video screen thanks to fibre optics, and a prototype mobile phone for Japanese brand KDDI.

Yoshioka is now considered one of Japan's most promising young designers. Born in Saga Prefecture in 1967, he studied at Kuwasawa Design School in Tokyo and then worked under legendary designer Shiro Kuramata and equally legendary fashion designer Issey Miyake, for whom he designed retail interiors. He set up his own design office in Tokyo in 2000. In his native Japan, Yoshioka is best known for his interior and exhibition designs. These include his ongoing interiors for Miyake as well as product launches for Peugeot and Hermès.

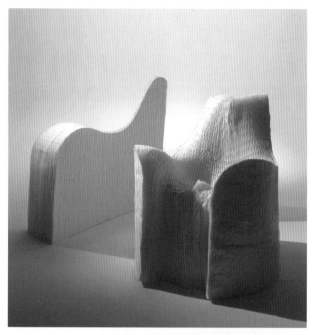

Tree Trunk Bench

Date **1999**
Designer **Jurgen Bey**
Material **Wood and bronze**
Manufacturer **Droog, Netherlands**

Consisting of a tree trunk impaled by traditional chair backs cast in bronze, this bench by Dutch designer Jurgen Bey is one of the most famous examples of Dutch conceptual design. It was first exhibited by Droog at the Milan furniture fair in 1999 and put into production the following year. It epitomizes the philosophy of "form follows concept" that was the rallying cry of Dutch design during the 1990s, and is typical of Bey's work, which often involves taking existing found objects and giving them new life by putting them together in unexpected ways.

In this project, created as part of a conceptual garden furniture project, Bey has cross-bred two very different types of seating – a fallen log that one might rest upon in a forest and antique dining chairs – to create a hybrid indoor-outdoor bench. The product is clearly somewhat impractical and absurd, lacking both the comfort of a real chair and – since it is designed to be used inside – the rustic context of the fallen log. Essentially Bey is playing a game with the notion of seating and the concept of comfort by using bronze – a rather luxurious material – on such an uncomfortable object.

Bey is one of the Netherlands' leading designers but also perhaps one of least celebrated, since his provocative designs often push at the boundaries of acceptable taste. His Kokon (cocoon) series of chairs, for example, takes traditional wooden chairs and re-covers them in stretchy PVC in lurid shades, making a familiar object seem weird and disorientating. His 2005 Dust series involved stuffing armchairs with recycled household dust – a waste material that has hitherto not been considered useful for anything. Born in 1965 and a 1989 graduate of Design Academy Eindhoven, he was one of the first designers to have his designs produced by Droog in the early 1990s.

Industrialized Wood

Date **2004**

Designer **Jeroen Verhoeven/Demakersvan**

Material **Plywood**

Demakersvan is a Dutch design team consisting of three young designers – Joep Verhoeven, Jeroen Verhoeven and Judith de Graauw – who all graduated together from Design Academy Eindhoven in 2004 and went on to set up a studio together in Rotterdam the following year. Their work concentrates on exploring different ways of combining seemingly contradictory influences, such as function and decoration, technology and craft, and historic and computer-generated forms.

Along with fellow recent Design Academy Eindhoven graduates, they are at the forefront of a new wave of Dutch design that builds on the conceptual work of "Droog generation" figures such as Jurgen Bey (see page 162) and Richard Hutten (see page 276) to produce work that is more flamboyant and expressive. This, coupled with the Academy's skill at marketing its students to the design press, is producing a steady stream of talented young designers who are achieving international recognition the moment they graduate.

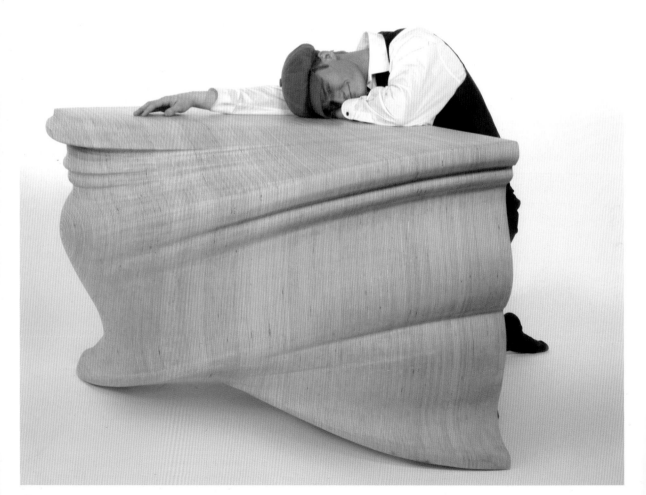

Jeroen Verhoeven's Industrialized Wood table was developed as his graduation project and explores how mass-production techniques can be harnessed to create unique objects. He began by sketching the profiles of two different antique sideboards – the front of one and the side of another. He then digitized the sketches and used computer-aided design software to morph one shape into the other, creating a virtual three-dimensional form that is a hybrid of old and new. He then set about building this fluid form in a manner that harnessed both the fine craftsmanship of the original pieces of furniture and high-tech manufacturing: the computer file was sliced into 57 thin layers and translated to a CNC (computer numerically controlled) mill, which precisely cut each layer from a sheet of plywood. Verhoeven then glued all 57 pieces together to create a solid object, which measures 120 by 75 by 80 cm (47 by 30 by 32 in) and which required a day of sandpapering to finish. The table is now in production as a limited edition.

Low Res Dolores Tabula Rasa

Date **2004**
Designer **Ron Arad**
Material **Corian**
Manufacturer **DuPont Corian, USA**

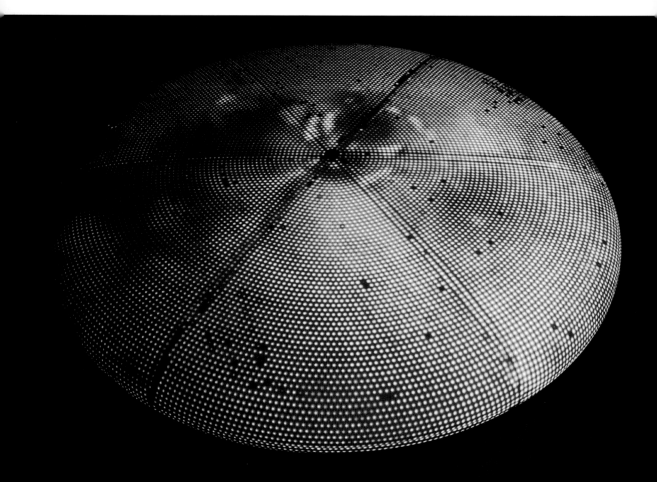

Israeli-born Ron Arad has been one of the world's leading avant-garde designers for almost 30 years, pioneering the use of uncompromisingly industrial materials in pieces such as his Rover chair (1981) – which used seats from old Rover cars – and his 1986 Well Tempered chair, made of sheet steel. More recently, Arad has exploited advanced materials and production processes, as with the Low Res Dolores Tabula Rasa collection he first exhibited at the Gio Marconi gallery in Milan during the 2004 furniture fair. The highlight of the show was the white lens-shaped table, the surface of which displayed moving images projected from within. The table, and a projection wall constructed using the

same materials and technology, was the result of a collaboration with the manufacturers of Corian – a composite material with a translucent quality. Arad wanted to explore ways of integrating moving displays into furniture and create pieces capable of displaying images or even films. Both the table and the wall contain a digital projector connected to around 200,000 m (656,168 ft) of optical fibres embedded in the Corian surface of the table. Each individual fibre projects a part of the image onto the inner surface of the table, creating a pixilated pattern of dots and causing the table to glow mysteriously. Unlike traditional cathode ray or plasma screens, which turn black when

they are switched off, Arad's pieces are pristine white when the projectors are not operational.

Arad was born in Tel Aviv in 1951 and is based in London. One of the most fêted and collected designers in the world, he has worked for major brands such as Vitra, Moroso and Kartell, yet has always retained an individualistic stance. Seminal pieces by Arad include his plastic Bookworm shelving (Kartell, 1994) and the injection-moulded Tom Vac chair (Vitra, 1998). Arad is a qualified architect and is working on building projects including a design museum for Tel Aviv and a hotel for crystal manufacturer Swarovski.

Table 1 and Table 2

Date **2002**
Designer **Fredrikson Stallard**
Material **Wood and steel**

London-based designers Patrik Fredrikson and Ian Stallard
produce powerful and often shocking furniture that contains
strong conceptual narratives. The result is that their work crosses
the boundaries between design and contemporary art, provocatively
challenging conventional orthodoxies of how furniture should look
and function and deliberately exploiting unlikely materials in its
manufacture. Like many other contemporary designers, Fredrikson
Stallard's work is hand-crafted and produced in relatively small
quantities rather than being mass-produced, but the duo go further
than most of their peers to justify their position intellectually, arguing
that the start of the twenty-first century is witnessing the breakdown

of the Modernist view of design as a union of form and function achieved through mass production. This, they argue, has led to a world overflowing with meaningless objects. Instead, they propose objects that are mysterious and emotional.

Table 1 (above left) and Table 2 (above right) consist of untreated, split birch logs bound together by a steel band of the type used to secure industrial goods for transportation. The first version has a diameter of 90 cm (35 in) and a height of 32 cm (13 in), while the second is 45 cm (18 in) across and 40 cm (16 in) high. The crudeness of the materials and the primitivity of the construction method recalls Tejo Remy's Chest of Drawers – a collection of wooden drawers salvaged

from old pieces of furniture and bound together by a cloth strap – which became one of the seminal examples of Dutch conceptual design when launched by Droog in 1991.

While Dutch design in the 1990s strove to make you smile, Frederikson Stallard's work is intended to stir darker emotions. Their Rug 1, for example, is a pool of black polyurethane literally poured onto the ground and allowed to harden; it is intended to resemble a puddle of crude oil – something totally inappropriate for a domestic interior. The Lovers, meanwhile, is another rug consisting of two pools of blood-red polyurethane that have merged together and contain 4.8 litres (5 quarts) of fluid – the amount of blood in the average human being.

Miura Stool

Date **2004**
Designer **Konstantin Grcic**
Material **Polypropylene**
Manufacturer **Plank, Italy**

Konstantin Grcic's Miura stool is a natural progression from his pioneering Chair One (see page 154), sharing the latter's strikingly angular aesthetic yet pushing the technical envelope even further. It features a shovel-like seat, supported by two forked supports connected by a V-shaped footrest. Grcic compares its sinewy, top-heavy profile to that of a bull – it is named after a breed of Spanish fighting bull and also the powerful sports car of the same name manufactured by Lamborghini, which has a raging bull as its mascot. Designed for the contract market for Italian furniture brand Plank in 2005, the lightweight, stackable barstool is made of a single piece of flexible, fibreglass-reinforced moulded polypropylene – a composite material that is 2.5 times stronger than aluminium. Softer and more overtly sculptural than the highly pragmatic and skeletal Chair One, Grcic again worked with physical models to develop the overall geometry but made greater use of computers to realize the complex intersections of its chamfered struts. A series of full-sized, rapid-prototyped models were produced from the computer aided design files to test the proportions.

Grcic, born in 1965, studied carpentry and cabinetmaking at Parnham College in England and then furniture design at London's Royal College of Art. He worked for leading minimalist Jasper Morrison in London before returning to Munich to set up his own studio in 1991. He is known for his collaboration with Authentics, the German manufacturer of plastic homewares, from 1996, and his iconic 1998 May Day hanging lamp for Flos. This interior product resembles an industrial safety lamp and features a translucent conical shade attached to a moulded plastic hook and cable winder. In 2004, he was appointed by German kitchen appliance company Krups to help it reinvent the design language of its products.

Fresh Fat

Date **2002**
Designer **Tom Dixon**
Material **Provista copolymer**

In recent years, plastic furniture has started to lose its connotations of cheapness and poor quality, as sophisticated new manufacturing techniques have allowed designers to produce highly affordable yet extremely well-made pieces such as Jasper Morrison's Air Chair (see page 152). Yet plastic is still largely seen as a material for mass production – a view Tom Dixon has challenged with his Fresh Fat range of tables, chairs and bowls. These are individually hand-crafted objects woven or twisted from spaghetti-like extrusions of warm, molten plastic, produced by a machine that is normally found in a factory. Thus the technology of mass production is subverted to produce unique one-off objects. The concept has much in common with Jerszy Seymour's use of polyurethane foam in his Scum products (see page 230).

Working with Provista – a type of polyester produced by the Eastman company – Dixon has produced a range of five products: an easy chair, a dining chair, a coffee table and a large and small bowl. To create each one, the molten plastic is manipulated by hand into moulds in overlapping loops. The nature of the plastic is such that it does not stick to the operator's hands but immediately bonds when it comes into contact with another piece of plastic, the multiple "welds" that give each object its shape and strength.

When the range was launched, Dixon demonstrated the process with live installations in both Milan and London, inviting other designers and the public to try their hands at creating objects. Dixon says he conceived the idea as part of an investigation into futuristic retailing, imagining that customers might one day be able to visit factories and specify exactly what kind of product they wanted, which would then be made in front of them.

Long one of the leading lights of the British design scene, his work is typically characterized by a fascination with materials and manufacturing processes. He has no formal training in design, instead teaching himself skills such as welding. He came to prominence in the 1980s as a pioneer of the Creative Salvage movement that took scrap metals and welded them into expressive, baroque forms.

Ordinairy

Date **2005**
Designer **Ineke Hans**
Material **Recycled plastic**

This range of chairs and tables is designed to look as if it was not designed. Inspired by the anonymous objects she had seen in folk art museums, Ineke Hans wanted to produce furniture that looked as ordinary as possible. Seemingly made of roughly cut timber boards that have been nailed together, the chairs and tables of her Ordinairy furniture collection deliberately evoke the unselfconscious objects that ordinary people once fabricated from the materials they had to hand, responding to a direct and pressing need and discovering which combinations of material and form worked by trial and error. They also provide only basic levels of comfort, offering the minimum required of a table or chair. However, the pieces are actually made of black recycled plastic with a wood-grain finish. This relatively new material, which is used in the Netherlands to create canalside boardwalks, gives away the fact that the furniture is contemporary. It also has the advantage of being wind-, water-, salt-, acid- and UV-resistant, making it extremely long-lasting and suitable for indoor and outdoor

use. Although a relatively cheap material, the range is sold as a luxury product in upmarket designer furniture shops.

This combination of ancient and modern, luxury and anti-luxury, rich and poor is typical of Hans' work, as is the use of black: she has experimented with using the colour on children's toys, ceramic tableware and other unexpected applications. Ordinairy furniture began in 1997 when Hans produced a simple picnic table and bench but in 2005 she expanded the range, adding a barstool, lounge chair, coffee table and a Deluxe chair (so-called in jest because, unlike the earlier benches, it has a back).

Hans is one of the Netherlands' leading young designers. Much of her furniture explores archetypal forms, like a child's stick-like pictograms of a table, chair or house. The Ordinairy furniture pieces, like her other designs, have a toy-like quality and attempt to reduce chairs and tables to an essence that conforms to people's unconscious expectations of what such items should look like.

Sponge Chair

Date **2004**
Designer **Peter Traag**
Material **Polyurethane and polyester**
Manufacturer **Edra, Italy**

With its wrinkled upholstery resembling elephant skin, Peter Traag's Sponge armchair is intended to look as if it has been in use for a long time. Each chair features a unique pattern of folds and creases, deliberately setting the design apart from the perfection and uniformity of most manufactured objects. In fact, the chair's crumpled surface is the direct result of a novel manufacturing process that Traag developed while still a student. It involves producing an oversized polyester-fabric chair cover – which is 130 per cent bigger than the final chair will be – and placing it inside an upside-down, chair-shaped mould.

As the mould is smaller than the polyester skin, the fabric bunches and folds when it is placed inside. The mould, which is suspended on a wooden frame, is made of PVC and Lycra so that it is flexible, thereby giving the final chair its distinctive bulging form. A structural steel frame, which will form the base of the chair and give it rigidity, is inserted into the mould. Traag then fills the mould with polyurethane foam, which expands, forcing the fabric against the mould and creating the characteristic wrinkles. A lid is placed on the mould and the foam is left to set for around 10 minutes, after which the chair is ready and can be removed.

Traag was born in the Netherlands in 1979 and developed the process while studying at the Royal College of Art in London. His prototypes were spotted by Italian furniture manufacturer Edra, which refined the production method and put the chair into production in 2004. As one of many young designers exploring ways of allowing accident and chance to affect the outcome of products, together with others such as Front (see pages 144 and 149)) Maarten Baas (see page 151) and Kram and Weisshaar (see page 184), he is at the forefront of a new movement that has arisen in reaction to the banality of mass-produced items, and combines technology and new materials with traditional craft attitudes to create unique items with personality and character.

Brosse Container

Date **2003**

Designer **Inga Sempé**

Material **Polypropylene**

Manufacturer **Edra, Italy**

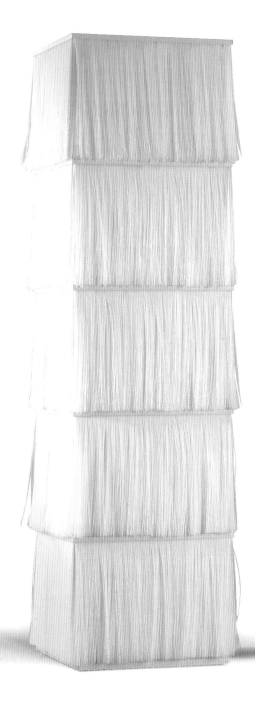

French designer Inga Sempé is one of the rising stars on the furniture scene, achieving international recognition in 2003 with her Brosse (Brush) storage units designed for Italian brand Edra. These consist of lacquered aluminium shelves screened by overlapping rows of bristles that act as an alternative to door or walls. The coloured polypropylene bristles, identical to those used in domestic brooms, are set into the underside of the shelves using industrial bristle-setting techniques. The result is a storage system that is both open and closed – to store or retrieve items, you pass your hands through the rows of bristles. The units come in two sizes – a tall, narrow version with five shelves and a shorter, wider version with four shelves. Black and white versions are available.

At a time when much furniture design is simply a reiteration of existing forms, Sempé is developing a reputation for developing new design typologies – a trait she shares with fellow French designers the Bouroullec Brothers (see pages 139 and 144) and Matali Crasset (see page 112). Her 2003 Long Pot is an extended flowerpot with legs that resembles a miniature, elongated bathtub; her 2000 Digital Analogue clock is a hybrid of old and new technologies, consisting of two hands mounted directly on the wall, each containing a circular display panel at the ends that showed the minutes and hours in LED lights. The displays rotated as the hands moved, meaning that the numbers were always upright.

Sempé was born in Paris in 1968. After completing her degree, she worked for Marc Newson and legendary French designer Andrée Putnam, setting up her own studio in 2000. Like so many upcoming designers, she owes her career to Giulio Cappellini, head of Milanese furniture manufacturer Cappellini, who has spotted and nurtured dozens of talents including the Bouroullec Brothers and Jasper Morrison. In 2001, Cappellini spotted a lamp she had designed – her 0203 floor lamp – and put it into production.

Solid

Date **2004**
Designer **Patrick Jouin**
Material **Liquid resin**
Manufacturer **Materialise, Belgium**

It is rare for designers to be presented with an entirely new manufacturing technology; the advent of rapid prototyping represents perhaps the most exciting opportunity for them since plastics were introduced. The method allows designers to "print" three-dimensional objects directly from computer-aided design files. It was developed in the 1980s as a way of rapidly producing prototypes (hence the name) for testing and evaluation of mass-produced objects such as components for the car industry.

It is only in the last few years that designers have started to experiment with rapid prototyping as a way of making finished objects, exploiting the technique's potential to create hitherto unrealizable new forms and creating what is fast becoming an entirely new aesthetic that is highly complex yet often organic in inspiration. However, due the high cost of the machinery involved, most of the resulting products have been small-scale objects such as lamps and bowls. But in 2004, French designer Patrick Jouin, working with Belgian rapid prototyping company Materialise, became the first person to produce full-size items of furniture from stereolithography – a type of rapid prototyping that involves using a precision laser beam to solidify liquid resin into three-dimensional objects.

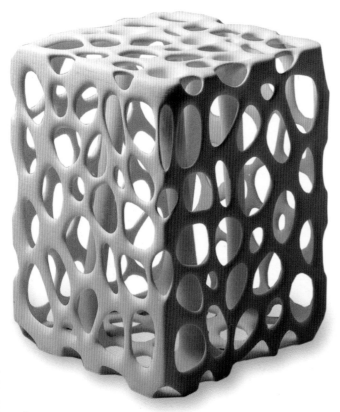

His Solid range shows the radical new shapes the technique allows and includes the Solid C2 chair, which is made from what appears to be a continuous, zigzagging solidified ribbon of resin; and the Solid S1 stool, which resembles a hollow sugar cube riddled with worm-holes, some of which are connected to create bone-like forms that give the item its strength. Jouin has also produced Solid T1, a glass-topped table supported by a forest of intersecting reed-like forms, and Solid C1, an ethereal, translucent chair that looks as if it is made from a single piece of massively scaled-up, microscopic mineral fibre and which is based on a two-dimensional pattern extruded into three dimensions.

Aqua Table

Date **2005**
Designer **Zaha Hadid**
Material **Polyurethane**
Manufacturer **Established & Sons, UK**

Designed by architect Zaha Hadid, the huge Aqua table exhibits the same seamless geometry and flowing forms as her architecture. It was designed as a limited edition piece in 2005 as part of the inaugural collection of new British furniture brand Established & Sons. Established & Sons was formed to capitalize on the burgeoning market for contemporary products – in particular for collectable, pieces by high-profile designers. The company have produced limited edition examples of most of their product range, including an aluminium version of Barber Osgerby's Zero-In coffee table and a rusty Corten steel version of Alexander Taylor's Fold light (see page 221).

Design has long been viewed as the poor cousin of the art world but in the early years of the twenty-first century the two markets began to merge, with art collectors increasingly showing interest in both twentieth-century and contemporary furniture. Prices began rising correspondingly fast. Auction houses such as Phillips in New York have capitalized on this, holding sales of collectable items by leading figures such as Ron Arad and Marc Newson. The 420 by 145 by 75 cm (165 by 57 by 30 in) Aqua table was produced in a limited edition of 12. A prototype version was sold at auction by Phillips de Pury in New York in December 2005 for US$296,000 – a record for a contemporary piece of furniture.

Like most architects, Hadid occasionally designs furniture, notably a collection of interlocking sofas and tables called Z.Scape for Sawaya & Moroni in 2000. Designed using advanced architectural modelling software, the table was manufactured using CNC (computer numerically controlled) techniques. Made of a single piece of matt-finish polyurethane, it features an undulating top resting on three fluid forms akin to waves, and resembles the form of Hadid's Phaeno Science Centre in Wolfsburg, Germany (see page 31), which opened in 2005. The tabletop is made of a sheet of silicon gel that moulds itself to the form beneath, forming shallow pools above the three hollow legs. The piece is available in both black and white.

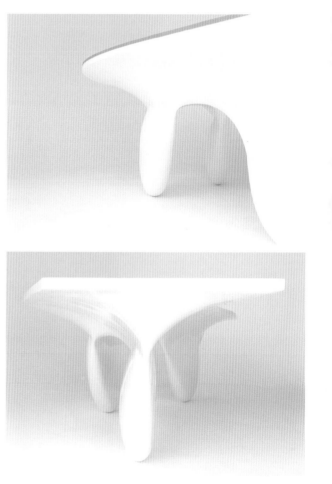

Breeding Table

Date **2005**
Designer **Kram/Weisshaar**
Material **Steel**
Manufacturer **Moroso, Italy**

Many contemporary designers use computers to design furniture but Reed Kram and Clemens Weisshaar have gone a step further with their Breeding tables, programming their software to suggest designs for them. The project was born of their frustration at the conservatism of the furniture industry, which they feel fails to fully exploit the potential of computer-aided design and manufacture. They began by adapting the Rhino software package – used extensively by furniture designers – to generate an endless stream of variations on a basic steel table frame akin to genetic mutations. The designers then weeded out the proposals that were impractical or aesthetically inferior – a process they compare to natural selection – and fed the digital files into computer-controlled laser cutting and bending machines. The resulting steel components were then hand-finished by skilled artisans. The result is a potentially infinite series of tables, each of which is unique. The Breeding table proves that state-of-the-art manufacturing and traditional craft techniques can co-exist, suggesting a way in which designers can exploit technology to produce one-off objects with the speed and affordability of mass production while retaining the uniqueness and quality of one-off pieces. The outcome is comparable to that offered by manufacturing technologies such as rapid prototyping (see pages 149, 180 and 197) and high-tech garment manufacturing techniques such as A-POC (see page 342). The table was put into production in 2005 by Italian manufacturer Moroso under the name T-Countach.

Kram, born in 1971, started out as a video game designer and later studied at the prestigious Media Lab at MIT in Cambridge, Massachusetts. Weisshaar, born in 1977, is a product designer who studied at Central Saint Martin's in London and worked for industrial designer Konstantin Grcic for several years. They met in 2001 while working for AMO – the research consultancy of architect Rem Koolhaas – where they developed digital display devices for Koolhaas' Prada stores in New York and Los Angeles.

Rock

Date **2004**

Designer **Job Smeets and Nynke Tynagel/Studio Job**

Material **Aluminium**

Resembling props from a fairytale, this series of chair, chaise and sofa by Studio Job deliberately flaunts just about every convention attached to practical furniture design, teasing the viewer by appearing to make visual references to history and mythology that are never explained. Yet each piece still manages to be functional and beautiful.

Studio Job consists of Belgian designer Job Smeets and Dutch designer Nynke Tynagel. Like many in their field, they recognize that their profession is no longer driven by the need to solve functional problems, thus their work hovers between art, design and burlesque. The duo have stated that their aim is to create antiques for the future rather than practical, affordable items.

The Rock chair, chaise and sofa are all cast in solid aluminium, making them both impracticably heavy and extremely expensive – they are aimed at serious collectors, selling to galleries and museums, rather than the average consumer of designer furniture. Indeed, the fact that they are cast in metal triggers associations with sculpture

although, visually and functionally, they are resolutely piecesw of furniture rather than works of art. Each piece appears inspired by a different historical period. The chair resembles a baroque dining chair; the chaise is reminiscent of a Modernist lounger; the sofa looks like a Pop-era inflatable seat. Apart from the smooth seats and backs, the chairs' surface is covered in a jagged crust that resembles a rock face or rough-cut crystals. This gives the impression that they may have been hewn out of the side of a mountain, or have been subjected to some strange oxidization process.

The series was unveiled in the Dilmos art gallery during the 2004 Milan Furniture Fair as part of a Studio Job show called Zoom. The title refers to both the bizarre time-traveller nature of Studio Job's work, which moves between different historical eras, and the notion of zooming from micro to macro scale – the crystallized surface of the chairs appears to be massively magnified, while the chairs themselves are slightly undersized, adding to their disorientating, but seductive, effect.

Scrapwood Sideboard

Date **2005**
Designer **Piet Hein Eek**
Material **Wood**

Piet Hein Eek is one of the pioneers of a new tendency towards using recycled materials to create furniture. In Eek's case, this is not so much due to a concern for environmental issues but rather an appreciation of the beauty of materials – particularly scrap timber – that would otherwise be considered waste. A graduate of Design Academy Eindhoven in 1990, he first came to prominence when one of his recycled chests of drawers was exhibited in Milan by the then-fledgling brand Droog. In common with other young Dutch designers at the time, Eek was bored with conventional notions of beauty and the sleek perfection of most contemporary furniture design at the time. He started to use wooden floorboards and planks salvaged from demolished or abandoned buildings, treating the worthless materials as if they were precious and lovingly crafting them into new pieces.

Yet Eek was overshadowed by fellow Droog exhibitors including Marcel Wanders, Hella Jongerius and Jurgen Bey, who went on to become pivotal figures in international design, while the bundle of found wooden drawers held together by a leather belt designed by Tejo Remy – another recycled piece that had much in common with Eek's work – became one of the icons of Dutch design.

Based in Geldrop in the Netherlands, Eek has continued to craft his unmistakable furniture ever since and has recently experienced something of a revival of popularity as recycling and customization returns to fashion. In 2005 he exhibited in London and Tokyo and his pieces – which are renowned for their exquisite carpentry – have started to become highly collectable, selling through art galleries. Besides salvaged timber, Eek works in a variety of materials, producing ranges of aluminium, polycarbonate and steel furniture. He continues to make one-off pieces himself while serial production and commissions are carried out by a partnership business called Eek & Ruijgrok.

Lighting

Nowhere is design's new spirit of experimentation and playfulness more evident than in lighting. Here, the return to decoration is highly evident, with designers largely abandoning the technically advanced, architectural forms that began to dominate towards the end of the twentieth century, and are instead taking a more romantic, low-tech approach. For example, Tord Boontje's 2002 Wednesday light – consisting of a perforated, floral garland made of a thin sheet of acid-etched metal that is draped around a bare light bulb – has proved to be highly influential and shows how a simple idea can create a striking effect. Boontje's light also has the advantage of being extremely cheap to make, thus giving consumers the chance to buy a genuinely affordable "designer" item.

Perhaps inspired by this, young designers today often put their efforts into producing elaborately hand-crafted lighting products as a way of getting their work seen by both the public and potential manufacturers. This means that they can make dramatic design statements with just a small capital outlay, and experiment with unlikely or even perverse ideas with abandon. The result is a return to an almost artisanal, cottage-industry situation, with designers working alone or in small teams to produce small numbers of luxury (expensive) products. As in other design disciplines, though, the notion of luxury is being turned on its head – such as Stuart Haygarth's Tide chandelier, which is constructed of discarded plastic items found on a beach, or Committee's seminal Kebab light, compiled of kitsch ceramic objects unearthed at junk shops and markets.

Surprisingly, given the rapid pace of technological development in other areas, lighting technology has remained static for decades, with the inefficient and

unreliable incandescent bulb still almost ubiquitous. There are a few exceptions to this: Yves Behar's Leaf light exploits new developments in LED technology, while Rachel Wingfield's Digital Dawn blind employs electroluminescent materials that are commonly used in electronic display panels but have only recently been used for lighting products.

The most significant technical advance in the lighting arena is rapid prototyping, the technology that allows three-dimensional objects to be printed in plastic. Belgian company Materialise is leading the way in this area, commissioning designers to create light shades using rapid prototyping techniques and producing an expanding range of dramatic products including Freedom of Creation's Lily light and Lionel Theodore Dean's Creepers. Elsewhere, though, there has been a widespread rekindling of old-fashioned lighting devices, such as candles (Frederickson Stallard's Candle No 1) and gas lights (Chris Kabel's Flame). Even chandeliers, the ultimate bourgeoise object, have enjoyed a revival, in no small part thanks to crystal manufacturer Swarovski's Crystal Palace initiative. Other young designers are exploring materials and forms that, rather than striving to achieve beauty, flirt with notions of ugliness and danger. Jerszy Seymour's Scum light is a deliberately grotesque accrual of dripping polyurethane foam; Julia Lohmann's Ruminant Bloom/Flock is made out of sheep's stomachs; Flood light by Michael Cross and Julie Mathias of Wokmedia consists of glowing bulbs submerged in water. Meanwhile, stalwart superstar Philippe Starck has ventured into territory where few designers dare go, creating a collection of lights made from weapons.

Wednesday

Date **2001**
Designer **Tord Boontje**
Material **Stainless steel**

Tord Boontje's Wednesday light is one of the most influential products of recent years and has become an icon of design's new decorative spirit. Boontje, like so many of the current generation of Dutch designers, studied at Design Academy Eindhoven before attending the Royal College of Art in London. He is one of the leading figures in the recent return to more romantic and decorative themes in design. His delicate floral patterns have been wildly successful, being applied to fabrics, wallpapers and crockery and spawning a host of imitators. Yet Boontje made his name with his lighting designs. In 2002, he was commissioned to produce a chandelier for Swarovski, to be shown as part of an exhibition at the Milan Furniture Fair. Boontje's design, called Blossom, resembled a jewel-encrusted tree branch with pulsating LED lights for leaves. It was a critical success but the real breakthrough was his Wednesday light of the same year – a spectacular but extremely simple product fabricated from a single sheet of wafer-thin stainless steel that has been acid etched with a filigree pattern of flowers and leaves.

The product is sold as a flat sheet in an envelope along with instructions showing the user how to manipulate the flimsy metal and drape it over a bare light bulb. This ensures that each light is unique, since it is impossible to hang any two versions in exactly the same way. The notion of involving the user in the design process – rather than dictating the final form of the object – is something Boontje has in common with a number of contemporary designers, including the Bouroullec Brothers (see pages 139 and 144).

Wednesday was a runaway success, with a cheaper, brass version, called Garland, produced for UK store Habitat in 2003, making it one of the most affordable of all design classics. Boontje's work appears to be hand-crafted but it is in fact rooted in technology. The floral forms of the Garland were drawn on a computer and advanced production techniques are employed in its manufacture.

Midsummer

Date **2004**
Designer **Tord Boontje**
Material **Tyvek**
Manufacturer **Artecnica, USA**

Following the success of his Wednesday and Garland lights (see page 192), Tord Boontje designed his Midsummer light in 2004 – another simple and affordable design that creates an equally spectacular effect. The light was launched in Milan during the furniture fair as part of a dramatic show for Moroso, called Happy Ever After, which saw Boontje deck out the Italian furniture brand's showroom in festoons of multicoloured, perforated fabrics to create the effect of an enchanted forest.

His Midsummer light consists of two sheets of Tyvek – a tough industrial paper used, among other things, to make the envelopes for international courier companies – that have been stamped with a delicate floral pattern, creating a perforated light shade. As with Wednesday and Garland, these are sold flat-packed and the user is invited to take part in the design process by shaping the draped shade over a bare bulb, creating a diaphanous multilayered effect, in a manner similar to the way flowers are arranged in a vase. The only component besides the paper is the discreet plastic cone that slips over the light fitting to prevent the bulb scorching the material.

The light, manufactured by American brand Artecnica, is available in a range of colour combinations, including yellow and red, yellow and green and plain white. The runaway success of the product has led to a wide selection of Boontje products based on similar principles, including Until Dawn, a curtain made of Tyvek perforated with an intricate pattern of flowers and forest creatures. Surprisingly, given his leading role in reintroducing romantic florals into design, Boontje's early work was austere and minimal, but when his daughter was born in 2000 he says he started to think about the kind of environment he wanted her to grow up in and developed his distinctive decorative language. Having made his name in London, Boontje relocated to the south of France in 2005, where he works for an increasing number of brands as well as pursuing his own projects.

Lily

Date **2003**

Designer **Jiri Evenhuis and Janne Kyttanen/Freedom of Creation**

Material **Polyamide and stainless steel**

Manufacturer **Materialise, Belgium**

Young Amsterdam-based duo Jiri Evenhuis and Janne Kyttanen of Freedom of Creation caused a sensation at the 2003 Milan Furniture Fair with a series of strikingly beautiful floor and table lights that exploited a manufacturing technique called rapid prototyping. The technique is sometimes known as three-dimensional printing, as objects are created from layer after microscopic layer of plastic material deposited by a machine that works in a similar way to a giant computer printer, albeit printing in three dimensions rather than just two. It was developed some years ago to create component prototypes and moulds in large industry sectors, such as car production, but has recently been adopted by designers as a way of manufacturing objects for the home.

Rapid prototyping is a slow process – it can take a day to make a complicated light – but has the advantage that it can be programmed to make every object unique. Simply tweaking the parameters on the computer screen can vary each object's shape. It has allowed Evenhuis and Kyttanen to produce three-dimensional shapes that would be impossible using a mould or any other manufacturing technique. Some, such as the Lily lamp, which consists of concentric layers of petals that seem impossibly fragile, are based on natural forms; others are complex geometric shapes, or shapes within shapes. FOC have also worked on concepts for clothes produced by rapid prototyping techniques and tailored to the exact size of the buyer (see page 362).

To produce the lights, FOC teamed up with Belgian rapid prototyping company Materialise, who were interested in finding new applications for their hitherto unglamorous technology. FOC designed the lights on computers using modelling three-dimensional software and emailed the files to Materialise's machines, which then made them in polyamide plastic. The partnership was a huge success and has spawned an ongoing series of collaborations between Materialise and a host of young designers that have resulted in increasingly complex lighting products being shown at Milan each year, usually featuring organic forms.

Digital Dawn

Date **2000**
Designer **Rachel Wingfield**
Material **Electroluminescent fabric**
Manufacturer **EL printed by Elumin8 Systems**

This window blind, by designer Rachel Wingfield, responds to the amount of daylight filtering through the window, becoming brighter as it gets dark and progressively dimmer in the morning. The eerie blue glow is produced by a film of electroluminescent (EL) material printed onto the blind in a series of concentric floral swags, and controlled by light sensors within the blind. EL material emits light when an electric current passes through it and is widely used to produce backlights for digital display panels on hi-fis, car instrument panels and mobile phones. However, in the hands of young designers like Wingfield, it becomes something magical.

Wingfield studied textile design at Loughborough University, then the Royal College of Art where she came up with the concept for Digital Dawn in 2000. She set up her company, Loop pH, in London and now works on numerous commissions, including Weather Patterns, an installation at York Art Gallery, which linked highly decorative EL-printed screens placed over windows to a weather station, so that the patterns on the glass varied according to weather conditions. Her first EL product to gain attention was the Light Sleeper duvet cover and pillows, which featured thin filaments of electroluminescent fibres woven into the fabric, causing them to glow at night. She has also used the technology in her Walls With Ears wallpaper, which features a flock pattern incorporating areas of EL material attached to sound sensors so that they glow strongly when noise is detected nearby.

Much of Wingfield's work explores the way products can be designed to change according to external factors. Her Temporal light is a concept for a public lighting system featuring wall tiles that, thanks to movement sensors, illuminate when people are near. Other designers to experiment with EL include Sam Buxton (see page 312), whose 2003 Surface Intelligent Objects table features EL place settings printed onto a circular glass top that light up when plates, cutlery and glasses are placed on them.

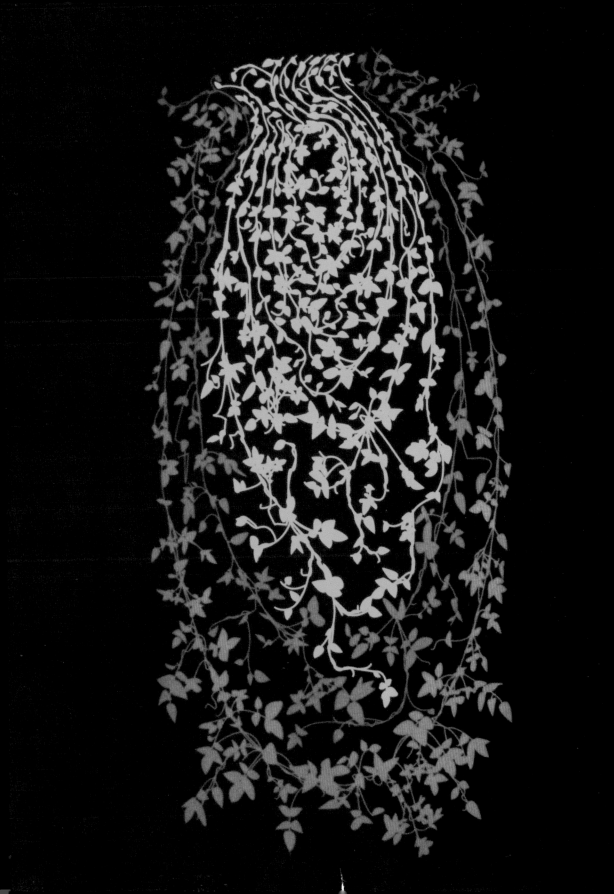

Kebab

Date **2004**
Designer **Harry Richardson and Clare Page/Committee**
Material **Found objects and fabric shade**
Manufacturer **Committee, UK**

A subversive interpretation of a traditional standard lamp, Committee's Kebab lamps have been exhibited around the world and take the vogue for reutilizing abandoned objects to a new extreme. Each consists of a vertical column of bric-a-brac drilled with a diamond-tipped bit, threaded onto a steel shaft and topped with a coloured shade.

Committee's Harry Richardson and Clare Page, born in London and Northampton respectively in 1975, devised the lamps partly as a joke, but also as a deliberate reaction against the slick form-making of much contemporary design. Yet, far from being random assemblies, each lamp is painstakingly and artfully composed of objects that tell a story or address a theme, and each is given a name. "Poacher", for instance, is a musing on the mythical English countryside and includes a ferret, an ornamental urn, a small silver hunting boot and a plastic hedge trimmer. "Mountain Rescue" invites you to invent your own surreal, fairytale-like narrative: a white ceramic stiletto is precariously balanced on a large plastic rock while an Eastern European peasant doll lies crushed between a cactus and a pink elephant. The assemblage is capped with a small Hungarian china pot featuring a picture of a peasant girl dancing on top of a radio.

Richardson and Page studied fine art at Liverpool Art School and moved to Deptford, South London, in 1998, where they founded Committee in 2001. They scour junk shops and flea markets – notably the anarchic Deptford Market near their studio – for their incongruous materials, selecting worthless items, such as single shoes or broken toys, but also occasionally splashing out on pricier antiques.

NeON

Date **2003**
Designer **Paul Cocksedge**
Material **Glass**

British lighting designer Paul Cocksedge shot to prominence in 2003 when he exhibited in Milan at the invitation of German maestro Ingo Maurer. Cocksedge's show upstaged that of Maurer and he was hailed as one of the most exciting prospects around. The highlights of Cocksedge's show were a cluster of small, mysteriously glowing glass pendants called NeON.

NeON features small hand-blown glass phials containing neon gas that glows a pale red when electricity is passed through it. It works on the same principles as the neon tubes employed in advertising displays, but Cocksedge uses an old technology to create something enigmatic and nostalgic. The phials are reminiscent of the valves used in early radios while the insipid glow of the neon brings to mind the experiments of some mad Victorian scientist, giving the lights an air of vintage familiarity.

Born in London in 1978, Cocksedge studied industrial design at Sheffield Hallam University before studying at the Royal College of Art under Ron Arad. In 2004 he was shortlisted for the Design Museum in London's Designer of the Year award for a range of lighting designs including NeON, Styrene (a light shade made of heat-shrivelled polystyrene cups) and Bulb, an internally illuminated glass flower vase that is switched on when a flower is inserted and off when it is removed. A fourth design, Watt, featured a desk light standing on a sheet of paper with a circuit drawn on it: by completing the circuit with a pencil stroke, the light is turned on. In 2004, Cocksedge was again the talk of Milan when he exhibited his Crystallise chandelier as part of Swarovski's Crystal Palace show (see page 209).

Light Shade Shade

Date **1999**
Designer **Jurgen Bey**
Material **Found chandelier and plastic mirror film**
Manufacturer **Moooi, Netherlands**

Nothing symbolizes the spirit of recent Dutch design more than this light by Jurgen Bey. Designed in 1999 at the height of the Dutch design renaissance, it features a found or salvaged light – usually a chandelier or a piece of 1970s casino kitsch – suspended in a sleeve of semi-transparent mirror film. When the light is off, the sleeve is opaque and reflective, shading the chandelier from view. But when the light is switched on, the shade becomes transparent and the illuminated chandelier becomes visible.

The light was designed for the highly influential Droog collective and first shown at the 1999 Milan Furniture Fair, but later went into production with upstart Dutch brand Moooi. It epitomizes the Dutch liking for designing products that aren't quite what they seem and which have a narrative: in this case, the way an object that, at first sight, looks highly contemporary becomes nostalgic, kitsch and humorous literally at the flick of a switch. Light Shade Shade is one of the most enduring and popular lighting products to come out of the Droog era, although the 85 Bulbs chandelier – designed by Rody Graumans in 1993 and which consists of 85 standard light bulbs hanging in a cluster – is also regarded as a Dutch classic.

Jurgen Bey is one of the leading lights on the Dutch scene, working mainly in furniture and interiors (see pages 102, 109 and 162). His work often involves re-covering discarded items to give them new life: his 1997 Kokon series featured old wooden chairs with tight new skins of PVC that resembled cocoons, while his St Petersburg chairs for Droog use similar pieces, covering them in a carapace of glass fibre painted in floral patterns. Light Shade Shade similarly gives new life to an old object, in this case making an unwanted light fashionable again.

Lolita

Date **2004**
Designer **Ron Arad**
Material **Crystals, LEDs and cable**
Manufacturer **Swarovski, Austria**

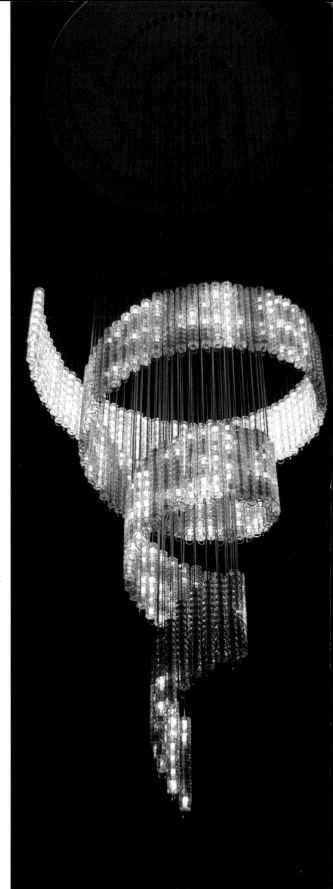

Crystal manufacturer Swarovski has successfully positioned itself as
a chic fashion and lifestyle brand in the last few years, despite the
fact that most of its business comes from making industrial glass
products and crystal giftware. Its annual Crystal Palace exhibition
began in 2002 as a branding initiative but has become a highlight of
the design calendar. Each year, the company commissions a string of
leading designers to produce a one-off chandelier that incorporates
its crystals. The series was initiated by creative director Ilse Crawford
and has managed to make chandeliers – until recently regarded as
the height of bourgeois bad taste – fashionable once again.

Initially held in Milan during the April Furniture Fair, the Crystal
Palace exhibition now tours the world and has produced a string of
designs that are regarded as classics, including this chandelier by
London-based designer Ron Arad, which was created in 2004. Lolita
features a suspended tapering spiral made up of 2,100 large crystals.
LED lights concealed between each of the crystals are connected by
1,000 m (3,300 ft) of wires to a computer controller hidden in the
ceiling. A mobile phone attached to the circuitry allows anyone who
has the number to send text messages to the chandelier. The LEDs
light up to display the messages, which scroll down the spiral.

The following year, Arad designed Miss Haze, a variation on Lolita,
which consisted of a screen of LED-backed crystals suspended face-
down from the ceiling. The chandelier's computer was connected
wirelessly to a Palm Pilot, recreating in real time on its crystal matrix
what was being drawn onto the device's screen. Both Lolita and Miss
Haze are named after Dolores Haze, the main character in Vladimir
Nabokov's classic novel *Lolita*, and are a private joke by Arad, who sent
so many text messages during the chandelier's development phases
that people suspected he had an illicit lover.

Voyage

Date **2005**
Designer **Yves Behar**
Material **Crystal, LEDs and steel frame**
Manufacturer **Swarovski, Austria**

Measuring 4.5 m (15 ft) long and weighing 1 tonne (2,200 lb), this enormous one-of-a-kind chandelier was designed by San Francisco-based industrial designer Yves Behar to hang in the newly completed Terminal 4 at New York's JFK airport. As much a work of sculpture as design, Voyage was commissioned as part of the airport's ongoing public art programme and represents the way that the boundaries between what constitutes art and design are blurring in the twenty-first century.

Prior to its installation at JFK, Voyage was exhibited at Swarovski's Crystal Palace exhibition in Milan during the 2005 Furniture Fair. Taking the form of a double loop, the chandelier is intended to express both the fluidity and the circuitous nature of air travel; Behar's visual inspiration is an ocean wave frozen in time but it can also be read as the solidified vapour trail of a circling aircraft. The soft blue glow of the chandelier is created by 2000 LED lights, which are set among the 52,000 crystals that cover Voyage's surface. These are mounted on a hidden framework of steel rods. Motion detectors embedded within the chandelier cause the LEDs to vary in intensity in response to the movement of people within the airport terminal.

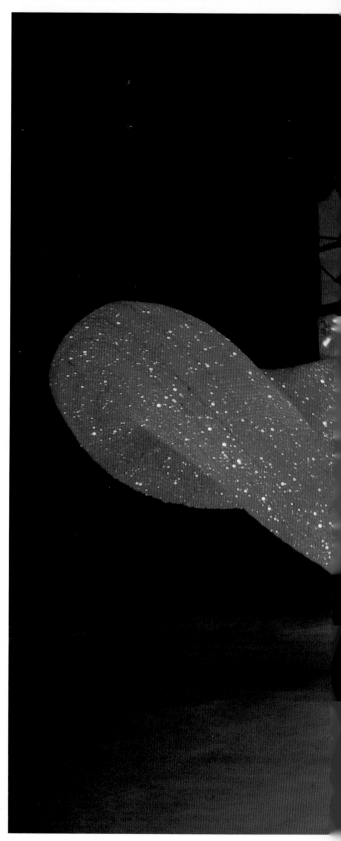

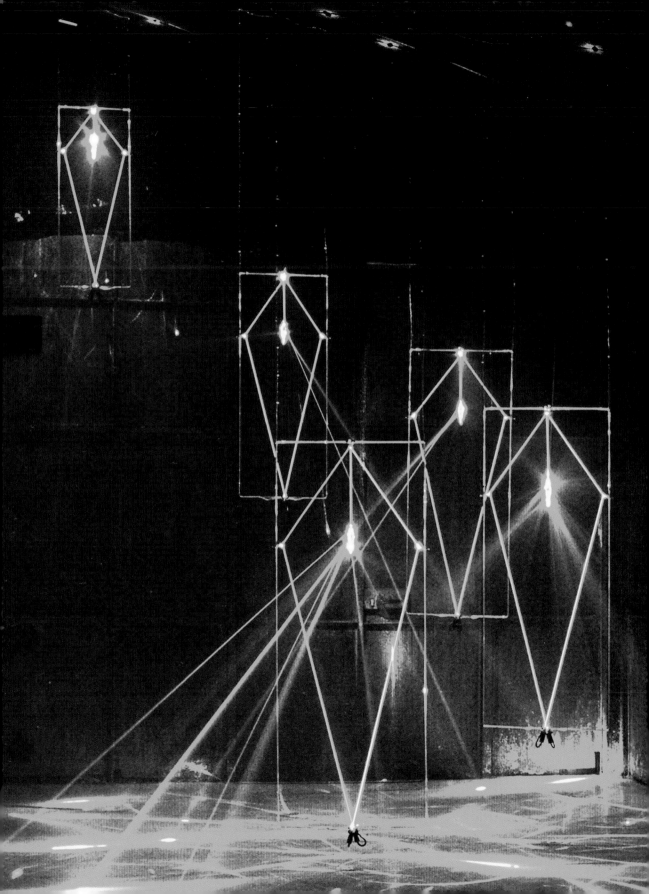

Crystallise

Date **2005**
Designer **Paul Cocksedge**
Material **Crystal glass and laser**
Manufacturer **Swarovski, Austria**

British designer Paul Cocksedge subverts the notion of the chandelier as an ornate, decadent object with Crystallise, a chandelier that contains just a single crystal. It was commissioned for Swarovski's Crystal Palace exhibition held during the 2005 Milan Furniture Fair and the sponsor nearly cancelled Cocksedge's contribution, feeling it didn't use enough of the crystal manufacturer's products. Cocksedge, however, pointed out that the green laser beam traces the outline of a giant crystal as it passes around the light, thereby saving his project.

Crystallise comes in a variety of sizes ranging from 90 cm (35 in) to 180 cm (71 in) in height. It consists of a glass crystal suspended on a monofilament within a rectangular frame of thin glass tubing. A laser module mounted at the top of the frame is precisely aimed at the first of four tiny mirrors mounted midway along one side of the frame; this reflects the laser light onto the next mirror, and so on until the beam returns to the top of the frame, having traced the shape of a trapezium on its way. The laser is then directed by the fourth mirror downwards onto the top of the suspended crystal, which shatters the beam. Despite its minimal components, the visual impact of the light, when displayed in a darkened room, is magical.

Random

Date **2002**
Designer **Bertjan Pot**
Material **Glass-fibre yarn and epoxy resin**
Manufacturer **Moooi, Netherlands**

Made of glass-fibre yarn dipped in epoxy resin and wound around a balloon-like inflatable mould, this light is typical of Dutch designer Bertjan Pot's fascination with structural surfaces – forms in which the outer skin doubles as the structure. Born in 1975, Pot studied at Design Academy Eindhoven, setting up a company called Monkey Boys with fellow designer Daniel White in Rotterdam in 1999. Random was an early Monkey Boys' project, although Pot subsequently set up his own design studio and continued producing the light. It is one of a series of lighting and furniture products created by Pot that employ fibres wrapped around moulds, starting with his Knitted lamp of 1998, which involved stuffing balloons inside a resin-soaked stocking: when the resin hardened, the balloons were removed, leaving a diaphanous, cluster-like form that was different each time. His Carbon chair (see page 156) , Random chair, and Carbon Cloud living pod are all constructed using a similar technique.

Like many contemporary Dutch designers, Bertjan Pot's work relies on a high degree of handcrafting rather than industrial processes. He eschews designing on a computer, preferring hands-on contact with materials. His products are usually the result of a great deal of trial and error. It took Pot three years to perfect the Random light technique, trying out a variety of materials and adhesives, and initially attempting to knot the fibres, until he found a process that worked.

The light – which resembles the coloured, string-wound shades popular in the 1970s – contains a circular hole through which the mould is removed and the bulb is changed. Unlike most shades, this hole is not located at the top of the lamp but is randomly placed at the side, hence the light's name. The bulb housing is suspended on a stiff metal rod with a circular bolt at the top that clamps on to the glass-fibre shell. The design was an instant hit and was put into production by Dutch furniture brand Moooi in 2002. It comes in three sizes – 50 cm (20 in), 85 cm (33 in) and 105 cm (41 in) – and is available in both black and white.

Bobbin Lace

Date **2001**
Designer **Niels van Eijk**
Material **Glass-fibre**

Niels van Eijk's Bobbin Lace lamp combines traditional Dutch lace-making techniques with fibre-optic technology and is an example of the current fascination with giving ancient production methods a contemporary twist to create surprising new effects. A light without a bulb, it is woven from glass-fibre threads so that the shade doubles as the light source. The shade is constructed of knotted glass-fibre cords, each of which contains 400 extremely thin light-transmitting filaments, meaning there is a total of around 500 m (1,640 ft) of filament in each light. A small, ceiling-mounted black box contains a light source, which is attached to the bunched ends of the cords. Where the knots are formed, a number of the glass-fibre filaments in each cord snap, allowing light to leak out and meaning the whole shade is illuminated by a constellation of pin-pricks. Van Eijk produces the lights to order in a variety of sizes and shapes.

The cords are hand-knotted, using traditional lace-making techniques, into a three-dimensional shade. The bobbin lace method is thought to have originated in Flanders in the fifteenth century and involves the manipulation of threads wound on bobbins to create highly decorative trims that were used to decorate cuffs, napkins and the like. It allowed extremely delicate patterns to be created in linen fibres and, in particular, metal threads of gold and silver wire wound around silk threads.

Van Eijk was born in 1970 in Someren, Netherlands, and studied at the Design Academy Eindhoven, later attending the post-graduate programme of the Sandberg Institute in Amsterdam. Together with fellow designer Miriam van der Lubbe, he set up a design studio in 1998. The two work both together and individually on furniture, lighting and other design projects that often exhibit a high degree of craftsmanship.

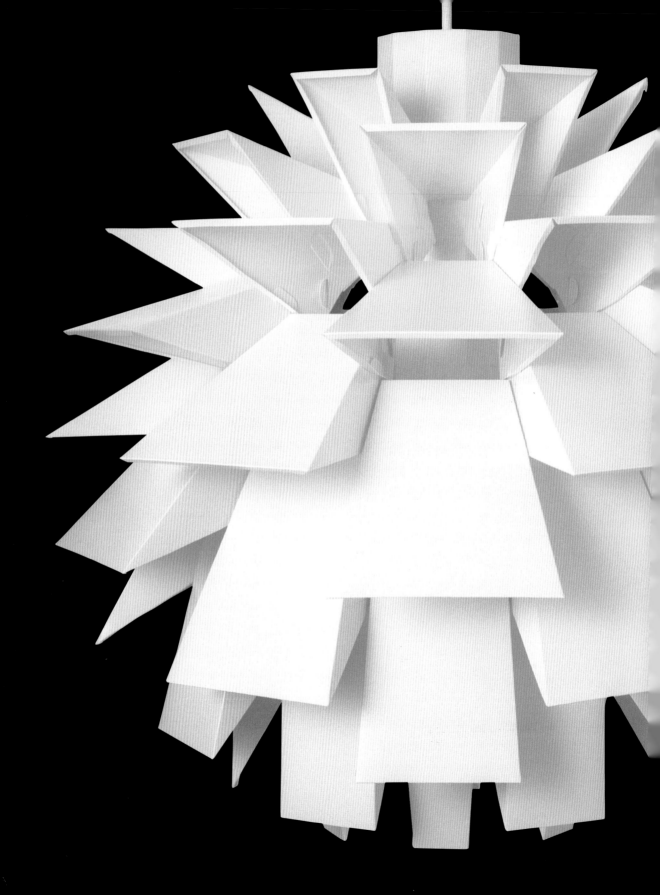

Norm 69

Date **2002**
Designer **Simon Karkov**
Material **Polypropylene**
Manufacturer **Normann Copenhagen, Denmark**

This spectacular pendant light was designed in the 1960s but only put into production in 2002. Its designer, Danish architect Simon Karkov, came up with the concept for the light, which is inspired by flowers and pine cones, in 1969 but had to wait over 30 years before he found a suitable material – polypropylene – to make it from, and a manufacturer – Normann Copenhagen – to put it into production.

Norm 69 is a self-assembly light consisting of 69 pieces of die-cut polypropylene that comes flat-packed in a box along with a set of instructions. It takes around two to three hours to fully assemble but does not require glue, scissors or any other materials. The thin sheets of polypropylene have little stiffness, so the light's strength comes from the way the pieces are folded along pre-scored lines and joined together with tabs and slots. It is available in both white and cream and in four different sizes with diameters of 42 cm (17 in), 51 cm (20 in), 60 cm (24 in) and 78 cm (31 in). The complex geometry of the shade ensures that maximum amounts of light are cast in all directions without glare. Although the light looks sturdy and architectural, it is in fact a delicate, lightweight product that has more in common with paper engineering than traditional lighting design.

The design recalls the iconic PH Artichoke light designed by fellow Dane Poul Henningsen in 1958 and manufactured by Louis Poulson & Co. This product, made of copper, steel and enamelled metal, is considered one of the all-time classics of Scandinavian design yet has always been extremely expensive to manufacture. The affordable Norm 69 is therefore a far more democratic descendent and has led to a host of imitators: there are now dozens of self-assembly polypropylene lights on the market in increasingly complex shapes.

Gun Collection

Date **2005**
Designer **Philippe Starck**
Material **Gold-plated aluminium alloy**
Manufacturer **Flos, Italy**

French-born Philippe Starck was the most famous designer in the world throughout the 1980s and 1990s and the first to become a genuine celebrity, combining a prolific output with a genius for self-promotion. He shot to fame in the "designer decade" of the 1980s with iconic products, such as his rocket-shaped Juicy Salif lemon squeezer, which became a must-have status symbol for a new generation of design-savvy young consumers. Although his influence has waned recently – he has been upstaged by younger talents such as Marcel Wanders and Thomas Heatherwick – Starck proved he could still make headlines when he exhibited a range of lamps made out of gold-plated guns at the Milan Furniture Fair in 2005.

Unlike artists, designers have traditionally avoided using the imagery of war or violence in their designs and steered clear of making political statements through their work. With this collection of prototype lamps, designed for Italian lighting brand Flos, Starck became the first high-profile designer to break this taboo with a bedside light, a table light and a floor light called Beretta, Kalashnikov and M16. Each featured a replica gun hand-plated in 18-carat gold leaf and featuring a black shade printed with crosses. The collection was then exhibited in New York at the emporium of influential design retailer Murray Moss. Later in 2005 the lights went into production, this time made of gold-plated aluminium alloy cast from the original guns.

Inspired by television images of Saddam Hussein's gold-plated gun cache broadcast during the war on Iraq, the range was presented in Milan arranged in ranks on plinths to look like a weapons cache. Starck claims his design is intended to raise awareness of consumers' political responsibilities at a time of rampant consumerism and celebrity-obsessed culture. Some critics, however, dismissed the venture as a publicity stunt.

Bourgie

Date **2004**
Designer **Ferruccio Laviani**
Material **Polycarbonate**
Manufacturer **Kartell, Italy**

Bourgie was launched in 2004 at the Milan Furniture Fair by Italian manufacturer Kartell – which specializes in affordable, translucent injection-moulded plastic furniture – and became an immediate icon. It is named after the French colloquialism *"bourgie"*, which is an affectionate term for a discerning person who appreciates the finer things in life.

With its decorative base recalling an antique candelabrum or the scrolling stonework of the Santa Maria Della Salute church in Venice, Ferruccio Laviani's Bourgie table light takes the formal language of the Baroque era and remakes it in contemporary materials. It consists of two pieces of moulded transparent polycarbonate plastic – the base and the shade – with a finish of such high quality that it appears luxurious. The outside surface of the tapered shade is ribbed, creating prismatic patterns of light that recall cut crystal, while the tripod base features opulent curves and scrolls. It comes in clear and black plastic and in limited-edition chrome- and gold-plated finishes. The lamp is perhaps the most elegant example of the contemporary trend for historical references in design, borrowing heavily from the past yet avoiding pastiche by reducing forms to their essence and employing cutting-edge manufacturing methods.

Like the majority of Italian designers, Laviani, who was born in 1960, studied architecture. During the 1980s he worked with Italian greats, such as Michele de Lucchi, Achille Castiglioni and Ettore Sottsass, becoming associated with the hugely influential Memphis collective and exhibiting in Memphis exhibitions in 1986 and 1987. In 1991 he designed the Orbital lamp – a Memphis-inspired piece, of irregular-shaped coloured glass shades mounted on a steel column – which was one of the outstanding lighting designs of that decade.

He was not the first designer to recast antique furniture in transparent plastic: in 2002, Kartell stablemate Philippe Starck launched his Louis Ghost armchair, which approximates the classical form of a Louis IX chair in a single piece of injection-moulded polycarbonate. This hugely successful design was a technological and aesthetic breakthrough and led to a rash of similar designs, including a large number of "ghost" versions of historical typologies by Starck himself.

Flames

Date **2003**
Designer **Chris Kabel**
Material **Powder-coated copper tubing and camping gas canister**
Manufacturer **Moooi, Netherlands**

Resembling a gas-powered candelabrum, the Flames table light by Chris Kabel employs old-fashioned technology while remaining strikingly contemporary. The light consists of a trident-shaped arrangement made of off-the-shelf copper pipes and fittings that are brazed together in the same way that domestic gas pipes are assembled. The trident is attached to the top of a standard camping gas canister. Both the candelabrum and the canister are finished in white powder coating.

Kabel, who was born in the Netherlands in 1975, studied at the Design Academy Eindhoven between 1996 and 2001. He achieved immediate success with his graduate project, Sticky lamp – a light with a peel-off sticky back that allows it to be stuck to the wall, which was put into production by Droog. Kabel also designs jewellery and furniture and is currently developing a chair made of folded and welded steel mesh.

Kabel's idea for the Flames light began with his fascination with public water fountains. Since he is a smoker, he wondered whether it would be possible to provide a constant supply of flames in a similar way, as this would mean that people would no longer have to remember to carry cigarette lighters around with them. He began experimenting with ways of producing small, constant flames from gas canisters and soon realized he had stumbled on an unusual yet romantic light source akin to a candle. It was a logical step therefore to arrange the gas pipes into the form of a candelabrum and paint them candle-white, creating a light ideal for the dinner table or window sill that has the advantage of not dripping wax. The result is an extremely honest design that does not pretend to be anything more than an assembly of standard gas-fitters' components and which has become a big success for Moooi, the Dutch brand that now manufactures Kabel's product.

Fold

Date **2005**
Designer **Alexander Taylor**
Material **Steel**
Manufacturer **Established & Sons, UK**

The Fold series of lights began as an exploration in how to create a product from a single sheet of material. Having set himself this brief, designer Alexander Taylor started experimenting with paper and card, cutting, folding and glueing it until he worked out a way to form a light shade, column and base from one piece. From there he moved on to prototypes made from sheets of 3 mm thick (¹/₁₀ in) acrylic, which he heated along straight lines in his studio and folded into shape. Later he began developing ways of fabricating the product from sheets of steel or aluminium, eventually producing a table lamp himself in small quantities.

In 2004, new British furniture manufacturer, Established & Sons, approached Taylor and offered to help him develop the product. This resulted in a family of lamps – a 120 cm (47 in) high bedside version,

a 2.6 m (8 ¹/₂ ft) high table version and a 4.5 m (15 ft) high floor version – manufactured in very thin powder-coated aluminium. The aluminium is punched from a sheet then folded in stages using metal presses. Despite this, the light's silhouette is deliberately reminiscent of the most ordinary, un-designed lamps on the market, and the use of a braided flex is a nod to old-fashioned domestic lights.

Born in 1975 in County Durham, Taylor studied furniture and product design at Nottingham Trent University and, after a period spent working for an architect, he set up his own design studio in 2002. He achieved early success with Antlers, a coat hook resembling a rack of antlers made of 8 mm diameter (¹/₃ in) steel wire formed on a computerized bending machine – a design inspired by memories of the hunting trophies used in ski lodges for hanging up coats.

Mirror Ball

Date **2003**
Designer **Tom Dixon**
Material **Plastic polycarbonate**

This hugely successful product range came about when British designer Tom Dixon decided to introduce a new light that would be almost invisible. As part of a self-conscious attempt to create products that were not over-designed, he imagined a simple, glowing sphere that reflected its surroundings and blended into the background. In fact, as Dixon admits, he achieved precisely the opposite: the shiny silver Mirror Ball light is as conspicuous as its mirror-clad disco namesake. Yet the light has become one of the best-selling lighting products of recent years and has proven particularly popular in bars, restaurants and retail outlets, where it is often hung in spectacular clusters.

Consisting of a lightweight ball of moulded transparent plastic, the inner surface of the light is coated with a microscopically thin layer of aluminium. This is applied using a technique known as vacuum metallization: the light is placed inside a vacuum tank and the air is extracted. An electrical charge is then passed through a filament containing a tiny amount of pure aluminium, which vaporizes and evenly coats the surface of the plastic.

Dixon has also produced a copper-coloured version of the series, which consists of three different sizes of lights with diameters of 50 cm (20 in), 40 cm (16 in) and 25 cm (10 in). The Mirror Ball comes as a pendant light but can also be placed on the floor or on a 120 cm (47 in) high tubular steel stand, which converts it into a floor light. There is also a wall version which comes in the form of a flattened blob.

Alquimista

Date **2003**
Designer **Robert Stadler**
Material **Tulle, Lycra, aluminium foil and steel wire**
Manufacturer **Coopa Roca, Brazil**

Besides designing a wide range of furniture, lighting and products
under his own name, Austrian Robert Stadler, who is now based
in Paris, is also a founder member of French design house Radi. His
Alquimista light is named after the Portuguese word for alchemist,
and this one-off ceiling light literally turns everything placed beneath
it to gold, thanks to the gold-coloured aluminium foil that lines the
inside of the 65 cm (26 in) diameter shade. The name also refers to
Stadler's experiences in Brazil, which he visited as part of an artist-
in-residence programme, and where the light was constructed.

Inspired by the Brazilians' ingenuity at creating beautiful objects
from cheap or worthless materials, especially for the annual carnival
celebrations when fantastic costumes and floats are created by hand,
Stadler bought all the materials for his design from a carnival supplies'
shop in Rio de Janeiro. The light consists of a dome-shaped wire-frame
shade covered in strips of tulle and Lycra knotted together and fixed
to the frame, creating a curious rug-like effect. It was hand-crafted
by members of Coopa Roca, a crafts cooperative based in the Rocinha
– one of the largest and most notorious of Brazil's favelas (shanty
towns). The cooperative was founded in the 1980s to allow women
in the favela to earn money working from home, while preserving
traditional craft techniques, such as appliqué, crochet, knotwork and
patchwork. Initially Coopa Roca's members used recycled fabric scraps.
They are increasingly undertaking commissions for leading Western
fashion houses and designers.

Delight

Date **2004**
Designer **Nahoko Koyama and Alex Garnett/Mixko**
Material **Felt**

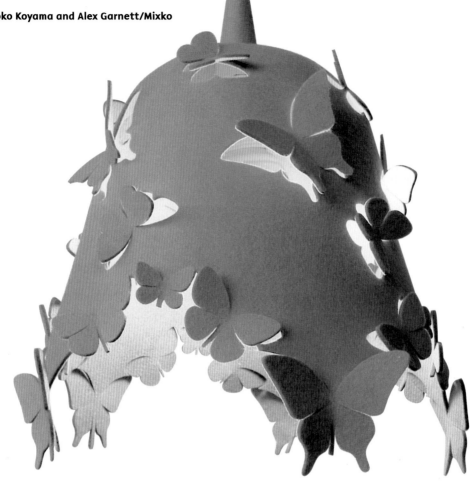

The recent revival of interest in decoration, pattern and natural forms among designers has seen a rash of products featuring butterflies, moths and other similar motifs. This light by British-based design duo Mixko is one of the most successful of such products. With its felt shade of unbleached wool and hand-punched butterfly motifs, it employs centuries-old hat- and shoe-making techniques, while still managing to appear undeniably contemporary.

Its designers, Tokyo-born Nahoko Koyama and the British designer Alex Garnett, met while studying at Goldsmith's College in London. Working together as Mixko, they are now based in Exeter, Devon. Koyama tends to work in felt, and other products she has designed include Coron – a simple lightshade constructed from a sheet of felt

twisted into a cone. Garnett's work involves playing with the scale of familiar objects and includes seating made from superscaled whistles, computer keys and mugs.

The soft, flexible, bell-shaped Delight shade is manufactured on a hat-maker's mould by traditional craftsmen, while the butterfly shapes are punched with tools that Koyama and Garnett discovered being used by shoemakers in Tokyo. The product comes in a range of colours and is 26 cm (10 in) high, with a diameter of 23 cm (9 in).

Made of highly flammable felt, this design has been made feasible by the introduction of low-energy bulbs – as have other potentially flammable products, such as Tord Boontje's paper Midsummer light (see page 195).

Candle 1

Date **2002**
Designer **Fredrikson Stallard**
Material **Wax**

With both the candle and the ornate candle holder cast in wax, Candle 1 is a temporary object that destroys itself as it burns. To its designers, London-based Patrik Fredrikson and Ian Stallard, the piece undermines the notion of the candlestick as a precious, beautiful artefact, instead deriving aesthetic pleasure from the manner of its destruction. The original pressed glass candlestick used to make the mould for the lower part of the object belonged to Fredrikson's great grandmother and was badly damaged. The designers restored it and combined it with the wooden handle of their studio broom to create a mould for the candle.

The mould was produced in the autumn of 2003, but due to the difficulty of casting wax into the intricate form, it took a further year to make just a handful of prototypes, which were exhibited at the 100% Design show in London in September 2003. Candle experts suggested that the designers simplify the mould by using a turned candelabra shape but they refused, preferring to stick with Fredrikson's family heirloom.

To protect the fragile product, it is sold in packaging that consists of a block of foam with the profile of the candle laser-cut from it, thereby reinforcing the ironic connotations of value. The product has proven highly successful, selling well around the world and serving as the centrepiece at many high-profile parties and dinners, where the sight of the burning candles melting en masse into a thick, dripping pool of wax is a spectacular piece of theatre for the guests. The designers are most proud of the time when fashion designer Oscar de la Renta lit 100 white candles at a birthday party in New York, while in Dublin on the same evening, Madonna hosted a party featuring 100 of their black candles.

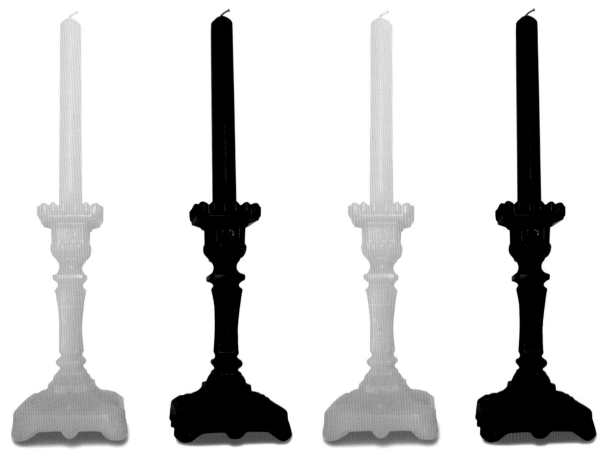

Tide

Date **2005**
Designer **Stuart Haygarth**
Material **Found objects**

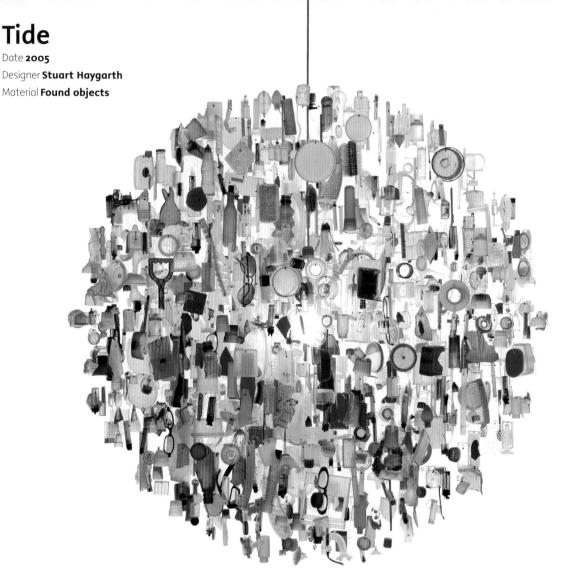

Stuart Haygarth's lighting designs involve the painstaking assembly of found objects, seeking beauty in – and giving new life to – discarded items. But unlike much salvage-based design – such as the Kebab lights by Committee (see page 200) – Haygarth handles the pieces of debris so expertly that at first sight his products appear to be made of bespoke components. His pieces also tell a story related to a specific time and place: his Millennium chandelier, for example, is made of 1,000 discarded plastic party poppers collected after the 1999 New Year's Eve celebrations in London. Suspended on monofilament line in the shape of a spinning top around a central light source, the multicoloured, semi-translucent poppers appear more like precious, specially crafted components than worthless rubbish.

Similarly, Haygarth's Tide chandelier records the manmade debris washed up on Dungeness Beach in Kent, southeast England. For over two years, Haygarth has collected and sorted objects discovered on the shore, reserving the small, translucent (and mainly plastic) items for his limited-edition chandeliers. Each 140 cm (55 in) diameter

chandelier contains roughly 1,100 objects – which include bottles, sunglasses, beach toys and industrial components – and takes about a week to assemble, not including the time it takes to collect and wash the refuse. The objects are suspended in a spherical formation, that Haygarth says refers to the moon, which controls the ocean tides.

Born in Lancashire in 1966, Haygarth came to design late, after forging a career as a photographer specializing in photo-montages used for book covers and magazines. His assemblage approach to design owes much to the way he arranged objects for his shoots. Other designs by Haygarth include Disposable chandelier, a 200 cm (79 in) high column constructed of 416 disposable plastic wine glasses surrounding a pink fluorescent light source, and Shadey Family, a series of ceiling lights made from groups of mismatching, discarded glass lamp shades. As with Committee's Kebab lights, the irony of Haygarth's work is that while his raw materials are worthless, his finished products are considered luxury items that sell for large sums of money.

Scum

Date **2003**
Designer **Jerszy Seymour**
Material **Polyurethane foam**

Produced in a limited edition of 100 in 2003, for a show at Paris exhibition venue Galerie Kreo, Scum light is part of a series of design projects by Berlin-based designer Jerszy Seymour involving sprayed polyurethane foam, a material usually used as insulation in the construction industry. Seymour, however, has taken the plastic material – which expands to many times its original volume and hardens when sprayed from a special machine – and treated it as a craft material, creating "live" objects in much the same way that a glass-blower manipulates molten glass. To create the lights, Seymour sprays foam over a hemispherical mould, a process that involves a great deal of skill. The unappealing appearance and name of the light belie the fact that Seymour is attempting to create a new visual language based on the honest use of an unusual material, rather than deliberately striving to create something ugly (he points out that the word "scum" has its origin in the latin word for "foaming"; the negative connotation is a later English introduction). In this way, Seymour questions accepted notions of beauty.

Born in 1968, in Berlin, Seymour studied at the Royal College of Art in London. He operates at the margins of the design world, producing installations that are more akin to artworks, such as his 2001 Bonnie & Clyde car – a full-size polyurethane foam cast of a Ford Cortina, which he hollowed out to create a seating environment that was halfway between furniture and architecture. His best known works include the 2000 Freewheelin Franklin table – a circular plastic tabletop mounted on the chassis of a remote controlled toy car – and Easy chair, a stacking, moulded plastic seat for Magis.

Other Scum projects by Seymour have included installations of lava-like flows of foam at design events around the world, a temporary Scum Skate Park in Tokyo and a self-build dwelling called House in a Box, which consists of an inflatable, removable mould complete with window and door voids, over which the user sprays polyurethane foam. Once the foam hardens, the mould is removed and the resulting domed structure can be inhabited.

Creepers

Date **2004**
Designer **Lionel Theodore Dean**
Material **Laser-sintered polyamide**
Manufacturer **Materialise, Belgium**

Manufactured by Belgian rapid prototyping company Materialise, which also produces Freedom of Creation's Lily lamp (see page 197), Creepers is a novel new type of decorative modular lighting system that exploits advanced manufacturing processes. It consists of vine-like tendrils with tiny leaves, which are set with flowers containing LED lights. The creepers are clipped to, and powered by, a grid of vertical cables, resembling the way a creeper grows across a trellis and creating an atmospheric screen that can be placed against a wall or used to divide a room.

Like many of the most interesting lighting products being developed today, Creepers is manufactured using rapid prototyping techniques which "print" solid objects directly from digital files. In this case, the product is made of polyamide (nylon) that has been laser-sintered – a process that involves firing a highly accurate laser beam into a vat of nylon powder. The laser traces the form of the required product into the powder, heating the nylon as it goes and fusing it into a solid. This process allows incredibly delicate and unique forms to be created: Creepers

consists of extremely thin stems and leaves that would be difficult to produce using traditional moulding techniques, and which come in an infinite variety of different configurations.

The product is an example of "parametric" design. The apparent simplicity of the naturalistic forms belies the sophistication of the design: the position of each leaf is precisely calculated to maximize the amount of light it reflects. Its British-born designer, Lionel Theodore Dean, gives his computer-aided design programme a set of parameters for each creeper and the computer then generates endless variations. This approach to design, which is extremely new, attempts to mimic the biological processes that ensure that each living entity is unique. Dean, who studied at the Royal College of Art in London and initially worked as an automotive designer, now runs his own project called Future Factories, which explores the potential of parametric design.

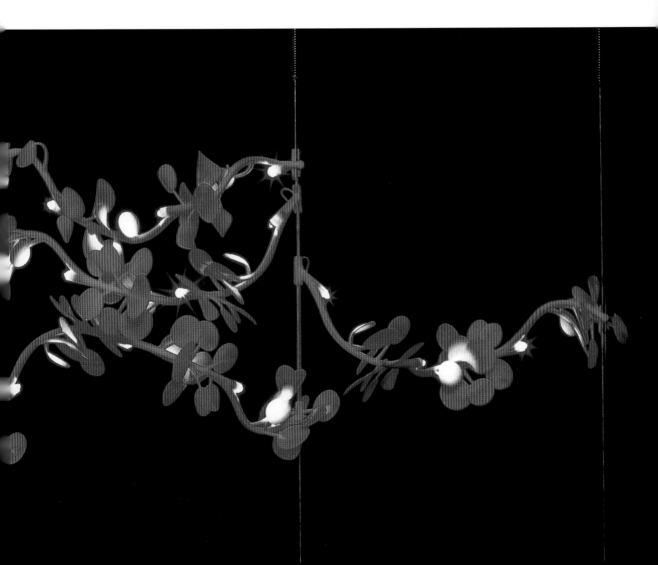

Cloud

Date **2004**
Designer **Jess Shaw**
Material **Polyamide, wire and fairy lights**
Manufacturer **Jess Shaw**

Born in Wales in 1967, lighting designer Jess Shaw studied fine art at Ruskin College, Oxford, in the UK. Her designs are often inspired by delicate and ephemeral natural forms and she works in a variety of unusual materials, both natural and artificial. Shaw's lighting designs include Hoar Frost – strips of white plastic attached to wire mesh surrounding a light source and resembling the thick frost that forms on leaves and branches – and Dancing Wood Anemones – delicate individual lights dressed with slivers of feather that recall both woodland flowers and shuttlecocks. Her best-known piece, the Cloud light, is produced by hand and made of twists of white nylon tube suspended on wires and concealing tiny light sources.

Shaw developed the light after exploring ways of creating forms that had no edges and which could theoretically be of infinite size. Cloud is as much an installation as a lighting product: each time Shaw is invited to create a Cloud light, the size, form and composition changes in reaction to its surroundings and Shaw's mood. The light's form – amorphous, three-dimensional clusters of twisted nylon, often with voids in them – most obviously resembles clouds, but has also been interpreted – among other things – as a sea anemone or some kind of micro-organism. In fact, to Shaw, the design is less about what it looks like than the way it triggers the imagination of the viewer. To her, it is a way of expressing ideas using form instead of words: conceptually, the light deals with the notion of aphasia, or the inability to understand language. Thus the light can also be read as a snowball, referring to folk tales of snowballs found in the Arctic which, when thawed, are found to contain frozen words.

Flood

Date **2004**
Designer **Michael Cross and Julie Mathias/Wokmedia**
Material **Hydroformed aluminium and LEDs**

Consisting of bare light bulbs attached to red and yellow flexes and submerged in vases of water, Flood light, by Michael Cross and Julie Mathias, was one of the outstanding pieces at the Royal College of Art degree show in London in 2004. The science behind the light is extremely simple, relying on low voltage (12v) bulbs that are specially made to resemble standard bulbs and which are more conductive than water, meaning most of the current flows through them rather than through the water. The seemingly dangerous combination of electricity and water is a deliberate provocation on the part of the designers, since much of their work starts with an urge to behave like a naughty child and break taboos about how objects should be used.

Cross, who is British and was born in 1979, met Mathias, born in 1978 in France, at the Royal College of Art in 2003 and they now work together under the banner of Wokmedia. Other notable pieces include Blow, a fan that is started by blowing on the blades and stopped by inserting your fingers between them, and Sprinkle, a rug consisting of individual tufts of wool set in small, non-slip silicon discs that can be scattered in clumps across the floor.

Flood Light represents the increasingly subversive tendencies of many young designers who are uninterested in simply churning out fancy new products for manufacturers and instead imbue their work with social commentary and narrative that was previously the preserve of artists. The design expresses the childish desire to ignore parental warnings and plunge live electrical devices into water. It is also a comment on Britain's obsessive safety culture which, for example, does not allow electrical sockets to be placed in bathrooms.

Leaf

Date **2006**
Designer **Yves Behar**
Material **Aluminium and LED lights**
Manufacturer **Herman Miller, USA**

The commercial lighting industry has proven surprisingly resistant to new lighting technologies, with most products on the market resolutely sticking with filament bulbs as their light sources. Yet these are inefficient, create vast amounts of heat, require bulky housings and need replacing frequently. They also lack versatility: if you want to change the colour or tone of the light, you have to change the bulb.

The Leaf task light, designed by Yves Behar for American contract furniture giant Herman Miller, exploits developments in LED technology. It features 12 LEDs that combine to provide an infinite variety of lighting effects. Besides varying the intensity, the user can also adjust the colour spectrum, choosing between cool lighting for efficient working to warm for a more atmospheric effect. The LEDs consume less than 40 per cent of the energy of traditional LEDs and less than half that of halogen or fluorescent bulbs. They also remain cool due to the fact that rather than burn continuously, they are constantly being switched on and off. This happens at such high speed that the flickering effect is invisible to the human eye.

Formally, the light is both visually dramatic and structurally simple, bearing a resemblance to a striking cobra or a praying mantis. Behar has dispensed with the mechanical complexity common to most task lighting – people rarely adjust the position of their desk lights, after all – and instead designed an articulated arm consisting of just two parts. These are blades of aluminium that have been hydroformed – a relatively new manufacturing process that allows for the precise forming of curved metal parts and which involves using a mould that is pressurized hydraulically. Each blade twists through 180 degrees, allowing the horizontal arm to be folded against the vertical to provide an ambient, rather than a direct, lighting effect. The flex is concealed within a seam running down the centre of each blade, much like the vein that runs the length of a blade of grass or a leaf.

Ruminant Bloom

Date **2005**
Designer **Julia Lohmann**
Material **Sheep intestines**

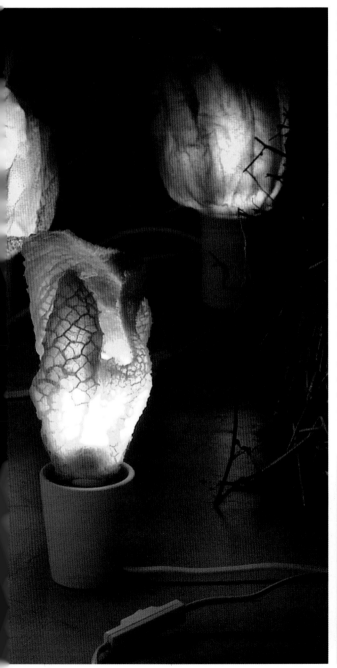

UK-based designer Julia Lohmann was born in Hildesheim in Germany in 1977 and became interested in design after the country walks she took with her father when, together, they would create strange creatures from the abandoned objects they found. She is now part of a new generation of designers who see design as being about more than just solving a functional problem. While her creations always have a practical use, they are also intended to provoke the viewer emotionally, triggering feelings of attraction, shock and disgust. Her Ruminant Bloom project achieves this through the use of an unusual material to create beautiful lights with strangely decorative surface patterns that glow mysteriously when lit from within.

The lights appear at first to have been constructed using rapid prototyping techniques or some other high-tech manufacturing process – but the viewer is often shocked to learn they are in fact made from preserved sheep stomachs. Lohmann began to explore the use of animal by-products when studying design products at the Royal College of Art in London, using worthless offal and leather off-cuts to create objects. Her choice of material is driven partly by the desire to explore people's complex emotional responses to animal husbandry, forcing them to make the connection between animals in the field and meat on the plate. Another project that achieves the same effect is Cow Benches: leather-clad forms that resemble the torsos of cows resting in a field.

Lohmann also views her choice of materials as a form of recycling, using animal off-cuts that would otherwise be thrown away. She collects the tripe from slaughterhouses and dries it over moulds to create the strange, ballooning forms, each of which is unique. A similar process is used to create Flock, a ceiling light made of a cluster of 50 inflated sheep stomachs, each with a light inside.

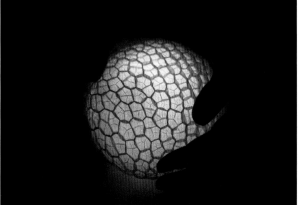

Homeware

If the tail end of twentieth century was largely characterized by functional homeware that displayed truth to materials and spare forms, designers in the twenty-first century seem to be busy overturning the tenets of minimalism and instead exploring ways of investing objects with colour, pattern and references from history and nature. Every generation reacts against the taste of the preceding generation and in many ways this is simply a return to how things were before Modernism became a ubiquitous style. It seems to be, at least partly, down to a yearning among designers to reconnect with the past and to create objects with idiosyncratic character and personal meaning.

But far from turning their backs on new materials and techniques, designers are embracing both and applying them in unexpected ways. Robert Dawson's After Willow plates, for example, use digital sampling techniques and photo-printing technology to create tableware in much the same way that a musician samples old records to produce an entirely new sound. Maxim Velcovsky's Digi Clock takes a traditional carriage clock body and replaces the analogue display with a digital one – an idea that has subsequently been much imitated and which acknowledges that there is no reason, beyond grounds of taste, why a contemporary clock mechanism needs to be placed in a contemporary housing. Hella Jongerius' Non-Temporary earthenware range re-examines ancient majolica glazing and decorating methods, but introduces deliberate "errors" that reveal the production techniques.

In fact, like Velcovsky, many designers are playing subtle games with the notion of taste, creating pieces that verge on kitsch or even downright offensiveness. Constantin Boym's Buildings of Disaster series, for example, takes one of the most derided object typologies – the souvenir – and creates mementos of some of the most taboo subjects imaginable, such as the 9/11 terrorist attacks. Timorous Beasties' Glasgow Toile design, meanwhile, takes the techniques and motifs of eighteenth-century toile de Jouy and replaces the bucolic imagery of peasant life with scenes from contemporary Glasgow low-life.

Other designers are deliberately undermining notions of mass production, elegance and even design itself by leaving the final outcome of their products to chance, such as Front's Rat wallpaper, which is patterned by gnawing rodents, or Fernando Brizio's Painting a Fresco with Giotto bowl, which features a simple unglazed ceramic dish stained by ink leaking from coloured felt tip pens balanced on the rim. Similarly, Ineke Hans' Black Gold tableware takes the concept of modularity to an almost absurd level, reducing the number of components to just five and employing clay that has been dyed black and which deforms during the firing process. As usual, it is Marcel Wanders who has taken the new fascination with randomness and unconventional beauty to the extreme by using advanced three-dimensional scanning techniques to capture the form of mucus globules flying through the air after a sneeze and turning the resulting shapes into flower vases.

Non-Temporary Ceramics

Date **2005**
Designer **Hella Jongerius**
Material **Ceramic**
Manufacturer **Royal Tichelaar Makkum, Netherlands**

The most important female designer in the world today, Hella Jongerius straddles the boundaries between mass production and craft, mixing references from history and technology and pioneering new ways of harnessing industrial processes to create objects with the character and uniqueness of hand-made pieces. She is at the forefront of the current revival of interest in employing craft skills to personalize and enrich otherwise soulless mass-produced objects. In an age where products are homogenous and disposable, she aims to create functional objects that will be cherished for years.

Jongerius is best known for her innovative work in ceramics. In 2000, she produced a range of vases and plates decorated with patterns of cotton threads, hand-stitched through holes in the porcelain. Her Long Neck and Groove bottle range of the same year featured vases and bottles constructed of hand-crafted glass and porcelain, joined together with plastic packing tape. Her 2005 Non-Temporary tableware range for Royal Tichelaar Makkum – shown here – offers a contemporary take on traditional majolica earthenware, employing traditionally inspired patterns but leaving areas of the plates and bowls unglazed as if due to a production error, showing the raw ceramic beneath the glaze and revealing an element of the manufacturing process that is usually hidden from view.

Much of Jongerius' work is aimed at the collectors' market, including her 2004 Nymphenburg Sketches series for German porcelain manufacturer Nymphenburg, which featured kitsch animal figurines, such as hippos and hares, set on plates and decorated with fragments of patterns selected from the company's archive. In 2005, however, she was commissioned by IKEA to design a series of affordable vases for mass-production. Called Jonsberg, the four identical vases are decorated with different patterns and glazing techniques derived from different parts of the world and are hand-painted in China. This range brings Jongerius' work to the masses for the first time.

Repeat Fabrics

Date **2002**
Designer **Hella Jongerius**
Material **Various fabrics**
Manufacturer **Maharam, USA**

Hella Jongerius' 2002 Repeat series of upholstery fabric designs for New York textile company Maharam combines motifs borrowed from vintage patterns she found in the company's archives with elements derived from the manufacturing process itself, such as scribbled technical information and patterns of dots derived from the punch cards that control the looms in the company's factories. The textiles have a 3 m (10 ft) repeat – an unprecedented length for a manufactured product – meaning that items of furniture upholstered in the fabric will appear unique.

Jongerius was born in De Meern in the Netherlands in 1963 and studied industrial design at the Eindhoven Design Academy, graduating in 1993. Like so many fellow Dutch designers, such as Marcel Wanders and Jurgen Bey, she came to prominence during the 1990s thanks to the influential Droog collective, which manufactured and exhibited many of her early pieces. She now runs her own studio,

JongeriusLab, in Rotterdam, designing homeware, fabrics and furniture for brands including Maharam, Royal Tichelaar Makkum, Vitra and IKEA. Yet Jongerius' dislike of the media circus that surrounds the contemporary design world means that she keeps a low profile and, as a result, her work is not as well known as that of lesser designers.

Her early pieces were austere and experimental in their use of materials, such as her Bath Mat – a rectangular piece of polyurethane with a pattern of bubbles resembling water droplets – which was exhibited in the first ever Droog show in Milan in 1993, and her 1996 Folded Washtub – a flexible washbasin made of moulded polyurethane. Since then, her work has gradually become richer, more detailed and more daring in the way it challenges the norms of mass production. In particular, she is known for introducing deliberate errors and hand-crafted elements into manufactured goods, subverting the perfection and uniformity of industrial products.

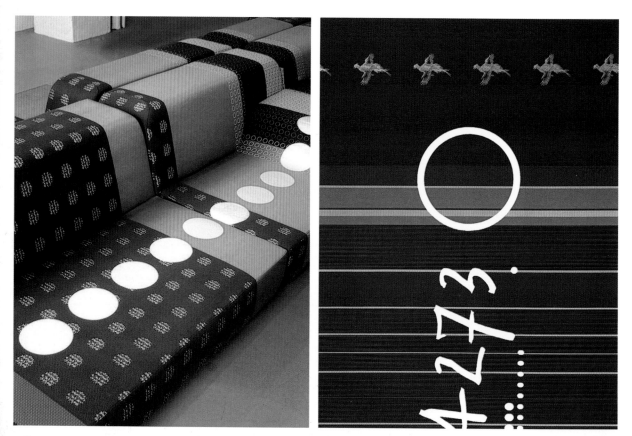

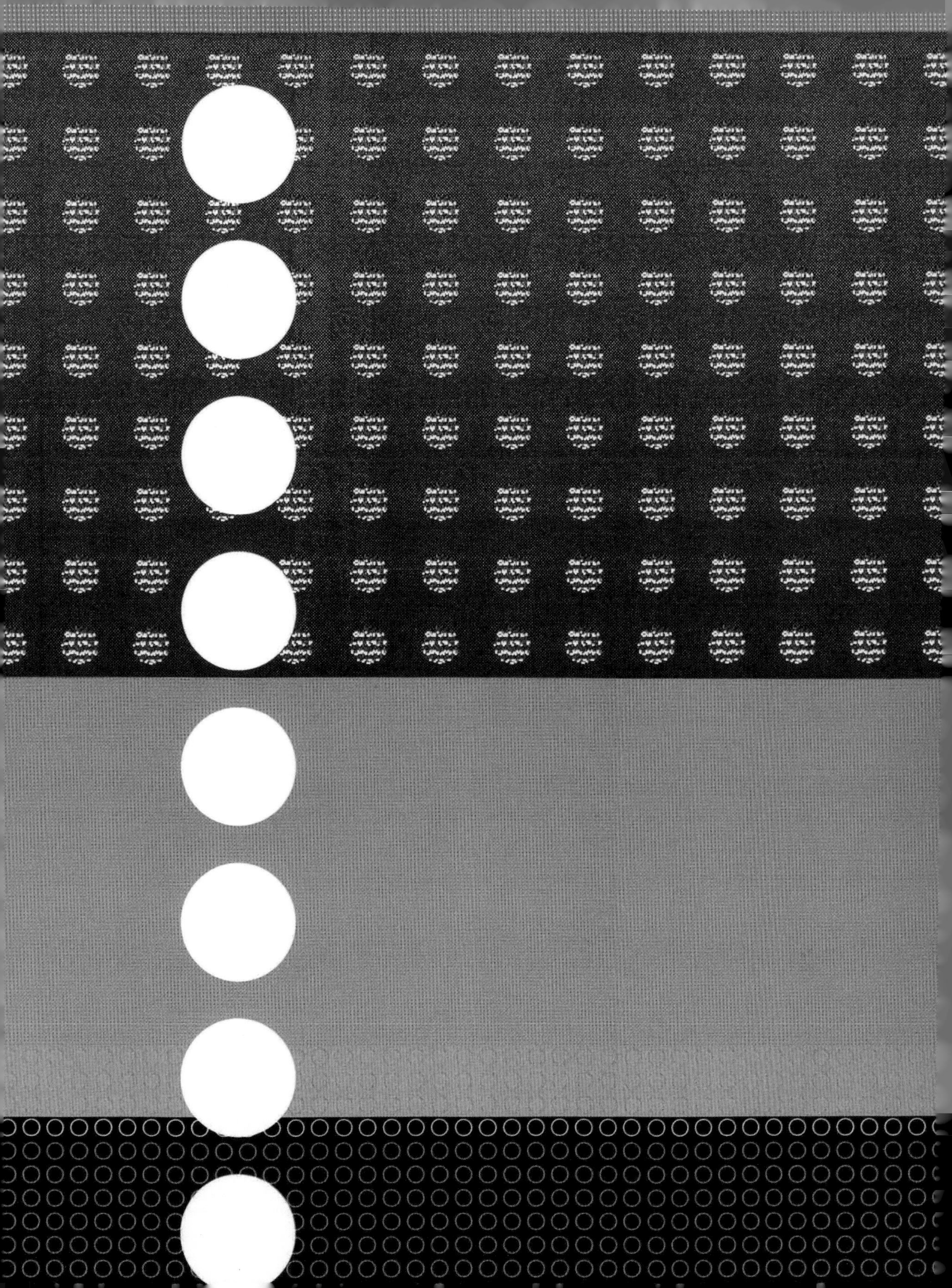

Glasgow Toile

Date **2005**
Designer **Timorous Beasties**
Material **Textiles and wallpaper**

Glaswegian textile and wallpaper designers Timorous Beasties introduced a strong dose of social realism into the twenty-first century vogue for all things decorative and historic with this 2005 fabric pattern. Glasgow Toile is based on the toile de Jouy fabrics produced in the French town of Jouy-en-Josas in the 1770s, which depicted often grimly realistic scenes of rural folk going about their work and leisure.

Timorous Beasties have borrowed the illustrative style and printing techniques of toile de Jouy but updated the motifs to include images of drunks sitting on park benches, teenagers urinating against trees and other low-life, nightmarish scenes from contemporary Glasgow. The design helped Timorous Beasties founders Alistair McAuley and Paul Simmons earn a place on the shortlist for the Design Museum's Designer of the Year 2005, which secured them international attention. Later that same year they produced a version called London Toile, which featured similar scenes enacted against a backdrop of famous London landmarks.

The company takes its name from a line in the Scottish poet Robert Burn's poem 'To a Mouse'. McAuley and Simmons met at the Glasgow School of Art in the 1980s and established their company, Timorous Beasties, in 1990 to design and hand-print their textile and wall-covering designs. They started out by working on interiors projects for local bars and restaurants. Their eclectic portfolio includes romantic florals and bold geometric designs, but much of their work – such as Insects, a wallpaper that mixes creepy-crawlies in with more traditional butterflies and tropical birds, and Oriental Orchid, a rich floral fabric themed around the sexual life of plants – gently subverts traditional styles.

Other examples of the company's designs also show irreverence and humour. Force 10 features a design based on the symbols that are used on meteorological charts, and Euro Damask approximates the traditional symmetrical motif with a design that is made up of the outlines of European countries.

Missoni Home Collection

Date **2004**

Designer **Rosita Missoni**

Material **Ceramics and textiles**

Manufacturer **Missoni, Italy**

Italian fashion house Missoni has long been renowned for its unmistakable, kaleidoscopic knits and prints. In 2003 Missoni Home – its offshoot homewares line – began releasing a seasonal range of soft furnishings and tableware, introducing bright colours and bold patterns from the catwalk to what had previously been the relatively austere world of tableware. The 2004 Home Collection, which borrowed floral patterns in both colour and black and white from Missoni's spring 2003 fashion collection, was by far the most successful of these. The range proved highly influential, coinciding with the general revival of interest in colour and pattern in design and interiors, and leading to a glut of copycat tableware ranges.

Missoni Home came about when Rosita Missoni, who co-founded the brand with her husband Ottavio "Tai" Missoni in the 1950s, retired from the fashion side of the business to concentrate on the homeware range, leaving the fashion lines to her daughter Angela. Rosita and Tai Missoni met at the Olympic Games held at Wembley Stadium in London in 1948 – she was a spectator while he was a member of the Italian team and competed in the 400 m hurdles. Tai had already established himself as a clothing entrepreneur, having invested in some newfangled knitting machines and designing and producing the Italian Olympic team's uniform.

Missoni's hippy-chic clothes became extremely popular in the 1960s, when the brand's ethnically inspired stripes and florals established it as one of the most influential names in global fashion. The company's venture into homeware came at a time when many international fashion houses – including Armani, Fendi and Donna Karan – started to do the same, as their increasingly corporate business structures demanded growth into new markets. However, most of these ventures resulted in rather bland furnishings and the much-predicted merging of the fashion, furniture and homeware products has yet to materialize.

Particularly notable are the products designed in collaboration with New York designer Stephen Burks. His Patchwork Collection vases are covered in scraps of patterned fabric rescued from Missoni's factory while the Missoni Mogu Fun Fun! range consists of stools and cushions fashioned from Japanese manufacturer Mogu's Styrofoam bead-filled sausages and blobs, which Burks has covered in similarly patchworks of Missoni off-cuts. Both ranges were launched in Milan during the 2004 Furniture Fair.

Rat Wallpaper

Date **2005**
Designer **Front**
Material **Paper**

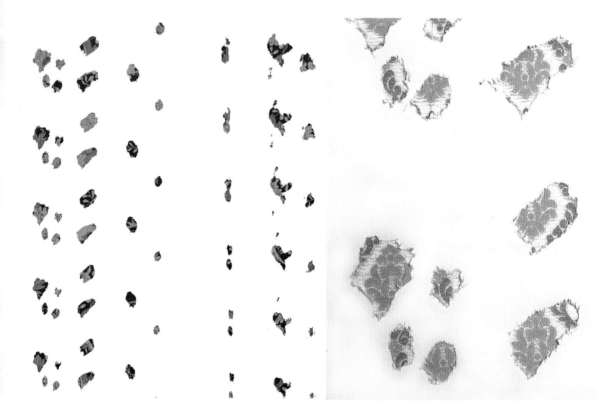

Rather than being the work of designers, the patterns on this wallpaper (shown above) are produced by the teeth-marks of hungry rats. Rolls of plain wallpaper were placed in a cage full of rats, which gnawed at the paper to create a random pattern of holes. When used to paper a room, the holes allow the original paper to show through. The design is part of a conceptual project by Swedish design outfit Front. The project, called Design by Animals, explores how accident, rather than intent, can be harnessed to create form and pattern.

The range includes Dog vase – a dog's footprint in deep snow that has been cast and hollowed out, and Snake hanger – a clothes hanger formed by wrapping a snake around a thin cylinder of clay. As the snake squeezes the clay, it creates indentations that become a pattern on the completed object. Another piece is Fly lamp – the path of a fly buzzing around a light bulb was recorded using motion capture technology. The path is then materialized using rapid prototyping technology to create a thin, random line that acts as an insubstantial shade. Front also used motion capture technology to produce their Sketch range of furniture (see page 149).

The Design by Animals range is completed by Rabbit lamp – a cast of a rabbit hole used to make a lamp – and Insect table – a wooden table with a top that is decorated with a pattern derived from the excavations of woodworm in old pieces of timber. The pattern was scanned and recreated on the surface of the object using a computer-numerically-controlled (CNC) router.

Interactive Wallpaper

Date **2002**
Designer **Rachel Kelly**
Material **Vinyl, foil and fabric**

Interactive wallpaper is an interior decor product that allows the user to create his or her own bespoke patterns. It consists of two parts: a patterned wallpaper and a range of patterned stickers that are applied to the background paper. The product, created by London-based designer Rachel Kelly, capitalizes on the recent revival of interest in both wallpaper and bold floral patterns after years of being considered the height of kitsch. It also reflects the growing interest in customizable products, where consumers add their own touches and the role of the designer is downplayed.

The wallpaper is manufactured in a range of simple patterns. The stickers – which are made of vinyl, foil and fabric – come in a variety of abstract floral patterns and a range of colours, which coordinate with the wallpaper patterns. The stickers can be removed and replaced, which means a room can be redecorated easily. The stickers can also be applied to other items, such as furniture, windows and floors.

Kelly, who was born in Edinburgh, Scotland, studied printed textile and surface pattern design at Leeds College of Art and Design, later completing a masters in textiles at Central St Martin's College of Art in London. She mostly produces her wallpapers for private commissions, creating bespoke background patterns upon which the client is encouraged to add their own choice of stickers. She has recently started producing a range of batch-produced wallpapers for general sale, and a range of transfers to complement the stickers.

Biscuit Ceramics

Date **2006**
Designer **Studio Job**
Material **Ceramic**
Manufacturer **Royal Tichelaar Makkum, Netherlands**

Decorated with a relief pattern featuring skulls, poodles and sperm, the Biscuit range of ceramics is a typically idiosyncratic and subversive work by Dutch-Belgian duo Studio Job. The range consists of nine plates and five centre pieces – a cake stand, lantern, candlestick, vase and a container. They were created in 2006 for Royal Tichelaar Makkum, the oldest ceramics' brand in the Netherlands, which was established in 1572. In recent years the company been reinvigorated by working with well-known avant-garde designers, such as Hella Jongerius (Non-Temporary

ceramics, see page 247), Jurgen Bey and Marcel Wanders. Yet the Biscuit range is perhaps the brand's bravest collection.

Studio Job, which is run by Job Smeets and Nynke Tynagel, works on the margin of good taste exploring subjects such as death, decay and decadence in their work. Made of unfinished, off-white ceramic, the Biscuit range takes its name from the industrial term for clay that has been fired but not glazed. The relief patterns decorating each object are made up of elements associated with the colour white: one

plate features a central motif of a skeleton, lambs and white flags surrounded by a border of bones, while a white, Pierrot-style clown adorns the underside. Elsewhere, sea shells, rockets, ambulances and even the White House appear. Studio Job's designs often incorporate elements most designers would consider unsavoury. The 2003 Bugs pattern consisted of silhouettes of insects applied to everything from clothing to porcelain. In 2006, they created a pattern featuring the skeletons of humans, Neanderthals and jungle animals.

Software as Furniture

Date **2002**
Designer **Daniel Brown**
Material **Digital media**

The merger of screen-based technology and interior design is something that has been endlessly mooted, but convincing applications have been thin on the ground. Movies such as 2002's *Minority Report* – in which the Tom Cruise character John Anderton strolled through shopping malls featuring wall-to-wall digital advertising that addressed him personally – posited a sinister vision of all-encompassing interactive surfaces that have resolutely remained in the domain of science fiction, and most attempts at producing interactive interior landscapes have been somewhat crude. The work of digital designer Daniel Brown is an exception and his breathtakingly beautiful creations led him to be named the Design Museum in London's Designer of the Year in 2003.

Brown's Software as Furniture project – which was instrumental in his winning the award – explores how digital animations could be transposed from the computer screen and into the home. The work consists of constantly growing images of blossom-like forms, resembling time-lapse photography of growing plants, which can be displayed on plasma screens or projected onto walls to produce digital canvases or wallpaper (see left). Called generative animation, the patterns mutate randomly but within a set of predetermined parameters, mimicking natural processes. Brown subsequently developed the Software as Furniture concept to create kaleidoscopic patterns that are designed to be projected onto plain white porcelain plates and tablecloths (see right).

Brown, born in Liverpool in 1977, is a leading figure in digital art and design, pioneering ways of exploiting the potential of the Internet as a vehicle for visual works of great beauty and complexity – rather than the sterile, flat imagery that dominated the web in its early years – through his websites noodlebox.com (which he launched in 1997) and play-create.com. He now works extensively for SHOWstudio, the online showcase for fashion and digital media.

Blossoms Vase

Date **2004**
Designer **Wieki Somers**
Material **Ceramic, glass and transfer print**
Manufacturer **Cor Unum, Netherlands**

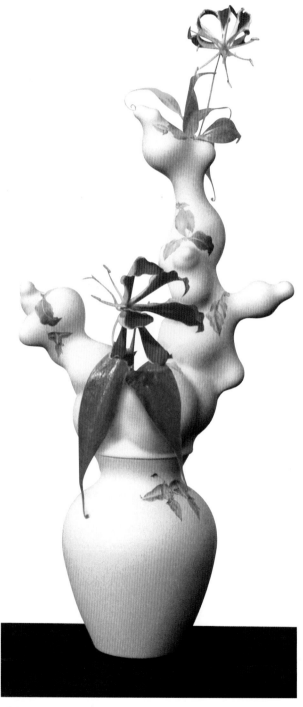

The aesthetic effect of Wieki Somer's work is often based on natural forms that are exaggerated and distorted until they are decadent and almost grotesque. Her Blossoms vase was designed in 2004 for Cor Unum, a Dutch ceramics company founded in 1953, which commissions a number of young designers each year to explore the potential of ceramics and presents the results in Milan during the Furniture Fair. It intended not just to contain flowers but also to complement – or perhaps even upstage – their beauty.

The ceramic vase resembles an abstract, globular, budding branch and is made of two cast sections – the base and the sculptural upper part – that are glued together. Flowers are held in three short glass tubes that slot into the ceramic branches. The vase, which stands 530 cm (210 in) high, comes in two versions – a black one printed with skeletal flowers in metallic white and a pale green one printed with green leaves. It is intended to be an object of unnerving beauty in its own right, but by inserting flowers in the glass tubes the vase is transformed into a strange blossoming tree.

Wieki Somers was born in 1976 in Sprang-Capelle in the Netherlands and now works in Rotterdam. She is part of what is being described as the second generation of contemporary Dutch designers who draw on the highly conceptual but somewhat austere approach of the "Droog generation" – designers who rose to prominence in the 1990s – but add a liberal dose of gratuitous aesthetics. Besides the Blossoms vase, Somers is known for her High Tea Pot, a teapot made of fine bone china in the form of a pig's skull with a teacosy made of rat fur. The unsavoury appearance of the pot is intended to make you reconsider how the tea might taste.

Digi Clock

Date **2002**
Designer **Maxim Velcovsky**
Material **Porcelain and digital display**

Maxim Velcovsky is one of the most exciting young design talents to emerge from the former Communist Bloc states of Central and Eastern Europe. Born in 1976 in what is now the Czech Republic, he is forging a new design language that both celebrates and makes fun of Czech traditions and tastes. Much of his work is in porcelain and glass – materials which have a strong craft tradition in his homeland. Yet production of both was industrialized and debased under Soviet influence, and Velcovsky is part of a movement to rediscover and reinvent lost traditions. His 2002 Digi clock features an ornate slip-moulded porcelain clock body with a digital liquid crystal display attached in place of the face and hands. The porcelain shells are rejects from a Czech factory that mass-produces Rococo-style carriage clocks, and which usually feature ornate cobalt blue decoration and rustic analogue hands.

Velcovsky instead takes the unadorned bodies, adding a playfully subversive touch to an already kitsch object. It is part of an expanding series of objects Velcovsky calls his White Collection, which take unpainted porcelain objects and give them new life. Other pieces in the series include his Moneyboxes, in which he turns rejected hollow porcelain wildlife figurines into useful objects by cutting a coin slot into them. The figures have to be smashed to get the money out.

Velcovsky's work also refers to the dramatic changes he has seen since the Velvet Revolution. His 2001 Coke XL is a ceramic cup cast in the form of the lower part of a plastic Coke bottle. It turns an item, synonymous with fast-food culture, into a luxury object and something disposable into something valuable. His 2005 Fast cup and wine glass made the same point, but in glass. The beaker is an extremely thin glass replica of a plastic drinks-dispenser cup.

Algue

Date **2004**
Designer **Ronan and Erwan Bouroullec**
Material **Polypropylene**
Manufacturer **Vitra, France**

This clip-together product by French designers Ronan and Erwan Bouroullec is ground-breaking as it constitutes a new design typology, sitting somewhere between homeware, furniture and architecture. The flexible, moulded polypropylene elements resemble seaweed or branches and feature poppers that enable them to be snapped together and suspended from a special track to create wall hangings, sculptures, room dividers or entire interior landscapes. They can even be used outside as screens or trellises for plants. Similar to an adult version of Lego, they are manufactured by Vitra and sold in boxes of either six or 50 identical pieces and come in a range of colours, meaning that people can add to or reconfigure their Algue collection. Joined end to end they create a permeable two-dimensional screen, but by adding more elements, a dense, multilayered effect can be achieved. The product comes without instructions or suggested uses: the brothers leave it up to the user to decide exactly what to do with the pieces.

This willingness to provide open-ended uses for their products is typical of the Bouroullecs and makes their creations among the most interesting of any available today. They reject the notion of design as a way of addressing specific problems and instead give the user the tools to create their own object. The concept subverts the notion of modularity – which, in the hands of most designers, usually only offers a pre-determined range of options – and is similar to that employed in the Bouroullecs' Cloud shelving system (see page 139) and Joyn desk system (page 144), both of which consist of elements that can be configured in an endless variety of ways. Algue builds on another project the brothers developed in 2002 called BETC. This was a system of identical polypropylene elements, resembling clothes pegs, which could be hung in a variety of ways on horizontal wires to create screens for roof terraces to protect against sun and wind.

Like so many promising young designers, the Bouroullecs were discovered by Giulio Cappellini, the legendary head of Italian furniture brand Cappellini, who spotted Ronan's Disintegrated Kitchen at an exhibition in Paris in 1997. This was a system that rejected the standard fitted, made-to-measure kitchen and instead proposed something more flexible: skeletal units that could be reconfigured like furniture and taken with you when you move.

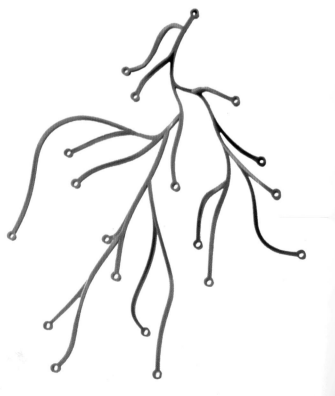

Airborne Snotty Vases

Date **2001**
Designer **Marcel Wanders**
Material **Polyamide**
Manufacturer **Cappellini, Italy**

Designers have always drawn on natural forms as inspiration for their products but this project by Marcel Wanders takes it to a new extreme. Using the latest digital-scanning technology it captures the form of mucus particles emitted during a sneeze and turns them into vases.

Called Airborne Snotty, the series consists of five vases named after five different diseases of the nasal cavity: ozaena (fetid discharge), pollinosis (hay fever), coryza (runny nose), influenza and sinusitis. The

project began by digitally recording a human sneeze with a three-dimensional scanner. The scanner, which resembles a magnifying glass without a lens, took a snapshot of the rain of microscopic mucus particles as they flew through the air. They were then transferred to a computer.

From the thousands of particles scanned, the design team then selected five individual particles that would form the basis of the vases. These were enlarged from their original miniscule scale to an

average size of 15 cm by 15 cm by 15 cm (6 in by 6 in by 6 in) and digitally edited to create hollows in which flowers could be placed to allow them to function as vases. The finished computer files were sent to a rapid prototyping machine, which printed the vases in polyamide. The five vases that were created as a result of this process were each named after one of the nasal diseases. They went on sale in 2001 and a complete set was purchased by Amsterdam's Stedelijk Museum.

With Airborne Snotty, Wanders is one of a number of designers exploring the potential of high-tech scanning techniques. Others include architect Frank Gehry, who uses three-dimensional scanners to digitize the sculptural cardboard and paper models he makes in his studio, while Swedish design outfit Front have produced a range of furniture formed by sketching chairs, tables and lamps in the air with a hand-held motion capture scanner (see page 149).

Do Break Vase

Date **2001**
Designer **Frank Tjepkema**
Material **Porcelain and rubber**
Manufacturer **Droog, Netherlands**

Every vase breaks eventually, reasons Dutch designer Frank Tjepkema – who also designed the Bling Bling pendant (see page 369) – so why not produce a vase that is designed to be broken? Called Do Break, Tjepkema's design consists of a simple, cigar-shaped porcelain object that is lined with a layer of rubber. The vase comes with instructions urging the buyer to smash the vase: on impact, the rubber lining holds the ceramic fragments together while the fracture lines create a random pattern on the surface of the vase. Thus the normally destructive act of breaking the vase actually increases its beauty and uniqueness. The lining also ensures that the product remains watertight after breaking.

The Do Break vase is one of several recent examples in which designers have used random, uncontrollable factors to create form or pattern: the Design by Animals series by Swedish group Front involves getting rats, snakes and other creatures to intervene in their projects (see page 254), while Dutch designer Marcel Wanders' Airborne Snotty vases (page 268) are based on scans of human mucus droplets flying through the air following a sneeze.

Tjepkema's product was designed for Dutch brand Droog in 2001 as part of a conceptual design project called Do Create. Droog, working with advertising agency Kessels Kramer, invited a number of leading designers to create objects where the user was invited to leave their mark on the product. Other examples of the series include Do Hit by Marijn van der Poll – a cube of thin steel sheet that is supplied along with a sledge hammer that the consumer uses to smash a seat-shaped indentation into the metal; Do Frame by Martí Guixé – a roll of adhesive tape printed with a decorative border, which the user employs to tape a favourite picture to the wall, creating a custom-sized frame in the process; and Thomas Bernstrand's Do Swing – a ceiling light fixture that can be swung on.

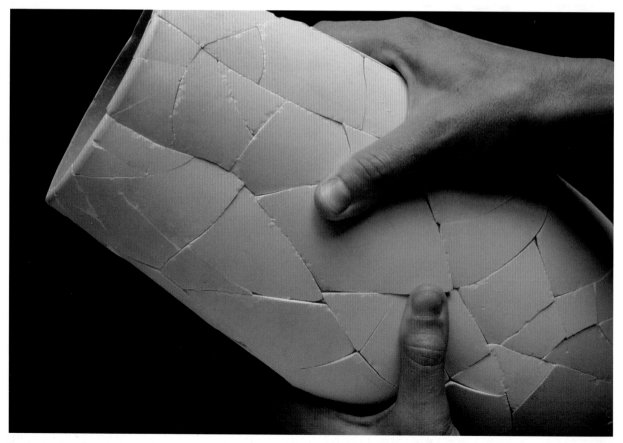

Black Gold

Date **2005**
Designer **Ineke Hans**
Material **Porcelain**

This range of porcelain ware by one of the leading Dutch designers, Ineke Hans, is as striking as it is unsettling. Using a black pigment that is not normally associated with ceramics, and that weakens the clay structurally, the pieces have a resultingly lopsided appearance. The range is the result of Hans' three-month residency at the European Ceramics Work Centre – a residential centre of excellence in Hertogenbosch in the Netherlands that invites designers to experiment with ceramic production techniques and which has done much to stimulate the revival of interest in ceramics among contemporary designers. While at the centre, Hans developed an interest in the way tableware is mass-produced from moulded elements – such as a mug and handle or a teapot and spout – that are "welded" together using slip clay. Her Black Gold range is an exploration of how to make the maximum number of different items from the minimum number of different moulded elements.

Hans, who was born in 1966 in the Netherlands and graduated from the Hogeschool voor de Kunsten in Arnhem in 1991 and the Royal College of Art in London in 1995, is now based in Arnhem. She produced a total of just five modular, moulded forms – tubes of three different diameters, a bent section and a funnel shape – that can be combined to produce vases, coffee pots, candelabras and so on. Each shape is designed to be used in various ways: for example, the narrow tube has an internal diameter suitable for holding candles and an external diameter appropriate for a handle. These elements are then manipulated, cut and joined together to produce the pieces in the range. Though entirely rational, the pieces have a primitive quality that is more akin to plumbing elements than fine dining ware, while the use of black pigment renders them even more unusual. Since it affects the strength of the clay, it also causes the larger elements to buckle during firing (see also page 174).

Eco Ware

Date **2003**
Designer **Tom Dixon**
Material **Biodegradable organic fibre plastic**

Although most contemporary designers profess concern about the environment and support the concept of sustainability, many recognize the paradox of their position: a large part of any designer's job is to encourage greater consumption by making objects look good and function well, so more people will want to buy them. This, inevitably, uses up more resources and creates more waste and pollution. The solution, of course, lies in the development of new non-polluting, biodegradable materials – but scientists have yet to produce sustainable materials that compete with plastics and metals in terms of performance and cost.

British designer Tom Dixon explores this conundrum with a range of cups, plates and bowls manufactured from a relatively new type of plastic made of organic fibres. Called Eco Ware, the rugged, earthy-looking range was launched at the Milan Furniture Fair in 2003. The material consists of 85 per cent bamboo-fibre – a by-product of the bamboo processing industry, which would otherwise be thrown away. It is ground to a powder and mixed with a water-soluble polymer to create a tough, durable thermosetting plastic material that resembles Bakelite and which can be moulded like traditional plastics. Similar materials have been developed using other organic by-products, such as coconut husks or rice fibres.

The drawback is that the material is biodegradable – it disintegrates over time as the products are used and washed, their shiny, smooth surfaces wearing away. But Dixon has turned this into an advantage, pointing out that the objects take on a new and more interesting character as they are used. Their lifespan is around five years – similar to the expected life of many more conventional items of tableware – and after this time they can be reused as plant pots or composted rather than thrown away. Eco Ware therefore represents one of the more successful attempts by designers to create genuinely sustainable products.

In future, as scientists develop better-performing organic-based plastics, domestic products with short lifespans may increasingly be produced from biodegradable materials.

Domoor Mug

Date **2002**
Designer **Richard Hutten**
Material **PPC plastic**

Richard Hutten originally designed this mug in 2000 for German TV station RTL+ to give away to the viewers of one of its children's programmes. However, the 26 cm (10 in) wide object became so popular that he put it into production, switching the ceramic of the original version to soft, pliable PPC plastic, which comes in blue, orange and purple. It is now recognized as a classic example of humorous Dutch design and is in the permanent collection of the Stedelijk Museum of Modern Art in Amsterdam.

Its name is a Dutch pun: *domoor* is a word used when someone does something daft and is a compound of *dom*, which means dumb, and *oor*, which means both handle and ear. Hutten designed the mug to be as wide as his then three-year-old son Abel, with its massively inflated handles exaggerating the movement of drinking, thereby turning an everyday action into a huge gesture. The mug has been extremely popular with disabled people, as the enormous handles are very easy to grip.

Hutten is best known for his furniture designs. Born in 1967 in Zwollerkerspel in the Netherlands, he graduated from Design Academy Eindhoven in 1991 and in the same year set up his own studio in Rotterdam to produce his furniture. His graduate collection included Chair table, a witty yet austere two-piece design that featured a square wooden stool and a separate four-legged arm rest. This piece was one of the earliest designs to be produced by Droog – of which he was a founder member – and remains one of Hutten's best-known works. The minimal simplicity of his work has made him extremely popular in Far Eastern countries such as Japan, and also Korea where he is due to open his own design academy in 2008.

After Willow Ceramics

Date **2004**
Designer **Robert Dawson**
Material **Ceramic**
Manufacturer **Wedgwood, UK**

Ceramic artist Robert Dawson's After Willow series pays cheeky homage to one of the most popular of all traditional English porcelain designs. With its blue-on-white patterns depicting oriental river scenes of birds, bridges and pagodas on islands, the Willow style was developed in the eighteenth century as a mass-produced imitation of fine imported Chinese porcelain ware and has been made by numerous manufacturers ever since. The design tells the story of two lovers who were forbidden contact with one another and whose souls, on their death, finally come together as two birds. However Willow, like decorative ceramics in general, went out of fashion in the latter half of the twentieth century, when it was seen as kitsch and old-fashioned. Manufacturers who produced Willow designs – notably Wedgwood, the venerable brand established in 1759 by Sir Josiah Wedgwood – found themselves struggling as a result.

Dawson, who was born in New York in 1953, studied ceramics and fine art at Camberwell School of Art and the Royal College in London, and now has his own studio called Aesthetic Sabotage. He first began experimenting with cutting and pasting elements of Willow designs in the 1990s as an act of subversion, employing photomontage techniques of cropping and pasting to create abstract designs, considered radical at the time.

With traditional designs undergoing a revival of popularity in the early twenty-first century, Dawson was approached by Georgina Godley, a former fashion designer and head of contemporary homeware retailer Habitat, who had been appointed creative director at Wedgwood to restore the brand's credibility. The result is a range of tableware based on Dawson's earlier designs and featuring traditional Willow elements that are cut out, blown up and rearranged on bone china dinner plates. The range has been hugely successful, helping rejuvenate the Wedgwood brand, and Dawson has recently designed a second range for the company. Called After Landscape, it similarly distorts the Italianate landscape engravings that were popular in the nineteenth century.

Origo

Date **1999**
Designer **Alfredo Häberli**
Material **Porcelain**
Manufacturer **Iittala, Finland**

Although Häberli specializes in furniture design, he is probably best known for his phenomenally successful and distinctive Origo table service range for Finnish company Iittala – a brand that is famous for producing the glassware design of legendary Finnish architect and designer Alva Aalto and his wife Eina Aalto. When first launched in 1999, the range consisted of plain white porcelain plates, bowls and cups – the patterns of horizontal stripes of different colours and widths only appeared on the smallest items. But the striped pieces proved so popular that Häberli introduced colour throughout the range. Origo now comes in a huge variety of pieces, with six different colourways – blue, pink, orange, beige, dark brown and petrol blue – which are designed to be mixed and matched.

While the cheerful stripes have made Origo one of the most recognizable tableware ranges of recent years, the colours and pattern have tended to outshine the inventiveness of the pieces themselves, which are designed around contemporary living and

eating habits. Häberli's deep bowls and handle-less mugs are designed to stack inside one another for efficient storage and rapid table clearance, while the high sides also mean they can be used for informal dining or even for eating from while walking around the kitchen. The multipurpose bowls in five different sizes can be used for everything from cereal and soup to tea or coffee, or as party snack servers. Besides Origo, Häberli has also designed two wine glasses – Essence and Senta – for Iittala.

Alfredo Häberli was born in Buenos Aires, Argentina, in 1964 and moved to Switzerland with his family in 1977. He studied industrial design at the School of Art and Design in Zurich (HGK, Höhere Schule für Gestaltung und Kunst) and graduated in 1991, when he won the diploma prize. He worked for several years as an exhibition designer at the Museum of Design in Zurich and set up his own studio there in 1993. Häberli has since designed furniture for leading companies, including Edra, Driade and Cappellini.

Painting a Fresco with Giotto Bowl

Date **2006**
Designer **Fernando Brizio**
Material **Ceramic and fibre-tip pens**

The ugly marks made by pens leaking in shirt pockets were the inspiration behind this bowl by Portuguese designer Fernando Brizio. Called Painting a Fresco with Giotto, it features an unglazed earthenware pot with 75 coloured felt-tip pens fixed, point downwards, around the rim. Over time, ink from the pens leaks into the porous ceramic, creating an irregular kaleidoscopic pattern. The name of the vase comes from the Giotto Turbocolor brand of colouring pens that Brizio used to make the bowl. He has employed the same technique on a vase, which features dozens of pens sticking out like cactus spikes, each leaving a circular stain of colour on the vase's surface. He has also created a cotton skirt, called Clothes Make-Up, decorated with large splodges of colour from leaking pens, which are attached to the fabric.

Born in 1968, Brizio is one of Portugal's leading designers. Along with others, such as Swedish group Front (see pages 146, 149 and 254), he is one of a number of young European designers who explore how accidental, uncontrollable factors can be harnessed to create magical effects.

Among his other creations is Journey, a series of unglazed white ceramic vases and bowls that were placed in the back of a van and taken on a bumpy journey immediately after being thrown and before being fired. The resulting deformities to the objects ensure that each one is unique and provides a strong narrative. When the pieces were exhibited in Lisbon during the city's Experimenta design festival in September 2005, they were accompanied by a video recording of their creation on a potter's wheel and their subsequent deformation.

Other works by Brizio, such as his salt and pepper shakers for Dutch ceramics manufacturer Cor Unum, employ a humorous approach. Their simple rectangular forms have been embellished by pressing standard café-style cruet pieces into their sides.

Buildings of Disaster

Date **2001**

Designer **Constantin Boym**

Material **Bonded nickel**

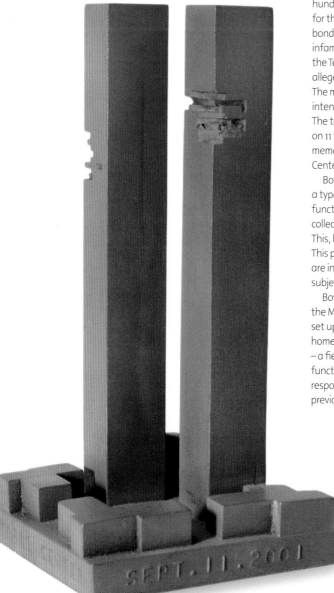

As the twentieth century drew to a close, New York designer Constantin Boym decided to produce a series of keepsakes immortalizing key events that had occurred during the previous hundred years. His Buildings of Disaster series – subtitled "Souvenirs for the end of the century" – consisted of a range of miniature, bonded-nickel figurines representing buildings synonymous with infamous events. These included the reactor number 4 at Chernobyl, the Texas School Book Depository (from which Lee Harvey Oswald allegedly shot John F Kennedy) and the Unabomber's mountain hut. The models were produced in numbered, limited editions, with the intention of ceasing production of the series on 31 December, 2000. The terrorist attacks on the World Trade Center and the Pentagon on 11 September 2001, however, led Boym to release a limited edition memorial set consisting of models of both buildings. The World Trade Center model stands 15 cm (6 in) high and quickly sold out.

Boym's motivation was to explore the concept of the souvenir – a typology of object usually shunned by designers as it is non-functional and kitsch, but which fulfils the very human desire to collect objects that remind them of things they have experienced. This, he believes, makes them valid subjects for designers to tackle. This provocative project recognizes that media-saturated tragedies are increasingly part of popular culture and therefore as worthy a subject for keepsakes as holidays or public events.

Boym, who was born in Moscow, Russia, in 1955 and studied at the Moscow Architecture Institute and the Domus Academy in Milan, set up his design studio in New York in 1986. He designs furniture, homeware and products and is an exponent of "critical design" – a field that frees designers from the need to justify their work on functional terms and instead allows them to produce objects that respond to emotional needs. This approach takes design into areas previously considered the preserve of artists.

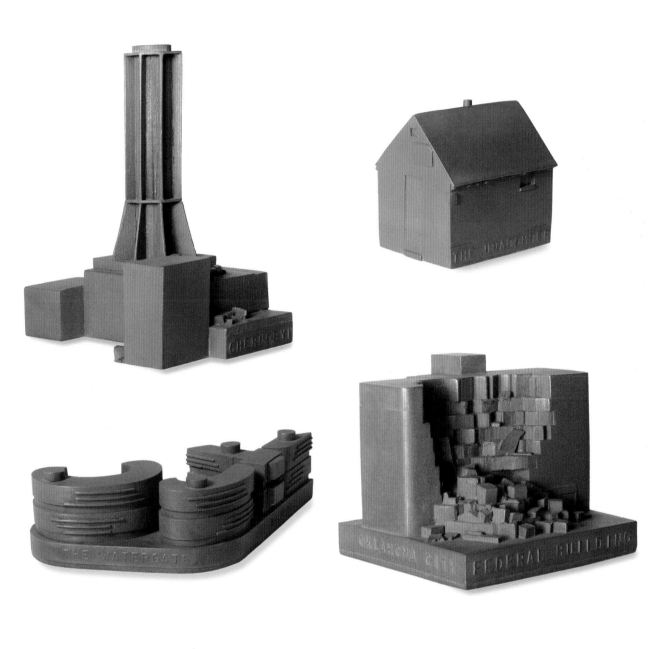

Warbowl

Date **2002**
Designer **Dominic Wilcox/Mosley Meets Wilcox**
Material **Plastic toy soldiers**

Made of hundreds of melted toy soldiers and resembling a lump of shrapnel, Warbowl is a fruitbowl with both attitude and humour. Dominic Wilcox, its designer, was still a student at London's Royal College of Art when he began exploring ways of combining existing objects to create new materials with unusual textures and properties as well as unexpected new meanings. His research led him to experiment with plastic toy soldiers, heating them up under a grill until they fused together in a deformed morass of melted limbs, creating a material that was reminiscent of both innocent childhood games and the horrors of war.

The next task was to find a use for this relatively crude new manufacturing technique. Further experimentation led to Wilcox arranging the plastic soldiers on a metal bowl, which he placed in a specially constructed oven for about 15 minutes until the components had melted smoothly on the underside yet still retained the details of

the original figures on top. After cooling, the plastic Warbowl could be removed from the metal form.

Wilcox teamed up with fellow graduate Steve Mosley – both studied the Design Products MA at the Royal College of Art, the course led by Ron Arad, which consistently produces many of the most interesting young design post-graduates in the world – to form design company Mosley Meets Wilcox. It now manufactures the Warbowl in small quantities using three types of plastic figures: soldiers, ninjas and knights. The bowls, which contain about 250 figures each, measure 10 cm (4 in) high and 44 cm (17 in) in diameter. The latest design features soldiers from the Battle of Waterloo, with roughly equal numbers of French infantry and British artillery figures. Mosley does not intend the product to have any particular meaning, with some interpreting Warbowl as an anti-war statement and others viewing it as a humorous use of an unexpected material.

Products

Today's throw-away consumer society leaves industrial designers with a dilemma: they have long aspired to produce goods that improve people's lives, but the sheer volume of cheap goods on the market means it is increasingly difficult to make a difference. Only rarely does a new product come along with a design attributable to an individual that is so brilliant it changes the market —Jonathan Ive's iPod is one such object, as is Max Barenbrug's Bugaboo Frog baby buggy.

These products are rare exceptions; most industrial designers have to be content with minor improvements to existing typologies. Meanwhile, innovation is increasingly provided not by designers in the traditional sense, but by technicians and scientists. Digital cameras, for example, represent a major technical advance over film cameras, but their exterior form is based largely on their predecessors.

Yet "design" is a valuable marketing commodity nowadays, and an elite band of talented designers are in demand to add their personal touch of magic to goods that can then be marketed as premium products, such as Jasper Morrison's Brunch range of kitchen appliances for Rowenta. Parallel to these developments, a new generation of young designers are attempting to move beyond the constraints of mass production, which, as mentioned in the introduction to this book, is increasingly viewed as being responsible for an avalanche of banal, meaningless goods. Joris Laarman's concrete Heat Wave radiator defies every convention of what a radiator should look like and, being composed of modular elements, allows the user to create their own unique form. Although the radiator is designed to be functional, the demands of mass production and distribution were not

foremost in Laarman's mind when he created it: as such it is as much a product as a declaration of war on the banality of most other radiators.

Other designers are also questioning why, given advances in manufacturing technology and the increasing fragmentation of consumer preferences, most mass produced objects look the same. Matthias Megyeri's Sweet Dreams Security products ask valid questions about the humourlessness and aggression of iron railings and razor wire, while Joep Verhoeven's Laced Fence similarly subverts the dull conformity of omnipresent chainlink fences. Megyeri and Verhoeven are both exploring ways of reintroducing artistry and craftsmanship into everyday objects that are usually taken for granted, but other designers are working within the framework of industry and

attempting to subvert it from within. Industrial Facility's Second Telephone for Muji challenges the lazy thinking visible in domestic handsets, reinventing the product from first principles and recognizing that much of the sophisticated functionality that comes as standard with contemporary electrical goods are unnecessary at best and counterproductive at worst.

Similarly, Doshi Levien's Mosaic cookware asks why, given the huge variety of different cooking cultures that exist around the world, manufacturers insist on selling exactly the same range of items in every country. And Nicolas Roope's Hulger phone questions the assumption that high-tech phones need to look like high-tech phones, suggesting that hefty, old-fashioned handsets actually inspire more meaningful conversations.

iPod

Date **2001**
Designer **Jonathan Ive**
Material **Stainless steel and plastic**
Manufacturer **Apple, USA**

The iPod is one of the most successful products of recent times, both commercially and critically. Designed by Jonathan Ive, the British-born senior vice president of design at Californian computer manufacturer Apple, the white stainless-steel-backed box has become an icon of the digital age. At the time of its launch in 2001, MP3 digital music players were a relatively new concept and had yet to supplant the portable CD player as the preferred mode of listening to music while on the move. But within a few years the iPod had utterly transformed the way people consume music, ushering in the digital music era.

In the same way that Hoover is used for "vacuum cleaner", iPod has become the generic term for all MP3 players. By allowing users to buy digital music online and store their entire music collection on an object measuring just 103.5 mm by 61.8 mm by 11 mm (4 in by 2 $^2/_5$ in by $^2/_5$ in) – at the time of writing, the top-of-the-range model has a 60 gigabyte hard drive, capable of storing 15,000 songs – it spelled the beginning of the end of the CD as a commercially viable format.

The success of the iPod perhaps owes less to Ive's design than to its ease of use and the seamless way it synchronizes with Apple's iTunes software and online music store, which make purchasing, storing and organizing digital music effortless. Yet Ive managed to express the iPod's functional simplicity with a pared-down, almost primitive external casing. With no visible screws, rivets or battery compartments, its seamless casing is more akin to perfume bottle or beauty product than a high-tech electronic device. The scroll-wheel interface, meanwhile, offers an intuitive means of selecting songs, adjusting the volume and fast-forwarding tracks. Early iPods featured a mechanical wheel surrounded by a series of buttons, but this has been replaced in recent models with an all-in-one touch-sensitive scroller.

Capitalizing on its commercial success, Apple has brought out new iPod models with bewildering speed, introducing the iPod Mini in 2003, the iPod Shuffle in 2004 and the iPod Nano in 2005. Video-playing capability has also been introduced.

Wall-mounted CD Player

Date **1999**
Designer **Naoto Fukasawa**
Material **Polypropylene plastic**
Manufacturer **Muji, Japan**

A simple plastic extractor fan was the inspiration for this wall-mounted CD player. Its designer, Naoto Fukasawa, had the idea while watching a CD starting to spin on a standard player and was reminded of the blades in the electric ventilator in his kitchen. The electrical flex that hangs from the bottom of the product doubles as a pull-cord that turns the device on and off, reinforcing the connection with the product that inspired it, while the speaker sits behind the disc cavity and faces the wall. This neatly gets round the fact that there is no space on the fascia for speakers. The device is also remarkable for having no visible controls or displays: besides the pull-cord, there is a simple volume control switch and track selector mounted on top of the moulded plastic housing.

Fukasawa came up with the idea for the product while running a design workshop in Tokyo that explored the theme "Without Thought". The aim of the session was to explore the subconscious ways people respond to products: although no CD player like this had ever been designed before, Fukasawa reasoned that people would intuitively grasp how it worked. Fukasawa describes people's response to the device as a "delayed wow", rather than the immediate "wow" elicited by a visually spectacular product. This instead first invites curiosity, followed by a visceral realization of how it works. Fukasawa believes this response is deeper and more rewarding.

Fukasawa later exhibited a prototype of the wall-mounted CD player at a design fair in Tokyo, where it caught the eye of Masaaki Kanaai, managing director of the Japanese "no-brand" home and office retailer. Kanaai immediately decided to put the product into production. It was an immediate success, selling 50,000 units in Japan alone in the first eight months.

VKB Virtual Keyboard

Date **2004**
Designer **Priestman Goode**
Material **Metallic spray finish on ABS plastic**
Manufacturer **Hutchison Harbour Ring, Hong Kong**

The VKB Virtual Keyboard is more an invention than a design. A portable device that uses advanced laser technology to project the outline of a keyboard onto a flat surface, it allows you to type anywhere. The product is an example of a virtual interface – a means of inputting data into a computer that requires no contact between the user and the device. This kind of project presents designers with a dilemma: since there are no moving parts or ergonomic factors to consider, the visual appearance of the product is entirely arbitrary. London-based industrial designers Priestman Goode, founded by Paul Priestman and Nigel Goode, chose to express the concept as a simple, mysterious grey monolith that gives nothing of its function away. It is only when the device is switched on that its function becomes apparent: then the product itself fades into the background and the projected keyboard, made up of a matrix of bright red dots, becomes the iconographic visual element of the design.

An alternative to mechanical keyboards, the VKB's casing contains a holographic infra-red illumination module that projects an optical QWERTY keyboard. As the user types, an image sensor works out which virtual keys are being touched and sends the information to the computer. Thus, a tabletop or airline meal tray becomes the interface. Since there are no moving parts, the product is less prone to malfunction and is especially suited to uses where the risk of damage caused by liquid spillages or dust is high, such as hospitals or factory floors.

The i-Tech branded VKB is manufactured by Hutchison Harbour Ring, an offshoot of Hong Kong telecommunications giant Hutchison. Avenir Telecom was the first distributor to market the VKB and worked closely with i-Tech on the development of the project and its associated software. VKB technology could be applied to any kind of interface but the first commercial version, produced in 2004, is intended as an executive gadget to replace portable mechanical keyboards used with PDAs and other portable digital devices.

Hulger Phone

Date **2005**
Designer **Nicolas Roope**
Material **Polycarbonate**

The Hulger phone is a comment on and a reaction against the disposability of many contemporary electronics products, which quickly become redundant as they go out of fashion, malfunction or become superseded by newer models with more features or greater degrees of miniaturization. Created by London designer Nicolas Roope in 2005, the Hulger is a chunky retro-style handset that plugs into a mobile phone or a laptop. Ironic and nostalgic, as well as being bulky and somewhat impractical to walk around with, it allows the user to replicate the experience of making a call on an old-fashioned landline, which Roope believes is more intimate and culturally resonant than holding a conversation on a tiny mobile phone or a hands-free device.

Roope began by soldering hands-free kits into vintage phones he picked up in second-hand shops and car boot sales, creating prototypes that he successfully sold on eBay. He then progressed to manufacturing his own handsets, modelled on a range of vintage designs, such as the hefty Bakelite models of the 1950s or the flimsy trimphone-style designs of the 1980s. He now produces wireless Bluetooth models and versions compatible with VoIP (voice over Internet protocol).

The handsets are designed to be timeless, allowing users to keep them for years, even if they regularly upgrade the rest of their technology. The name Hulger was inspired by Roope's Danish grandfather, a man who was not particularly interested in material possessions and who stuck with the same leather armchair, pipe and 1950s' Opel car until he died.

Finger Biscuit

Date **2004**
Designer **Paolo Ulian**
Material **Butter, sugar, flour, eggs and brandy**

Made of butter, sugar, flour and eggs, flavoured with brandy and moulded into a shape similar to a traffic cone, this biscuit is designed to indulge consumers' greed. It sits on the end of your finger and is used to dip into a jar of chocolate sauce or Nutella. It was created by Italian designer Paolo Ulian as part of a designer biscuit project organized by Bolzano University in Italy in 2004. The university's design and arts faculty invited 24 well-known international designers to create new biscuits with innovative flavours and appearances.

Other designers' contributions included the Spoon biscuit by British-based duo Shin and Tomoko Azumi – a chocolate-coated teaspoon that could be used to stir and sweeten coffee and then eaten – and the Modular Cookie Landscape System by German designer Werner Aisslinger. This featured thin, square biscuits topped with an abstract pattern picked out in icing sugar and chocolate powder, which fit together to create a table-top landscape.

The biscuits that were produced were then exhibited and their recipes published; the university even held an event at a bakery in Milan during the furniture fair at which the biscuits were freshly baked each day. The not entirely serious project attracted widespread media attention and comes at a time when designers are increasingly becoming involved in creating food products.

The success of "techno cookery" chefs, such as Ferran Adria of El Bulli in Spain and Heston Blumenthal of the Fat Duck in England, has led to a surge of interest in new ways of preparing and shaping food. Spanish designer Martí Guixé has invented a gamut of new food types and published a book called Food Design, and Design Academy Eindhoven in the Netherlands encourages students to experiment with food and has even opened a restaurant where students can prepare and serve their inventions.

AU Design Project

Date **2001**
Designer **Various**
Material **Various**
Manufacturer **KDDI, Japan**

Japan has emerged as a hotbed of industrial design in recent years, as intense competition in the consumer electronics industry has forced manufacturers to compete on design rather than price. The Infobar and the Talby, designed for Japanese mobile phone brand KDDI, are two of the most acclaimed mobile phone handsets of all time, and both are the result of a design programme the company initiated to differentiate its products.

KDDI launched the programme, called AU, in 2001 with the intention of hiring a leading Japanese or international designer each year to develop a phone concept that challenged conventional handset design. The first figure they chose was Naoto Fukasawa, already well known for his work for IDEO and Muji. The defining feature of Fukasawa's concept, Infobar, was a keypad of large, square tiles that extended right to the edges of the phone (below, right). This came in a variety of checkerboard colour schemes including *nishikigoi* – which represented a traditional Japanese carp pool – and *itchmatsu* – a

black and white kimono pattern. A slim 11 mm ($^2/_5$ in) thick and 138 mm (5 ½ in) long, its lightweight magnesium alloy case meant it weighed just 87 g (3 oz). The phone was the AU design project model to go into production in 2003 and became an instant classic.

Marc Newson's Talby phone enjoyed similar, if not greater, success (below). Named after a hippy character in 1974 sci-fi comedy *Dark Star*, it was introduced in 2004 and displays Newson's typical retro-futuristic styling. The keypad – available in the designer's trademark acid orange, green or black – features circular buttons that sit flush with the slim, rectangular magnesium alloy body, which measures 45 mm by 132 mm by 13 mm (2 by 5 by ½ in). It weighs just 79 g (2 ¼ oz). The oblong slot above the screen fits a woven cotton lanyard, also designed by Newson. The AU project has produced several more prototypes, including a pebble-shaped design called Ishicoro by Fukasawa (above, right), and Apollo 02, a phone designed by Ichiro Higashiizumi, inspired by the film *2001: A Space Odyssey*.

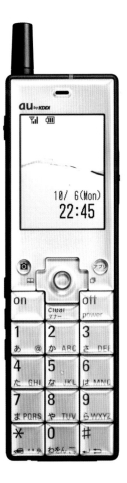

Second Telephone

Date **2004**
Designer **Industrial Facility**
Material **ABS plastic**
Manufacturer **Muji, Japan**

London-based product design company Industrial Facility is headed by Sam Hecht and Kim Colin. Hecht was born in London in 1961, studied industrial design at the Royal College of Art and worked for architect David Chipperfield (see page 111) and then for industrial design firm IDEO, alongside Naoto Fukasawa (see pages 291 and 296). Colin, a trained architect, was born in Los Angeles in 1961. She worked as an editor in architectural publishing and taught at the Royal College of Art before joining Hecht to form Industrial Facility in 2002. They design extensively for Muji – for whom they are European creative directors – as well as Epson, Lexon, Whirlpool and Droog.

The pared-down, minimalist aesthetic of the company belies the radical and often subversive nature of their design philosophy. Much of their work is a reaction against the marketing-driven approach adopted by most mainstream brands, which leads to row upon row of near-identical, over-specified and often ill-considered products lining the shelves of high street retailers. Their Second Telephone for Japanese chain Muji illustrates their methodology. Muji asked them

to design a cheap, simple phone that would be used in addition to the domestic user's main land-line.

Industrial Facility realized that this product need do nothing more than make and receive calls, and did not require any of the often superfluous and confusing additional functions of most telephones on the market. Thus, the device has only a numerical keypad and an "engage" button to initiate and end calls, and no screen. They also realized that the device would spend most of its time not being used, and so they designed it primarily to rest, face down, on a table or similar surface. Its simple, white, brick-like form reflects this, avoiding the pseudo-ergonomic styling of most other phones. When not in use the flush keypad is hidden, while the weight of the phone keeps the engage button disabled; when the phone rings, the act of picking it up releases the button, switching the device on. Similarly, the call is ended by placing the phone down. Industrial Facility calls this approach "product as landscape" – products designed to be part of the domestic interior rather than shouting about their function.

Heat Wave Radiator

Date **2003**
Designer **Joris Laarman**
Material **Concrete, glassfibre and plastic**
Manufacturer **Droog, Netherlands**

When young Dutch designer Joris Laarman completed his training at the prestigious Design Academy Eindhoven in the Netherlands in 2003, his graduation project became an instant media sensation. Within a matter of months it was featured in over 80 publications worldwide – an indication of the massive press interest in contemporary design.

Laarman's show-stealing design was a prototype radiator made from glassfibre-reinforced concrete, called Reinventing Functionality (since renamed Heat Wave). The product is made of identical concrete components, each about 60 cm by 70 cm (24 in by 28 in) in size, which can be linked together to create an infinite variety of forms. The moulded concrete parts contain plastic pipes usually used in underfloor heating, which do not expand as they heat up, thereby protecting the concrete from cracking. The scrolling Baroque forms of the components are radically different from the geometric austerity of most other radiators, yet Laarman claims the swirling design is highly functional,

as the relatively large amount of surface area means that the product radiates heat more efficiently. The radiator was subsequently put into production by avant-garde Dutch manufacturing brand Droog.

Laarman's work, like that of many contemporary designers, is a reaction against the dogmatic minimalism of Modernist design and represents a rediscovery of ornament. Yet Laarman, born in 1979, claims not to use decoration gratuitously but rather as a way of adding meaning and poetry to objects. His graduation show also featured a climbing wall, called Ivy, featuring Art Nouveau-type ceramic swirls that rambled up a wall like a creeping plant, while his later series of Limited vases explored the notions of beauty and decay: the curvaceous porcelain vases were mass-produced using a mould that was designed to degrade over time, meaning that the more vases he produced, the more deformed they became. Thus, the vases bloom, wither and die much like the flowers they are intended to hold.

PAL Radio

Date **2002**
Designer **Henry Kloss**
Material **Rubberized plastic**
Manufacturer **Tivoli Audio, USA**

The PAL (Portable Audio Laboratory) radio is something of a paradox, featuring old-fashioned technology, such as analogue radio reception, and a single monophonic speaker instead of digital, stereo sound. Yet the product has been a huge commercial success. This is partly due to its simple and intuitive design, which dispenses with the usual superfluous array of buttons and displays, and instead features just three controls: a tuner dial, a volume dial and an on/off/band switch. Thanks to the technological advances made by Henry Kloss, the legendary American audio engineer and designer who created the PAL, its exceptional sound quality has also contributed to its success. The radio is particularly praised for its reception: the AM/FM tuner has an automatic frequency control that locks into stations. Kloss, who died in 2002, was one of the last of the old-style designer-engineers, who combined technical flair with visual skills. In contrast, most designers operating today concentrate on appearance, and work alongside engineers, who take care of the technical side of things.

Visually, the PAL's minimal, brick-like form chimes with the techno-minimalist aesthetic of cult products, such as Apple computers and iPods. Its friendly, rubberized, weatherproof plastic case comes in a range of fashionable colours and its upright shape means it can be placed on bookshelves, among stacks of CDs or in other locations where you wouldn't think of putting a normal, horizontally configured radio.

The product is a development of Kloss' Model One table radio – a retro-style analogue design with a brushed-aluminium face and a polished wooden case. This product set the tone for later digital radio launches by rival brands, most of whom adopted the old-fashioned appearance of the Model One. The PAL, however, manages to look extremely contemporary despite its lack of high-tech credentials (the choice of single-speaker monophony instead of stereo is due to the fact that stereo speakers need to be placed a fair distance apart and so are redundant in small radios).

Priscila Huggable Atomic Mushroom

Date **2003**

Designer **Dunne & Raby**

Material **Fabric and polyester beads**

London-based designers Tony Dunne and Fiona Raby met at the Royal College of Art in London, where Dunne studied industrial design and Raby architecture. After graduating, they moved to Japan for three years, where Raby worked for architect Kei'ichi Irie and Dunne worked for Sony. They now both teach at the Royal College of Art, where Dunne is Senior Research Fellow for Computer Related Design and Senior Tutor for Product Design, while Raby teaches at the Architecture and Interaction Design departments.

The duo is at the forefront of a new approach to the design of products that respond to human emotional needs rather than strictly functional concerns. Their work, which can be categorized as "critical design", is born of a recognition that while industrial designers have been remarkably successful at solving technical problems, they have tended to shy away from dealing with the broader cultural issues. The point of Dunne and Raby's work is to stimulate discussion and explore new areas of design. Thus, they create objects that have a nominal use but which also delve into human anxieties, reclaiming back for design the creative territory that has recently been considered the domain of artists.

Their polyester-filled, fabric representation of a nuclear mushroom is typical of their work. Modelled on the mushroom cloud created by the detonation of a 37-kiloton test bomb in Nevada in 1957, it is a kind of anxiety-relief cushion that allows people to confront their fear of nuclear war by turning a horrific event into something cosy and domestic. The product is part of a series titled Designs for Fragile Personalities in Anxious Times. Another example of the series is Type 2, a beautifully crafted wooden box that is designed to contain a life-size version of *The Naked Maja* – Goya's famous painting of a reclining nude that is an allegory of sexual confidence. The idea is that people who fear abduction can climb inside the felt-lined box and assume the provocative position of the Maja, thereby feeling in control, proud and comfortable rather than paranoid.

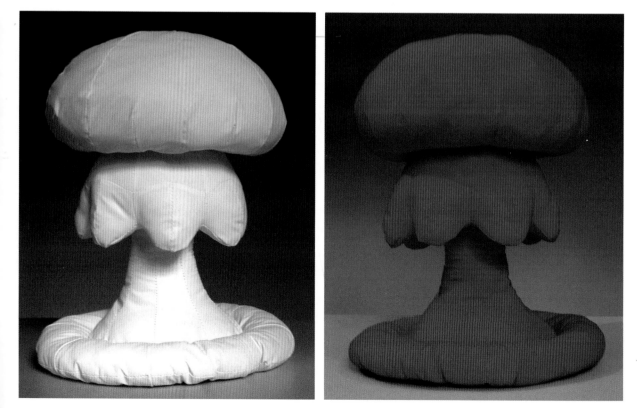

Sweet Dreams Security Products

Date **2003**
Designer **Matthias Megyeri**
Material **Cast-iron and cast-glass**

When young German-born designer Matthias Megyeri came to London to study at the Royal College of Art in 1996, he was immediately struck by the paradoxical nature of many of the British homes he saw, which were decorated with cute ornaments, lace curtains and garden gnomes but which simultaneously bristled with security devices such as CCTV cameras, iron railings and razor wire. He was fascinated by this contradictory combination of kitsch homeliness and paranoia and began to investigate ways of combining endearing and threatening qualities, producing a range of security products that are both humorous and ruthlessly functional.

Working under the name of Sweet Dreams Security, Megyeri has produced a set of railings topped with charming cast-iron cartoon rabbits, penguins and donkeys that nonetheless feature pointed beaks and ears; and a range of cast-glass "ornaments" in the form of trees and buildings that can be set on top of walls to deter burglars (and which are a substitute for the more traditional broken bottles, which are now illegal in the UK). He has also designed a quirky cover for CCTV cameras that features ears and whiskers, thereby disguising the camera as a cat, and a plastic cap that fits over the top of a standard ADT burglar alarm, transforming it into a giant daisy.

Megyeri's work is part of a new movement in design that couples utility with social commentary and coincides with many designers' exploration of the theme of fear in the wake of September 11 and the widespread threat of terrorism. His Mr Smish & Madame Buttly razor wire – which features butterflies and love hearts instead of barbs – graced the cover of the New York Museum of Modern Art's catalogue for its major 2005 exhibition SAFE: Design Takes on Risk, which explored this theme.

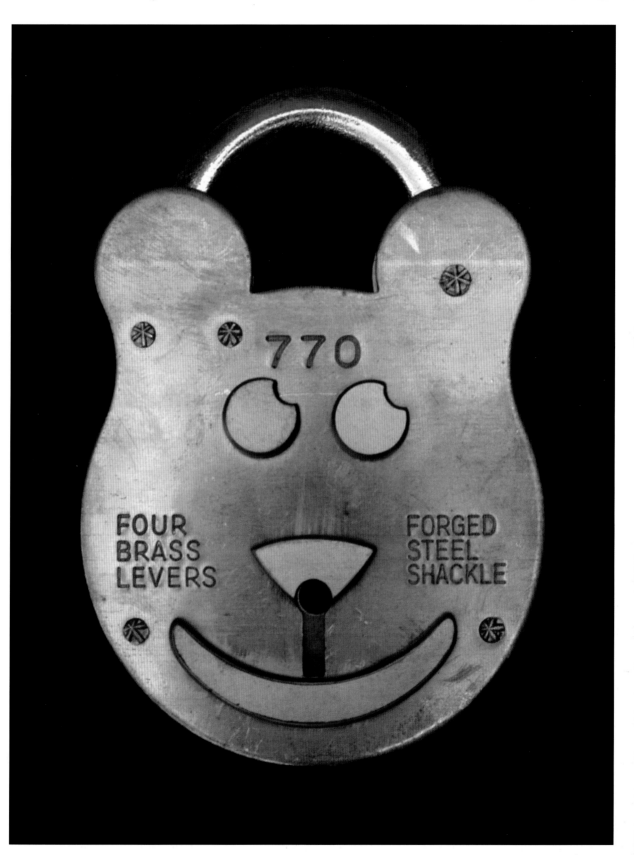

USB Saint

Date **2005**
Designer **Luis Eslava Eloy**
Material **Plastic**

Advances in computer technology have spawned a whole host of new product types, including data storage peripherals, such as USB drives and external hard drives. These devices have tended to adopt remarkably similar – and generally bland and uninteresting – forms, often using a streamlined, high-tech visual language, or a solid, boxy visual syntax designed to give the impression of secure storage. Yet since they have no moving parts, USB storage devices could theoretically be any shape whatsoever. Young designer Luis Eslava Eloy has therefore produced a prototype USB drive in the form of the Virgin Mary. Although seemingly a novelty, Eslava Eloy's moulded plastic saint refers to the blind faith people put in technology and

their fervent hopes that their data will be kept safe – one prototype version features a halo around the Virgin's head with the legend "Oh Maria keep my data safe" embossed on it.

Eslava Eloy, who was born in Spain in 1976, designed USB Saint as part of his final project at London's Royal College of Art. He believes that computers have become almost religious objects of mystery and reverence, since few people understand how they work yet they often trust them implicitly – and invoke a higher being when they go wrong. Hence, the USB Saint is a token of both superstition and faith, akin to the wearing of a Saint Christopher medal when going on a journey or hanging a religious token in a car to ward off evil spirits.

Heineken Bottle

Date **2002**
Designer **Ora Ito**
Material **Brushed aluminium**
Manufacturer **Heineken, Netherlands**

In 2002, Heineken commissioned young French designer Ora Ito to create a new, fashionable bottle for the unglamorous beer brand. His design is a fusion between a beer bottle and a can yet despite this unpromising parentage, it appears extremely sophisticated. Made of brushed aluminium and featuring graphics printed directly onto the metal, the 330 ml (11 fl oz) bottle was launched in fashionable nightclubs and bars.

Ora Ito (real name Ito Morabito) was just 24 when he completed this project, and has since worked with Toyota, Davidoff and Swatch. His dramatic rise to fame is attributable to the ingenious and audacious way he marketed himself. In 1999, aged 21, the design school dropout son of Parisian fashion designer Pascal Morabito decided he needed to find a shortcut to success. He created a range of fictional products for multinational brands and presented them on his website. These included a rugged, camouflage-painted laptop for Apple, called the

"Hack Mac" (slogan: "think weapon"), a range of Swatch watches, and a backpack and table football game for Louis Vuitton, both in the brand's famous monogram pattern.

The site caused a sensation, with buyers inundating the brands with enquiries about products that did not exist. One enterprising Chinese manufacturer even started producing fake versions of some of Ora Ito's already fake designs. Soon, brands were approaching him with real projects, including some of the companies he had spoofed: he has since worked with Swatch on a watch design. He has also worked with leading Italian brands, such as furniture companies Cappellini and B&B Italia, and lighting house Artemide. He designed the grenade-shaped Ogo mineral water bottle, and he has worked on perfume bottles for Adidas and Joop! Interior projects include Toyota's flagship store on Paris' Champs Elysées and the redesign of Parisian nightclub Le Cab (both in 2003).

TAK Pushpin

Date **2004**
Designer **Scott Kochlefl**
Material **Plastic and stainless steel**
Manufacturer **Ideation Designs, USA**

The TAK pushpin is a rare example of a designer improving an everyday object that is seemingly already perfect. Invented by Chicago-based designer Scott Kochlefl, the product takes the standard plastic-headed metal pin used to temporarily fasten objects to a wall and successfully adds additional functionality. It consists of a moulded plastic head resembling a champagne cork with a notch cut into its lower half. Two sharp metal prongs are set into the base of the head.

By having two prongs instead of one, photos, postcards and other objects can be fastened with a single pin without swivelling. The concave sides of the plastic head allow items such as keys to be hung from the pin, meaning it can double as a hook. And the horseshoe-shaped channel in the head is designed to accommodate cables, so the pin can also be used to secure telephone cables, chains of Christmas lights and other types of flex. Thus, in addition to improved basic function, the design allows for two further uses.

Designed in 2004 and manufactured by Kochlefl's own company Ideation Designs, the TAK Pushpin won a host of awards including an IDEA Award and *International Design*'s Design Distinction Award.

Garlic Crusher

Date **2005**
Designer **Ineke Hans**
Material **Stainless steel**
Manufacturer **Royal VKB, Netherlands**

Garlic crushers tend to be over-complicated mechanical devices that are messy and hard to wash. With this simple object, Dutch designer Ineke Hans has completely rethought the process of this culinary activity. Her product is a rare example of a designer abandoning a well-known product typology in favour of something new – and the manufacturer's decision to back the idea is equally rare. Instead of the usual method of crushing garlic, which involves squeezing it through a die in a hinged, hand-held press, Hans' version involves crushing the clove beneath a roller.

Measuring 18 cm (7 in) long and with a diameter of 3.5 cm (1 ½ in), the crusher is made of solid stainless steel. The object is so self-explanatory and intuitive it hardly needs explaining: the cylindrical roller is used in the same way as a rolling pin, with a hand gripping either end and rolling the device back and forth while applying downward pressure with the wrists. The serrated section between the hands grips and pulverizes the garlic, a method which the manufacturer, Dutch kitchenware brand Royal VKB, claims leads to a more intense garlic flavour. It is certainly a lot easier to clean: you simply rinse it under the tap. Hans also claims that rubbing your hands against the device under a running tap removes the odour of garlic, thanks to the composition of the steel.

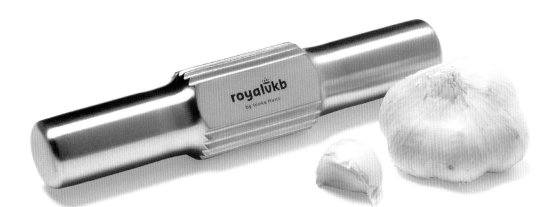

Ty Nant Water Bottle

Date **2002**
Designer **Ross Lovegrove**
Material **PET plastic**
Manufacturer **Ty Nant, UK**

Upmarket Welsh mineral water brand Ty Nant already had one of the most iconic bottles on the market before it approached industrial designer Ross Lovegrove to produce a new version for it. The company's 1989 teardrop-shaped, cobalt blue glass bottle had been hugely popular, subverting the Victorian tradition of storing poisonous liquids in blue bottles. In 1999, it decided to commission Lovegrove to produce a new plastic bottle in response to mineral water's surge in popularity thanks to the trend towards healthier eating and drinking, which took what had been an elite product away from the restaurant table to the refrigerator in the corner shop. Yet Ty Nant still wanted their product to have an air of exclusivity.

Lovegrove, whose work tends towards the organic and curvaceous, is one of the most successful industrial designers today, applying his trademark flowing lines to everything from furniture to lighting and products. For this project, he drew inspiration from a book of water studies by Leonardo da Vinci, choosing to make the bottle itself into a three-dimensional representation of flowing water. There are practical reasons for this, too: the rippling surface gives the bottle strength and allows thinner PET plastic to be used, and it makes gripping the bottle easier.

But the bottle also perfectly expresses the product contained within – so much so that a label is not necessary. Lovegrove's design is both packaging and logo. However, whereas the earlier cobalt blue bottle became a cult object in its own right and was kept by consumers and reused as a candleholder, vase or ornament, Lovegrove's bottle needs to be full of water to work: when it is empty, it becomes flimsy, lustreless and disposable.

Mikro

Date **2001**
Designer **Sam Buxton**
Material **Stainless steel**
Manufacturer **Worldwide Co, UK**

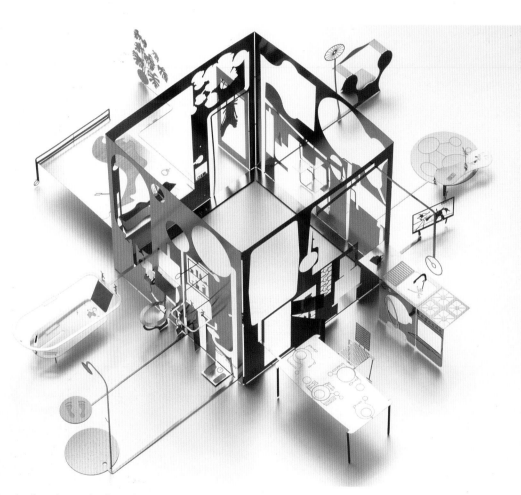

After graduating from the Royal College of Art in 1999, British designer Sam Buxton decided to design his own business card to promote his work. Eschewing the standard card type, he produced a design so attractive that people were prepared to pay for it.

Made of a sheet of extremely thin acid-etched stainless steel, the card featured a fold-up model of an abstract figure called Mikro-Man – who represented Buxton himself – working on a computer behind a desk. The card was exhibited as part of the Design Museum's 2001 exhibition Design Now – London, where it caught the attention of manufacturing company Worldwide Corp, and they decided to put the card into production.

Buxton soon expanded the range of Mikro products to include fold-up tableaux featuring Mikro-Man on a bicycle, in the jungle

and even on the moon. The products are produced from steel that is 150 micron (6 mm/⅕ in) thick using a technique known as chemical milling borrowed from the electronics industry. The process involves transferring a two-dimensional drawing onto sheet metal that has previously been coated with a substance called "photo-resist". The metal is then washed in a chemical bath, which removes the photo-resist from the areas covered by lines and solid parts of the drawing. A second bath of acid then eats away at the unprotected areas of steel, producing incredibly precise incisions and perforations.

Mikro products have proved incredibly successful as gifts and Buxton has since worked on scaled-up versions, including a Mikro-style skateboard park for Vauxhall. Buxton, born in London in 1972, now designs for international brands including Reebok and Siemens.

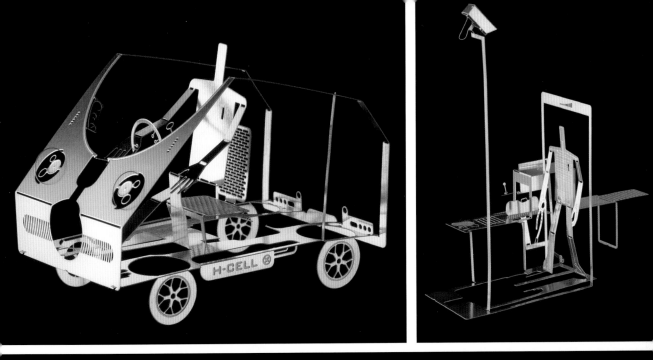
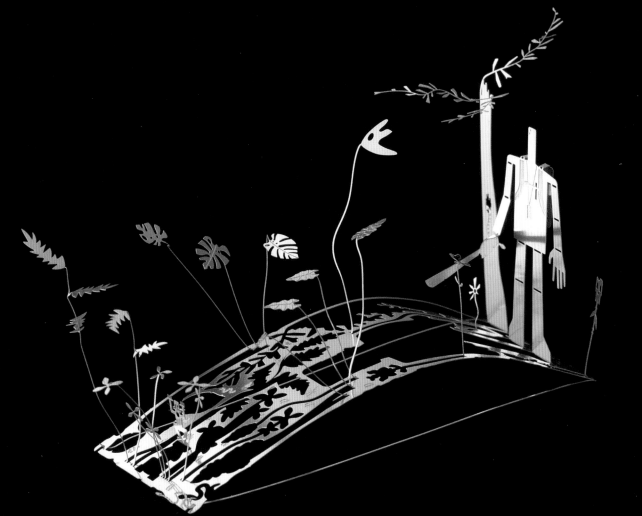

HE Design
Marcel Wanders

Date **2005**

Designer **Marcel Wanders**

Material **Various**

Manufacturer **Holland Electro, Netherlands**

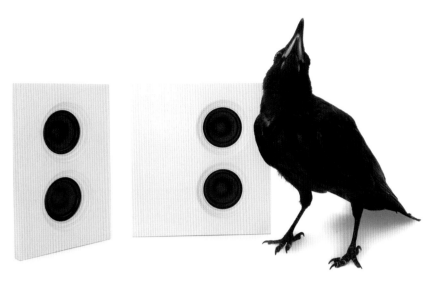

This range of six consumer electronic products explores new ways of integrating furniture and audio-visual equipment. Designed by Marcel Wanders for Dutch home appliances brand HE Holland and launched at the IFA Consumer Electronics Fair in Berlin in September 2005, it replaces the technical minimalist design language employed on nearly all domestic electronic products with styling that refers back to the decorative wood and Bakelite casings of early radios.

Key to the range are wireless transmitters that send signals from laptops, MP3 players and DVD players to screens and speakers. Wanders has designed two versions: Mathilda is a battery-powered, pebble-shaped transmitter made of moulded black plastic with a decorative embossed pattern (left, with lizards). This plugs into an MP3 player, allowing sound to be beamed to speakers around the home. Merlin is a much smaller transmitter that plugs directly into the USB port of a PC or laptop (with scorpion).

Wanders has also designed wireless speakers, called Egg, flattened sphere-shaped objects styled to match the transmitters. A subwoofer, also wireless and called Pandora, is integrated into a small, dark wood side table, while another pair of extremely thin, rectangular speakers, this time styled in minimal white and called Domino, is designed to be mounted on shelves or walls (above, with crow). Theatre, a home-cinema system, consists of a DVD player and speakers contained in a low coffee table (above left, with cat). The sixth product, Wave TV, is the only kitchen product in the range: this consists of a microwave oven with a TFT screen integrated into the door, which can show TV programmes or play DVDs on the integrated DVD player.

The range was launched with an intriguing marketing campaign that featured each product photographed with an animal. A scorpion appears to be attacking the Merlin transmitter, while a cockerel stands on top of Wave TV. Wanders intends these as cryptic jokes, with a link between each animal and product known only to him.

Brunch Kitchen Appliances

Date **2004**
Designer **Jasper Morrison**
Material **Polypropylene**
Manufacturer **Rowenta, Germany**

Multinational electrical goods companies usually employ anonymous in-house designers to style their products, so this range of Rowenta kitchen appliances is something of a departure. Designed by Jasper Morrison – a highly influential designer with a pared-down, essentials-only approach – the range is part of an attempt by German company Rowenta to position itself as a more up-market brand.

Called Brunch, the range consists of a toaster, coffee maker and kettle. Made of matt white polypropylene, with touches of grey to identify handles and switches, their minimal styling belies their intelligent design. The coffee maker, for example, has a flip-top lid that reveals a storage compartment for spare coffee filters and a coffee spoon, while the toaster features a photo sensor that can detect the correct brown-ness of the toasting bread. The latter also includes an electronically-controlled ejector system so that toast ascends and descends gracefully, rather than popping up with a twang of springs. The kettle, meanwhile, is devoid of all instrumentation, with the power switch and indicator light both mounted on the base.

With the product ranges of most volume manufacturers driven by marketing departments rather than designers, adventurous brands are hoping that by making their products stand out on the shelves, they can increase sales and foster greater brand loyalty among customers. Rowenta is owned by French electrical giant Groupe Seb, which also owns Tefal, Krups, Moulinex and other household names. Under Groupe Seb, the various sub-brands are being encouraged to reposition themselves through design. Tefal led the way with cooking implements designed by Marc Newson and Doshi Levien and objects such as corkscrews and bottle openers by the Bouroullec Brothers, while in 2003 Krups appointed Konstantin Grcic to create a design language for its products. However, the price premium that consumers are asked to pay for "designer" goods means that such products often fail to appeal beyond an elite core of design-literate buyers.

Laced Fence

Date **2005**
Designer **Joep Verhoeven/Demakersvan**
Material **Plastic-coated copper wire**

This project takes an everyday, factory-produced product that performs an important function yet is rarely considered, and reinvents it as a lovingly crafted object. The concept represents a reversal of the usual process of industrialization, in which the culture of hand-made objects is gradually usurped by industrially manufactured products. It also asks why notions of beauty cannot be applied to banal objects.

Laced Fence was produced by young Dutch designer Joep Verhoeven as his graduate project while studying at Design Academy Eindhoven. He is now part of young design team Demakersvan, which is based in Rotterdam. The idea is based on the anonymous chainlink security fences that are ubiquitous on industrial estates and sports grounds around the world. These are usually made of PVC-coated steel wire, which is woven into a continuous mesh by a process akin to giant-scale knitting, and then erected on posts.

Working with plastic-coated copper wire – which is more malleable than steel – Verhoeven wove intricate patterns, inspired by traditional Dutch lace-making techniques, into the fence, creating a delicate screen of foliage and flowers. Thus, a product that is a symbol of privacy, denial and even paranoia becomes something celebratory and strangely domestic.

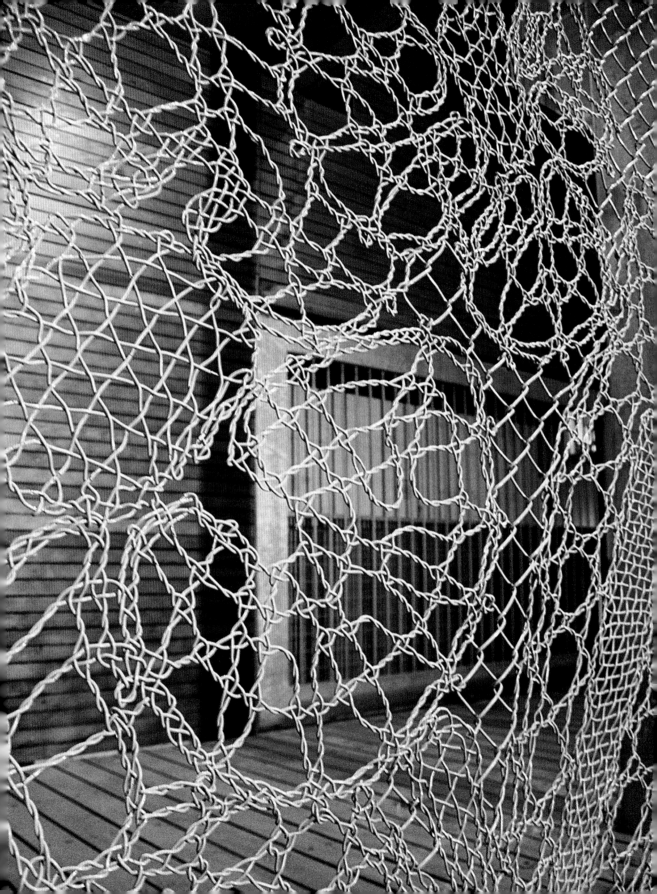

Bugaboo Frog

Date **2001**
Designer **Max Barenbrug**
Material **Aluminium and plastic**
Manufacturer **Bugaboo, Netherlands**

Since its introduction in 2001, the Bugaboo Frog has revolutionized the baby stroller market and turned what was formerly a pragmatic and style-free product type into a desirable status symbol. The Bugaboo concept came about in 1994 when Dutch design student Max Barenbrug (born 1964) developed a concept for a versatile pushchair for his graduation project at Design Academy Eindhoven in the Netherlands. Barenbrug's stroller was aimed as much at the needs of parents as it was at babies: he wanted to create a product that would give parents the freedom to continue with activities that were usually curtailed by the cumbersome nature of most pushchairs on the market at the time.

His prototype design consisted of a modular aluminium X-frame that could be reconfigured in a variety of ways. The baby seat could face either forwards or backwards. The combination of two rugged wheels and two smaller trolley-like wheels allowed it to be pushed over rough terrain, while its clever folding design enabled it to be stored in a car boot, attached to the back of a bicycle as a trailer or even converted into a backpack. The design helped Barenbrug win the Academy's award for best final project and, on graduating, he teamed up with his brother-in-law, Eduard Zanen, to develop the concept and attempted to find a manufacturer. They had little success at first as most stroller brands considered it too radical, so they funded the product themselves, gradually re-orientating the design away from the cycling and hiking sector and marketing it as a lifestyle purchase for style-conscious urbanites.

The first model went on sale in 1999 with the Frog following in 2001. Despite its high price compared to other products on the market, its versatility and its high-tech aesthetic (which made it highly appealing to men) meant it was a huge international success, appearing on the hit TV show *Sex and the City* and spawning a host of copycat designs.

Mosaic Cookware

Date **2003**
Designer **Doshi Levien**
Material **Aluminium, steel and terracotta**
Manufacturer **Tefal, France**

At a time when rampant globalization threatens to erase local traditions, the work of Anglo-Indian duo Doshi Levien proposes ways of creating new cultural hybrids and reconciling the often competing agendas of craft and industry. Nipa Doshi, who grew up in India, met British-born Jonathan Levien while they were both studying at the Royal College of Art in London. They set up Doshi Levien in London in 2000. Their work reflects their respective backgrounds and often explores how traditional objects can be reinterpreted for mass production without losing their emotional significance.

While on a research trip to India, Doshi and Levien noticed shops selling cookware by French manufacturer Tefal that was ill-suited to the culinary traditions of the country. On their return to London, they proposed to Tefal that they design a new range of cookware that reflected different ethnic food cultures around the world, and that could be used with contemporary cooking equipment. The result is a series of five implements: an Indian karhai skillet, a Moroccan tajine pot, a Mexican fajita pan, a Chinese wok and a Spanish paella dish.

Each is faithful to the spirit of the traditional implement yet updated with contemporary materials, such as non-stick surfaces (in brown, to avoid the cheap connotations of ordinary, black non-stick products) and heat-resistant handles. However, the designers resisted the temptation to style each object in the same way, instead creating a family of implements that feature a range of materials and forms. The tajine, for example, features a traditional terracotta lid, but the base is in cast aluminium so that it can be used on a modern cooker rather than an open fire. Each piece features a base screen-printed with a pattern derived from local decorative styles to enhance its cultural validity.

Office in a Bucket

Date **2004**
Designer **Inflate**
Material **Polyurethane-coated ripstop nylon**

British design company Inflate has been producing inflatable furniture and objects since 1995, but has recently started to develop products that are architectural in scale. Office in a Bucket is a portable, 2.2 m (7 ft) high indoor structure that can be used as an office, meeting room or den. Made of white polyurethane-coated ripstop nylon, the cocoon-like product was launched in 2004 and quickly became a fixture at exhibitions and trade fairs. It has an open top, but no doors or windows; the two ends can be simply pulled apart for access and then pulled together again for privacy. The fabric is supplied in a large plastic bucket that also has a low-noise electric fan set in its base. The fan is used to inflate the structure via a nylon umbilical cord that fits over the lip of the bucket: it takes around eight minutes to complete this process. The product comes in two sizes, 3 m by 4 m (10 ft by 13 ft) and 4 m by 5 m (13 ft by 16 ft).

Inflate, headed by Nick Crosbie, became well known in the 1990s for quirky inflatable products made of heat-welded PVC fabric that were characterized by blobby shapes and cartoonish colours. These included inflatable eggcups, lights, wine racks and fruit bowls, plus moulded plastic products, such as the Mr and Mrs Prickly salt and pepper shakers. Crosbie later moved into furniture, working with Ron Arad in 1999 to produce the acclaimed Memo chair – a plastic beanbag that moulds itself to the shape of the user and can be transformed into a hard seat. In 2001, he won the Peugeot Design Award for his Snoozy bed, made of stackable, air-filled plastic slats.

Since the success of Office in a Bucket, Inflate have produced a range of inflatable structures of increasing size and complexity, mainly for the conference market.

Lunar

Date **2004**
Designer **Barber Osgerby**
Material **ABS plastic**
Manufacturer **Authentics, Germany**

This range of bathroom accessories was designed in an attempt to produce a single, unified range of goods for the bathroom instead of the uncoordinated toilet brushes, soap dishes and bins that most people have in their homes. When researching bathroom accessories, designers Edward Barber and Jay Osgerby were surprised to discover that no such range existed.

Lunar was commissioned by German moulded plastics company Authentics, under the art direction of industrial designer Konstantin Grcic. The range consists of five products – a toothbrush holder, a lidded container (suitable for cotton wool swabs), a wastepaper bin, a soap dish and a toilet brush – and is a clever exercise in applying a coherent visual language to a range of diverse, and somewhat banal, everyday objects. Just two shapes – a circle and a short sausage shape – are used to generate the entire range.

Stylistically, the range is reminiscent of classic plastic products from the 1960s or '70s, with their cylindrical forms in white moulded ABS – a lightweight, rigid plastic with a tough, shiny surface that is also used to make Lego bricks. The range is given a distinctive flourish by the recessed lids that resemble lunar craters and give the range its name. Contrasting with the products' white shells, the lids come in a variety of colours – green, beige, orange, red, grey and dark and light blue. The visual coherence of the range extends to the detailing of these lids, with both the toothbrush holder and the bin featuring sausage-shaped openings rather than the usual round ones. The designers claim to have tested the bin and found that 90 per cent of standard bathroom waste could be dropped through the opening. The sausage shape also crops up on the soap dish – the only non-circular element in the range – and in the discreet air vent in the side of the toilet brush holder.

AQHayon Collection

Date **2004**
Designer **Jaime Hayon**
Material **Porcelain and stainless steel**
Manufacturer **ArtQuitect, Spain**

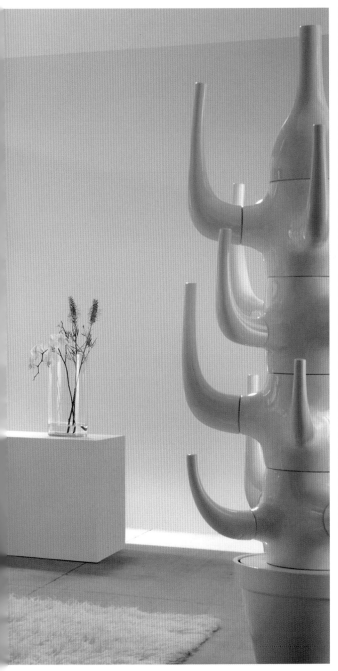

Bathrooms are not usually arenas for cutting-edge design, but this collection by Barcelona-based designer Jaime Hayon, is striking for both its formal and functional innovation. The range was commissioned by ArtQuitect, a Spanish bathroom products company established in the 1990s, to distribute design-led products within Spain. It recently began commissioning its own product range, starting with a collaboration with Hayon. Hayon, who was born in Madrid in 1974, studied industrial design in Madrid and Paris and worked at Fabrica, the design and communications research centre in Treviso, Italy, that is funded by fashion brand Benetton. Working across the boundaries of design and art, Hayon has developed a singular, Miró-esque aesthetic language that has been labelled Mediterranean Digital Baroque. He has created installations in galleries in London and Minneapolis and is best known internationally for the collectable cartoon dolls he has produced for Far Eastern manufacturer Toy2R. He is widely considered to be the most exciting and promising young designer in Spain.

Hayon's range, which was launched at the Milan Furniture Fair in 2004, consists of a washstand and basin, wall-mounted mirror and a range of modular peripherals, including a lamp, a vase and a shaving mirror. The striking form of these objects recalls antique furniture, '60s Pop and Dali-style surrealism. It adds a touch of sensual neo-baroque glamour to the bathroom and treats this neglected room as one that can be styled and accessorized like any other in the home, rather than simply being filled with functional equipment.

The integrated washstand and basin are made of high-quality porcelain, crafted by Bosa Italo in Italy, and come in a range of widths and combinations, including a double-sink version. They feature fittings that allow the boudoir-style lamp to be integrated into the stand – a radical move as these objects are usually considered separately. The lamp can also be mounted on the wall. All the interchangeable porcelain products in the series are available in a variety of colours, including black, white, yellow and metallic gold and silver. The highly decorative, frameless wall mirrors are backed in stainless steel and cut by laser. The range is completed by a wall-mounted towel hanger that resembles a flattened human head.

ENV Motorcycle

Date **2005**
Designer **Seymour Powell**
Material **Hollow-cast, aircraft-grade aluminium**
Manufacturer **Intelligent Energy, UK**

Powered by a non-polluting fuel cell, the ENV (Emissions Neutral Vehicle) motorcycle is a major step towards tackling transport's contribution to climate change. The ENV, which was launched as a prototype in March 2005, is the first, commercially viable, two-wheeler to be powered by fuel cells. Fuel cells convert hydrogen into electricity without creating pollution and have long been regarded as the most promising way of delivering clean energy. Created by London-based industrial design firm Seymour Powell for British fuel cell manufacturer Intelligent Energy, the ENV has a top speed of 80 kph (50 mph) and a range of 160 km (99 miles). The 6 kW electric engine is powered by a removable fuel cell pod mounted between the handlebars and saddle. This can be demounted and used to power other devices. The manufacturers claim each fuel cell, called a core, is capable of powering a motorboat or a small home.

The bike was designed to show that fuel cell technology has now improved enough for it to power vehicles. It takes five minutes to refill the 1 kW fuel cell with hydrogen, giving four hours of engine use. A battery pack stores power while the bike is idling or coasting, boosting power when required for acceleration or high speeds. The device is virtually silent and the only by-product of the chemical process that converts hydrogen and oxygen into electrical power is water vapour. The bike's frame and swinging arm are made of hollow-cast, aircraft-grade aluminium, meaning its total weight is just 80 kg (176 lb).

Fuel cells are not new: they were invented in the nineteenth century by Welsh lawyer Sir William Grove, then NASA developed them further in the 1950s and '60s. However, recent concerns over climate change, as well as fears about the dependability of global gas and oil supplies, have led to a surge of interest in the technology. The ENV motorcycle is due to go into production in 2007, by which time the manufacturer promises to have developed an infrastructure of hydrogen refuelling points.

MINI

Date **2001**

Designer **Frank Stephenson**

Material **Various**

Manufacturer **BMW, Germany**

The original Mini, designed by Sir Alec Issigonis, was one of the most successful cars of all time. Launched in 1959, it was a glamorous, affordable urban runaround that became a British icon and a symbol of the Swinging '60s. It was in continuous production until 2000, by which time 5,387,862 had been sold. At the dawn of the twenty-first century, however, the original design was an anachronism and when BMW acquired the rights to the Mini brand from struggling parent company Rover, it set about building an entirely new car that nonetheless reflected the spirit of the original.

Under BMW's American designer Frank Stephenson, the 3 m (10 ft) long economy car was reinvented as a luxury sports hatchback, with the high-performance Mini Cooper S – which won the Monte Carlo rally in 1964 – used as the benchmark. The design team was insistent that this would not be a "retro" car, but would instead be an evolution of the original, retaining the design "DNA" of details such as the large, eye-like headlights, the chrome front grille, the corner-mounted wheels and the two-tone paintwork.

Yet the new MINI differs significantly from its predecessor in many respects: at 3.5 m (11 ½ ft), it is longer while the horizontal lines of the original are replaced by diagonals that suggest the car is moving forward even when stationary. Roof-support pillars are hidden behind flush glass, giving the upper part of the car a highly architectural look that contrasts with the friendly, rounded styling of the lower parts. Unsurprisingly, given the sentimental attachment to the original, there was a lot of scepticism about BMW's version. However, the new MINI was launched in 2001 to rave reviews, and long waiting lists, and has proved to be the surprise hit of the decade, achieving a similar cult status to its predecessor.

Airbus A380

Date **2005 (maiden test flight)**
Designer **Airbus**
Material **Various**

The Airbus A380 is the largest passenger jet ever to go into production and possibly the largest mass-produced object ever built. The design challenge was to create an airliner that could carry more passengers further and in more comfort than any previous plane, while also reducing noise levels and per-passenger fuel consumption. The double-deck, four-engine airliner is capable of carrying up to 800 passengers in an all-economy configuration – although a three-class configuration seating around 555 is more likely when airlines take delivery of the first models in late 2006. This still means it can take 155 more passengers than the Boeing 747-400 – the previous record holder and which has 50 per cent less cabin space than the A380.

With air traffic doubling every 15 years, the A380 was developed in response to the massive rise in passenger demand and will work long-haul routes between major international hubs. It has a range of 15,000 km (9,320 miles), making it possible to fly non-stop from London to Sydney. For passengers, the A380 promises to offer unprecedented comfort and facilities. Standard seats will be 2.5 cm (1 in) wider than the industry norm and first class cabin mock-ups designed by industrial designers Priestman Goode (see overleaf) are more akin to luxury hotels or cruise liners, featuring libraries, lounge areas, coffee bars and luxury bathrooms. Airbus claims the jet will generate about half the noise of a 747-400 and that per-passenger fuel consumption is comparable to that of a small car. However, environmental campaigners have pointed out that the increase in passenger journeys the new Airbus will trigger will more than offset the increase in fuel efficiency, leading to more greenhouse gas pollution.

Airbus is a Europe-wide consortium with manufacturing plants in 16 countries. Components – including 38 m (120 ft) long wings fabricated in Wales – are transported by road, rail and sea to Toulouse, in south-western France, where the airliners are assembled. The A380 measures 79.8 m (262 ft) from wingtip to wingtip and is 73 m (240 ft) long. Its empty weight is 275,000 kg (605,000 lb) and it has a top speed of 1,000 kmph (620 mph). The purchase price is $280m. Costing around US$13 billion and taking over a decade to develop, the first A380 is due to go into service with Qantas in October 2006, flying between Melbourne and Los Angeles.

Clothing and Accessories

Fashion has long existed on a different plane from the rest of the design disciplines, being a multi-billion dollar global industry that must, thanks to the seasonal nature of the collections, completely reinvent its product lines twice a year. This has tended to mean that fashion designers endlessly recycle ideas and inspirations. Notions of timelessness, technical innovation and cultural relevance that occupy designers in other spheres are not so relevant. There are exceptions, notably Hussein Chalayan, whose technical innovation is matched by the conceptual content of his collections.

However, in recent years fashion and lifestyle brands have increasingly started to approach figures from the worlds of industrial design and furniture to ask them to create products for them – as much for the cross-pollination of ideas this brings as the marketing value. Marc Newson's Zvezdochka trainers for Nike are a striking example of this: Newson introduced materials and manufacturing techniques unheard of in sports clothing, as well as his inimitable visual style. The Campana Brothers' jelly shoes for Brazilian footwear brand Melissa is another such example. Similarly, watch companies are hiring the services of designers such as Philippe Starck, resulting in timepieces that are more in tune with aesthetic trends in other disciplines.

Fabric technology has evolved surprisingly slowly in the mainstream fashion industry, with most developments being

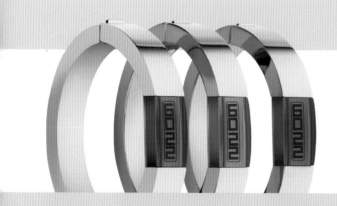

improvements in weave techniques for existing natural and manmade fabrics. Similarly, the rapid turnover of product lines has made it uneconomical for fashion brands to invest in advanced manufacturing technologies – it is cheaper for them to employ workers in low-cost economies to produce garments in time-honoured fashion. Designers, such as Manel Torres and Elena Manferdini, are attempting to challenge this. Torres has developed a technology that allows fabric to be sprayed from a can instead of woven while Manferdini is experimenting with computerized manufacturing technologies already widely used in other industries and that allow mass-produced garments to be tailored to individual customers.

The performance-driven sportswear industries are more reliable hotbeds of fabric innovation, with Speedo's Fastskin being one of the more interesting developments of recent years. By far the most innovative technology to come from the fashion industry itself is Issey Miyake's APOC line, which allows complete garments to be manufactured on an advanced loom; post manufacture, a few scissor cuts is all that is required to finish the dresses, T-shirts and sweaters. Rapid prototyping is another technology that could be adopted by the fashion industry, although the printed fabrics developed by Freedom of Creation, which use this process, are so far only being used commercially to produce accessories such as bags.

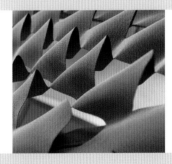

APOC

Date **1999**
Designer **Issey Miyake and Fujiwara Dai**
Brand/Manufacturer **Issey Miyake APOC, Japan**

Issey Miyake has long been one of the most innovative and influential forces in global fashion, but his APOC line – which stands for "A Piece of Cloth" – is widely viewed as the most important development in garment design and manufacture since the introduction of the Jacquard loom in 1801. Revolutionary in both concept and technology, APOC involves creating complete garments from a single piece of fabric that requires no pattern cutting or sewing. Highly advanced, computerized looms produce a continuous, flattened tube of fabric, containing both the structure and form of shirts, skirts or head-to-toe items. All that is required to make an item wearable is a pair of scissors, by cutting along lines woven into the stocking-like tube the embedded garment is liberated. The fabric contains an under layer of stretchy yarns that contract when cut, sealing the material and preventing it from unravelling.

APOC represents to the fashion industry what rapid prototyping promises to three-dimensional design: a complete break with traditional multi-stage manufacturing, allowing a single computer-controlled machine to do the work of an entire production line, and allowing unique, custom-made items to be produced to customers' individual specifications.

Miyake was born in Hiroshima in 1938. He studied graphics in Tokyo before heading to Paris, where he entered the Syndicat de la Couture and worked under legendary couturiers Guy Laroche and Hubert de Givenchy. After a spell in New York, he set up Miyake Design Studio in Toyko in 1970. Over the next 30 years he produced a series of highly inventive and internationally acclaimed collections including Pleats Please, a range constructed of body-hugging, permanently pleated fabrics that he launched in 1993. Miyake's work is inspired by – but does not imitate – traditional Japanese clothing, such as the kimono, creating loose, sculptural silhouettes that move with the body without fetishizing the figure, as is the norm in so much contemporary fashion. Hence his clothes are often described as architecture for the body.

In 2000, he handed over the reins of his label to his right-hand man, Naoki Takizawa, in order to concentrate on APOC with his partner Dai Fujiwara. Since then he has refined the manufacturing technique and expanded into the production of accessories and furniture.

Living Room Collection

Date **2000**

Designer **Hussein Chalayan**

Brand/Manufacturer **Hussein Chalayan, UK**

Unlike most other fashion designers, concept and process are more important to Hussein Chalayan than the end result. An intensely intellectual designer, Chalayan is not interested in the frothy glamour and celebrity obsession of the mainstream fashion industry and instead often bases his work on intensely personal political and cultural themes.

A Turkish-Cypriot born in Nicosia, Cyprus, and educated in London, Chalayan became the darling of the British fashion press with his groundbreaking Living Room collection, presented in spring 2000. Held at the Sadler's Wells theatre in London, it featured a plain white stage set with a range of tables and chairs that transformed into clothing. Armchair covers became dresses and a round table became a skirt as the models picked up the furniture, put them on and walked off. The show was based on the theme of enforced exile: the models represented families who had to flee their homes because of impending war or the threat of death. Chalayan says the idea is based on memories of the invasion of Cyprus in the '70s and the war in Kosovo in the '90s. Displacement and the collision of cultures is often a theme of his work: his spring/summer 1998 show featured six models wearing traditional Muslim chadors of diminishing length, so that the first was covered from head to toe and the last was naked. His spring/summer 2003 show, called Kinship Journey, mixed Armenian, Georgian, Byzantine and Viking influences.

Chalayan is perhaps too much of an individualist to work exclusively for a major brand, although he has produced ranges for Asprey, TSE and Top Shop. For all the conceptual theatrics of his early shows, Chalayan is a talented craftsman who increasingly produces highly wearable yet innovative collections each year. The cut and construction of his clothes are exceptional and he is regarded as one of the most important fashion designers of his time.

Birkis

Date **2004**

Designer **Yves Béhar**

Brand/Manufacturer **Birkenstock, Germany**

Founded by Konrad Birkenstock in Germany in 1896, Birkenstock was the first company to produce footwear with flexible arch supports. More recently, it has become famous for its ergonomic, cork-soled, leather-strapped sandals, which were first produced in 1964 and have enjoyed renewed popularity in the last few years. In response to its new-found fashionability, Birkenstock has launched several lines of more style-driven products in collaboration with well-known designers, including this 2004 range of plastic clogs by San Francisco-based product designer Yves Béhar.

Visually the Birki resembles a traditional wooden clog, although the flexible plastic means the shoe moulds itself to the form of the foot. Designed with gardeners in mind, the slip-on shoes are produced from a single piece of brightly coloured, moulded Alpro-Cell, making them totally waterproof, light and extremely durable. Grip is provided by a honeycomb pattern on the sole, which resembles the tread of a tyre. The inner features lateral ducts to ensure the circulation of air while the toe and front part is reinforced to protect the foot. To clean the shoe, you simply hose it down.

Béhar has also designed a second range for Birkenstock. His Architect collection for the brand's Footprints line is a range of urban footwear, which includes shoes and boots that combine leather uppers and moulded plastic soles.

Béhar is one of America's leading industrial designers. Born in Lausanne, Switzerland in 1967 to a German mother and a Turkish father, he studied industrial design in Europe and later at the Art Center College of Design in Pasadena, California. He worked at Frog Design in Silicon Valley and at Lunar, developing products for companies including Silicon Graphics, Hewlett Packard and Apple Computer. In 1999 he founded his own studio called Fuseproject. Besides Birkenstock, Béhar has designed computers and peripherals for brands including Toshiba and Microsoft and a range of leisure wear for car brand MINI. He is also developing perfume packaging for fashion designer Hussein Chalayan and a number of products for sportswear brand Nike.

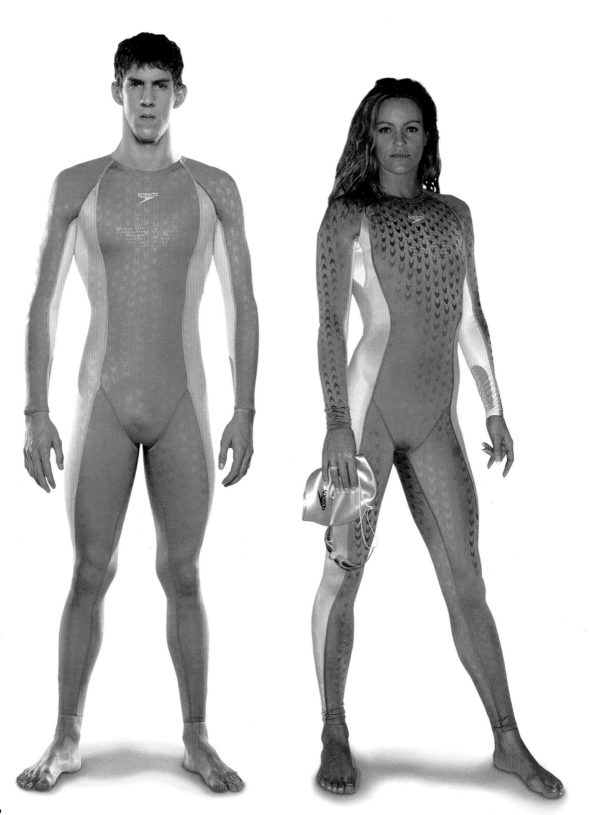

Speedo Fastskin

Date **2000**
Designer **Speedo design team**
Brand/Manufacturer **Speedo, USA**

Designed to mimic the skin of a shark, this swimwear fabric reduces drag to enable competitive swimmers to swim faster. Speedo's Fastskin is an example of biomimetics – the science of mimicking nature to produce advanced materials. Sharkskin is covered in microscopic v-shaped ridges called dermal denticles. These decrease turbulence, allowing water to pass more efficiently over the shark's body and reducing drag. Scientists and engineers at swimwear company Speedo sought to mimic natural sharkskin, creating a woven fabric with similar ridges on its surface. In addition, the highly elastic "superstretch" fabric compresses the athletes' muscles, helping them perform better. Launched in 2000, Fastskin was found to be 7.5 per cent faster than rival materials. Of all swimming medals at that year's Sydney Olympics, 83 per cent were won by athletes wearing Fastskin, according to the manufacturer.

In 2004, Speedo launched Fastskin FSII, a suit made of a more advanced fabric and containing a number of new innovations.

Whereas the original fabric was tested in a water flume, this was developed using Computational Fluid Dynamics (CFD) technology, which involves analyzing the performance of a virtual swimmer in mathematically modelled water. CFD is commonly used to develop Formula 1 cars and also in the aerospace industry, but it had never been used in the garment industry before. The new suit mimics the way dermal denticles vary according to the water flow at various points along the shark: those on the shark's nose are rough while those further downstream are smaller and smoother. Individual athletes' bodies were digitally scanned to optimize the fit of their suits.

However, fabricating a bodysuit entirely in this fabric would cause the swimmer to lose the "feel" of the water, so Speedo's researchers developed panels of titanium silicone featuring microscopic three-dimensional scales, which are applied to the inner forearms and neutralize the effect of the suit. The Fastskin FSII has up to four per cent less drag that the original Fastskin suit.

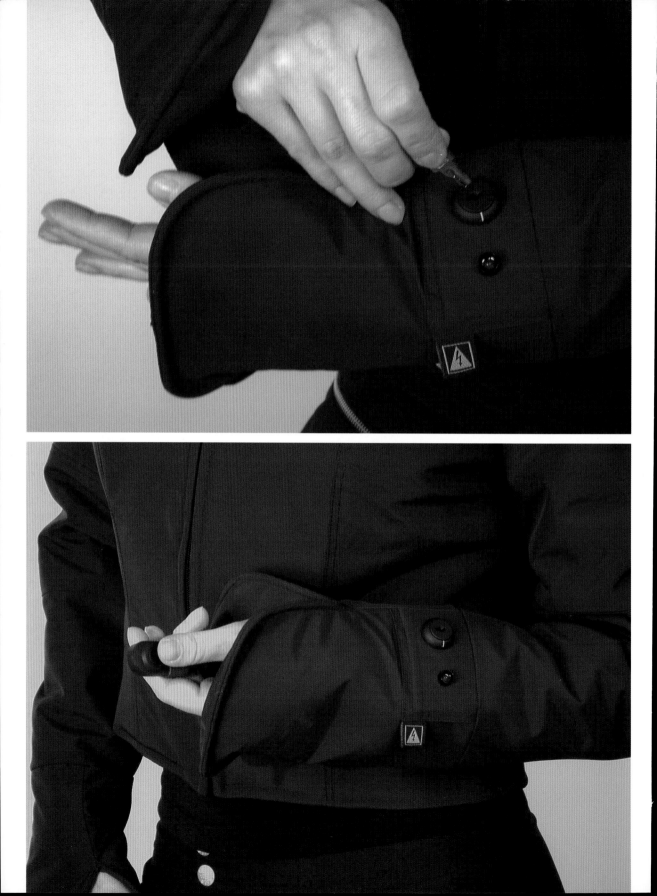

No-Contact Jacket

Date **2002**
Designer **Adam Whiton and Yolita Nugent**
Brand/Manufacturer **No Contact, USA**

Many designers are attempting to integrate electronics into clothing, but the No-Contact jacket is perhaps the most extreme manifestation yet. The jacket features a layer of electrically conductive fabric that, when activated, gives the assailant an 80,000 volt electric shock. Designed by Americans Adam Whiton, an industrial designer at the Massachusetts Institute of Technology, and Yolita Nugent, head designer at Advanced Research Apparel, it is intended to give women a means of defending themselves when attacked and was designed in response to a report stating that three quarters of all American women would be victims of at least one violent crime during their lifetime. Besides offering protection, the designers were also aiming to raise awareness of the levels of violence against women and reverse the fashion industry's tendency to exploit, rather than respond to, women's vulnerability.

The rugged garment resembles a waterproof motorcycle jacket. The outer layer of Teflon-coated waterproof supplex nylon conceals and protects the electrically conductive material, which is powered by a 9-volt alkaline battery. The shock administered on contact is enough to temporarily disable the assailant's neuromuscular system, causing short-term disorientation, loss of balance and pain. An electrically insulated rubber under-layer protects the wearer from electric shocks while insulated sleeves extending from the arms prevent her from accidentally touching the charged exterior.

When entering a potentially threatening area, the wearer activates the jacket using a keyed lock, causing a red warning LED to flash. The defence system is triggered by pressing either of two switches that extend from the arms to rest in the palm of the hands. An audible electric arc leaps between two projecting seams below the jacket's right shoulder, warning the assailant that the jacket is armed. Whiton and Nugent are currently patenting the design and plan to manufacture it in the near future.

Fabrican Clothing

Date **2003**
Designer **Manel Torres**
Brand/Manufacturer **Fabrican, UK**

Fabrican is an attempt to develop fabric that can be sprayed from a can rather than woven. It raises the possibility of "spray on" clothing that is created either directly on the body or on a mould, removing the need to cut and sew flat cloth into garments.

Developed by Royal College of Art graduate Manel Torres at Imperial College London, the patented idea involves mixing fabric fibres with a binding agent. When sprayed onto a surface, the mixture builds up in layers, allowing fabric of varying thickness to be created. The properties of the resulting fabric can be altered to make the material flexible or stiff, rough or smooth, and so on. Torres' early experiments used cotton fibres, but recent trials involve a wide variety of both natural and artificial fibres.

So far his trials have created complete garments, but the technology could also be used to create applied decoration or padding to traditionally produced clothing, or to make three-dimensional forms that are difficult to create with two-dimensional fabric. Sprayed fabrics could also be adopted by the furniture or automotive industries to produce upholstery.

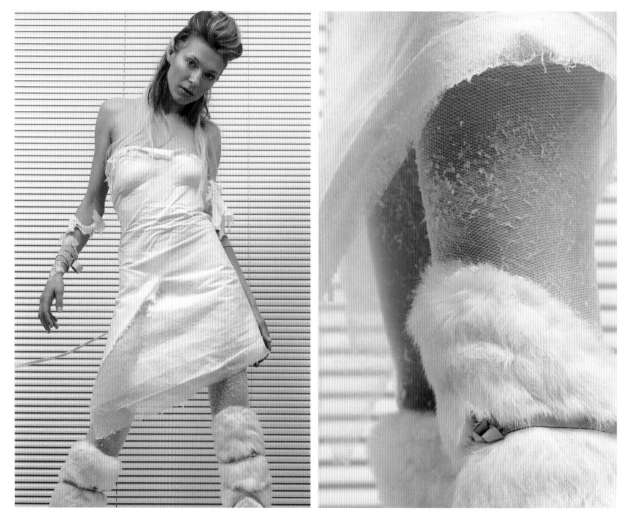

American Apparel

Date **2003**

Founder **Dov Charney**

Brand/Manufacturer **American Apparel, USA**

Since opening its first shop in Los Angeles in October 2003, casual clothing chain American Apparel has become America's fastest growing and most talked-about fashion brand. While the clothes it sells are simple, plain-coloured and logo-free, the company itself is highly unusual, both for its ethical manufacturing policy and its notorious marketing approach. The company's founder and senior partner, Dov Charney, was born in Canada in 1969 and began selling T-shirts in Montreal as a teenager, later manufacturing plain garments to be sold to companies that produced printed T-shirts.

At a time when clothing companies are increasingly outsourcing their manufacturing to factories in the Far East, American Apparel produces everything in a single, enormous building in downtown Los Angeles. This "vertically integrated manufacturing", the brand claims, allows it to take a garment range from conception to completion in a week, meaning it can respond extremely quickly to consumer demand. With 100 stores around the world and 5,000 employees globally, it is now the largest garment manufacturer in the USA. Because it doesn't outsource to local or developing-nation sweatshops (or to ad agencies, for that matter) the entire process is time-efficient, and responds faster to market demand. It proudly pays its workers above the minimum wage and provides above-average working conditions. The company trumpets these progressive elements in its stores and its literature.

Yet it has also been controversial, notably for its sexually charged advertising that some critics have compared to soft porn. Its adverts, which are a world away from the airbrushed glamour of most fashion imagery, often feature amateurish shots of young men and women in provocative or submissive poses. The models are often American Apparel employees and photos are taken by Dov Charney himself, as well as other photographers. The images here are from American Apparel's catalogue and also show some of the advertisements publicizing the opening of the company's store in Mexico City and London in 2005.

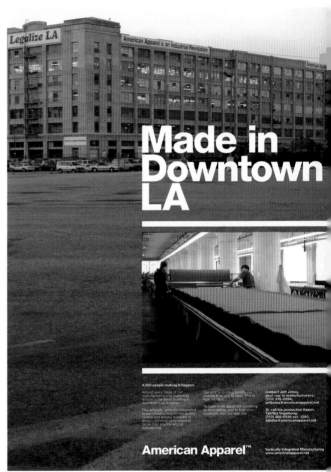

¡Viva México City!

Sofia, one of our original Mexico City store employees, also makes her way to Playa del Carmen sometimes to help sell bikinis from our year-round swim line. She's seen here wearing our Bandeau Bikini Top, available online and at our stores.

Next stop for her may be London, where we hear they could use a dose of Latin warmth. Word is that Mexicans are scarce over there, and we couldn't think of a lovelier messenger to spread the news about one of our favorite places.

Sofia is photographed here in our Mexico City apartment where, just five months earlier, the *Mexico City Monthly* was conceived. This new publication by us and some friends will be distributed for free at our stores worldwide.

To learn more about our company, to shop online, and to find store locations, visit our web site.

American Apparel®

Made in Downtown LA
Vertically Integrated Manufacturing
www.americanapparel.net

DANCE
by American Apparel®

¡Mamacita!

Manantia Lira, (aka Spring), was born in La Paz, Mexico. When she was 12 years old, she and her family moved to the United States. "My sisters and I bought some sunglasses and new clothes and tried to pass ourselves off as American girls at the Mexican/American border."

We met Spring at a pool party in the summer of 2003. She has since graced the pages (and covers) of many a catalog, as well as ads, billboards and store walls.

One of her most exciting contributions to the company though, was a small T-shirt stand that she ran on Venice Beach. In a sense, it was the first American Apparel store, and the success of that tiny operation was one of the inspirations for our move into retail. She has since opened and managed many of our stores.

We just found out that Spring is going to have a baby, and wanted to take the opportunity to celebrate her. To us, she's a reflection of what Los Angeles is all about. We look forward to welcoming this new addition to the family.

To learn more about our company, to shop online, and to find all store locations, visit our web site: www.americanapparel.net

American Apparel® Made in Downtown LA
Vertically Integrated Manufacturing

horts

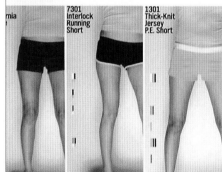

7301
Interlock
Running
Short

1301
Thick-Knit
Jersey
P.E. Short

Skirts

1303
Thick-Knit
Jersey
Skirt

8325
Stretch
Cotton
Skort

5303
California
Fleece
Skirt

RSA7300
High-
Waisted
Skirt

Shirts

4400
Baby Rib
Fitted S/S
T-Shirt

4408
Baby Rib
Tank

3408
2x1 Rib
Tank

2065
Fine Jersey
Muscle
T-Shirt

2456
Fine Jersey
S/S V-Neck

2406
Fine Jersey
Pocket
S/S T-Shirt

2410
Fine Jersey
S/S Ringer
T-Shirt

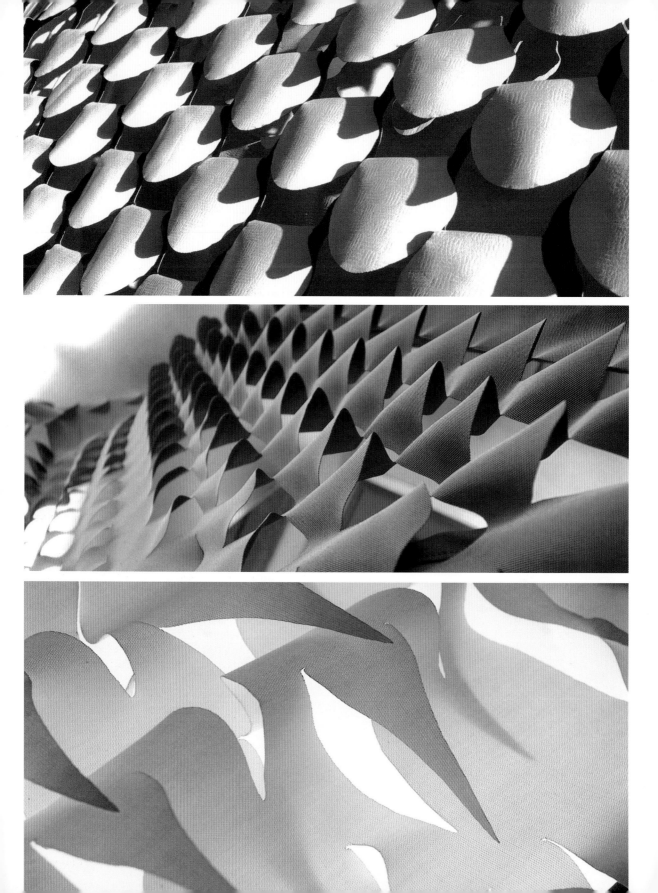

Clad Cuts

Date **2004**
Designer **Elena Manferdini**
Brand/Manufacturer **Atelier Manferdini, USA**

Developed by architect Elena Manferdini of California-based Atelier Manferdini, Clad Cuts takes design techniques used in other disciplines, such as architecture, product design and computer animation, and combines them to produce clothing that requires a minimal amount of hand finishing. This approach is an attempt to apply advanced computer modelling and manufacturing techniques to clothing, exploring how developments, such as three-dimensional modelling and mass customization, could be applied to the fashion industry.

Compared to the industrial design industry, fashion is still largely craft-based and relies on skilled sample sewers to produce prototypes and factories full of workers to assemble the garments. This is partly because of the vast range of sizes, styles and colours that are required and the rapid obsolescence of product lines. It is also because the complex, constantly moving geometry of individual human bodies presents a design challenge of such complexity that technology is only just beginning to be able to respond.

In the case of Clad Cuts, the garments are first created on screen using three-dimensional modelling software. The designs are then imported into animation software, where they are "worn" by moving models. This process is used to record the way the garment responds to movement and allows adjustments to be made. In theory, thanks to developments in body scanning technology, each garment could be tested on individual customers and an unlimited number of bespoke versions manufactured.

Once the garment's design has been finalized, the three-dimensional forms are unfolded to produce two-dimensional patterns. The patterns are engineered to require the minimum number of seams to reduce finishing time, and then sent to laser-cutting machines, which are capable of cutting many sheets of fabric at once. Fabrics with synthetic content such as cotton-polyester blends are used as these self-seal when exposed to the heat of the laser, meaning edges do not require seaming. Manferdini's collection also features decorative vents cut into the fabric during the cutting process.

Zvezdochka Trainers

Date **2004**
Designer **Marc Newson**
Brand/Manufacturer **Nike, USA**

Named after the fifth Russian dog to be blasted into space, Marc Newson's Zvezdochka trainers, for sportswear giant Nike, were inspired by photographs of cosmonauts wearing special socks while taking exercise by bouncing around in the zero gravity of their spaceship. Despite the Space Race nostalgia of their genesis, the trainers mark a technological and aesthetic step forward for footwear. The modular design consists of just four manufactured parts, rather than the dozens of components that are machine-sewn or glued together to create most contemporary footwear. This reduces waste and potentially allows for a more efficient production process.

The first part is the outer shell, which is made of a single piece of moulded TPU (thermoplastic urethane) – a recyclable, tear-resistant plastic with high elasticity and good resilience. This shell, which is perforated with a pattern of open circles to allow air to circulate, was created using three-dimensional modelling software and is manufactured on a highly complex, multi-part mould. A second part, an interlocking TPU sole, sits inside the shell to form the base of the shoe. Fitted inside the shell, a removable, slipper-like inner sleeve moulds itself to the wearer's foot, acting like a combined insole and sock. This sleeve can also be worn separately. The fourth part, a cushioned inner sole, sits in the base of the sleeve for additional support and comfort. Available in a range of colours, the shoe was initially launched as a limited edition and sold through leading design shops rather than traditional sportswear users, revealing its intended status as a fashion statement rather than a performance-driven purchase.

Nike's collaboration with Newson is just one of many recent joint ventures between designers and sportswear brands keen to increase their kudos among discerning consumers. For example, Adidas has long worked with Yohji Yamamoto, and Puma has recently created a line of shoes and sandals with Philippe Starck.

V-bag

Date **2004**
Designer **Freedom of Creation**
Manufacturer **Materialise, Belgium**

This shoulder bag is one of a range of garments and accessories produced by Dutch designers Freedom of Creation using rapid prototyping technologies – a new manufacturing technique that is usually used to create solid objects. The bag is constructed of highly flexible fabric made up of thousands of interlocking circular links of polyamide – a relatively lightweight, washable plastic. The fabric looks and feels rather like a very delicate chain-mail, although the links are solid and have no seam or join. Unlike traditional fabrics – that are made from strands of fibre woven together – the entire V-bag is "printed" in one go on an SLS (selective laser sintering) machine with the links already meshed together.

As with other rapid prototyping products, the bag is first modelled on a computer using CAD (computer-aided design) software. The digital file is then sent directly to the rapid prototyping machine. To remove the abrasive surfaces typical of SLS-produced plastics, the V-bags are placed in a rotating drum containing tiny ceramic particles, that smooth off the rough edges.

Rapid prototyping is still a relatively expensive and slow process so in order to improve efficiency, the computer software "bunches" the links of the fabric together in the most efficient way before printing. This means that the bag emerges from the rapid prototyping machine scrunched up rather than laid out flat, meaning that several bags can be printed at once.

Freedom of Creation, who designed the Lily lamp (see page 196) is also developing complete garments using rapid prototyping machines. Thus, by feeding data relating to size and preferred pattern into the CAD software, a tailor-made product can be produced. The designers have also proposed a mail-order system for their clothing and accessories, in which the product emerges from the rapid prototyping machine already encased in a box with the customer's address printed on it.

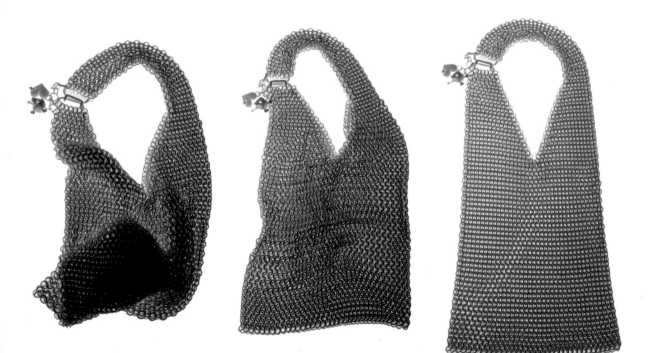

Melissa + Campana Shoes and Bag

Date **2005**
Designer **Fernando and Humberto Campana**
Brand **Melissa, Brazil**
Manufacturer **Grendene, Brazil**

Brazilian footwear label Melissa has been producing its trademark "jelly" shoes since 1979. Manufactured by footwear giant Grendene – the world's largest manufacturer of sandals – they have become one of the country's most successful and best-loved brands. To celebrate their 25th birthday, Melissa approached Brazilian design duo Fernando and Humberto Campana to create a new range of shoes and bags in their signature style.

The Campana Brothers have become international stars in recent years thanks to their exuberant furniture designs, such as the Favela chair (see page 142). These are inspired by the spontaneous creativity of the Brazilian people and employ unlikely materials, such as hosepipes, children's cuddly toys and scraps of fabric and wood. For their Melissa range, the brothers revisited a technique of weaving pliable, off-the-shelf materials, such as plastic tubing or nylon string, randomly back and forth across a frame. This was an idea that was inspired by the sight of tangled hoses lying in the gardens of suburban São Paolo. They had already used the technique, which they call "zigzag", to create a range furniture items, such as chairs, stools and screens, with loosely-woven seats backs and surfaces. The same process seemed appropriate to moulded "jelly" shoes, since the resulting fabric has numerous gaps that would allow air to circulate around the feet.

The brothers began experimenting with 3 mm ($^{1}/_{8}$ in) diameter aluminium wire, which they hand-wove into the shape of a shoe. This prototype was then refined by Melissa's designers to create the open-weave effect of the final product. The result is a range of three types of moulded plastic shoe – high-heeled, low-heeled and tennis – and a bag. All are in an range of primary colours plus black and white. The low-heeled shoes are moulded in one part, while the high-heeled version has a moulded upper fixed to a clear plastic heel. The bag is made of two circular side panels and a base that clip together.

Fossil by Starck

Date **2000**
Designer **Philippe Starck**
Brand/Manufacturer **Fossil, USA**

Designer watches are becoming something of a twenty-first century phenomenon, as fashion and lifestyle brands commission designers more used to working in the furniture and industrial fields to create timepieces for them. The result is a rapidly growing range of dual-branded watches that bear the names of both the designer and the brand. The objects tend to be more adventurous and futuristic than the traditional or retro-looking styles that most brands' in-house designers come up with.

One of the most successful of these collaborations is Philippe Starck's range for Fossil, which was launched in 2001 and now contains more than a dozen different models. The design language common to almost all of them is the way in which each watch is flattened, its edges rounded and its back arched so that it integrates seamlessly with the rubber strap. This unisex product comes in a variety of colours, with the face coloured to coordinate with the strap. Thus,

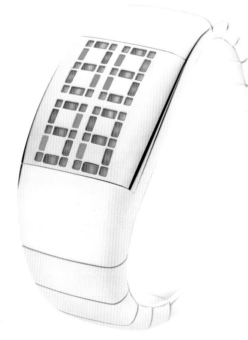

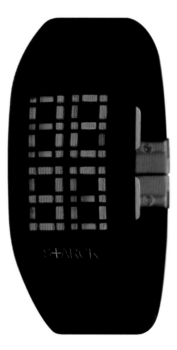

visually, watch and strap read as one, resembling a bangle or bracelet rather than a traditional timepiece. Buttons controlling the alarm, chronograph timer and countdown timer are set flush along the side of the face in early models, with later versions featuring a circular input panel set into the strap. The rectangular faces have a digital display consisting of thin, extended, square-edged LCD numerals – something of a Starck trademark, since his collection of barometric clocks for Oregon Scientific also employ similar grid-like numerals. More recent versions, launched in 2006, feature LED displays with the matrix of clear plastic housings that make up the numeric display exaggerated to create an abstract pattern akin to jewels.

Other collaborations between designers and brands include designs by Harri Koskinen, Tokujin Yoshioka and Naoto Fukasawa for Issey Miyake, Yves Béhar's designs for MINI and Marc Newson's work for Ikepod.

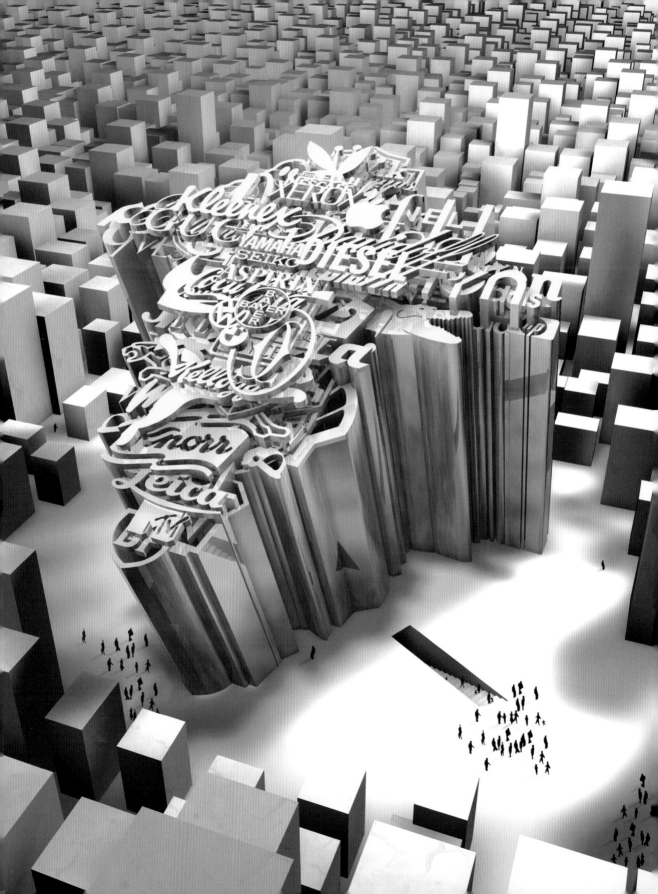

Bling Bling

Date **2002**
Designer **Frank Tjepkema**
Manufacturer **Che ha paura, Netherlands**

From a distance, this pendant appears to be nothing more than an elaborately decorated gold crucifix. However, on closer inspection, it turns out to be made up of the logos of hundreds of the world's best-known brands. Created by the Swiss designer Frank Tjepkema, Bling Bling is a piece of conceptual jewellery that comments on the contemporary obsession with brands. It makes the point that, according to some, shopping has become a replacement for religion and logos have replaced religious iconography as the preferred way of displaying allegiance.

The piece, which Tjepkema describes as "the most branded object in the world", measures 8 cm (3 in) by 9 cm (3 ⅕ in) and is made of gold-plated silver alloy. The cut-out logos, which include everything from lifestyle brands such as Diesel, Nike and Puma to McDonald's, Coca-Cola, Volkswagen and Michelin, are superimposed over one another to create a thick crust. The medallion's name, Bling Bling, refers to

the name given to describe the overtly materialistic taste of American hip hop artists, who favour chunky jewellery and clothing by luxury brands with prominent logos.

Bling Bling was created in 2002 for Che ha paura, a jewellery label based in Amsterdam. Founded in 1996 by Droog design founder Gijs Bakker and Italian jewellery retailer Marijke Vallanzasca, its aim was to create a new range of jewellery that was not merely decorative, but also had some kind of conceptual meaning. Che ha paura has commissioned designs from many leading contemporary designers.

Tjepkema was born in Geneva in 1970 and studied at Design Academy Eindhoven. He now runs Tjep, his studio, which is based in Amsterdam. His work includes furniture, interiors and industrial design. In 2004, he proposed a none-too-serious follow-up to Bling Bling called The Next Bling – a giant scaled-up version of the pendant, intended to house a shopping mall (left).

Bio Jewellery

Date **2003**

Designer **Tobie Kerridge and Nikki Stott**

Bio Jewellery is part of an ongoing project that explores ways of making tangible objects that exploit recent scientific advances in the field of biotechnology in order to provoke public discussion of the subject. Designers Tobie Kerridge and Nikki Stott developed the idea of producing jewellery using human bone tissue that has been grown in a laboratory. The project involves extracting bone cells from a couple and "seeding" them to produce bone tissue that would then be used to make a pair of rings. The bone is combined with precious materials (far right) and formed into rings. The rings, designed according to the donors' wishes, would then contain their combined DNA and serve as a unique symbol of their relationship. By exchanging rings, the couple would, in effect, be giving a part of themselves to each other.

The project was initiated in 2003 at the Royal College of Art in London, where lecturers Tony Dunne and Fiona Raby of Dunne & Raby set a brief called "Consuming Monsters" on the Interaction Design course. They worked in conjunction with Ian Thompson, a bioengineer at Kings College London.

Under the brief, students were asked to consider ways of encouraging debate about the ethics of biotechnology – a subject that is usually presented in the media as a futuristic and somewhat frightening branch of science. By using biotechnology to produce familiar objects, such as pieces of jewellery, Dunne & Raby hoped that they would generate discussions that had more resonance with the general public than abstract debates about human cloning or genetically modified crops.

Once a donor couple has been found, bone samples will be taken and cultivated at Guy's Hospital in London. The ideal couple would be two people who require operations to remove wisdom teeth, as this usually involves the removal of bone tissue from the jaw. The tissue would then be cultivated until enough bone had been produced to fashion the rings. The design would then be developed in discussion with the doners in much the same way that a jewellery maker discusses a one-off commission with a client. The bone could be used in conjunction with precious metals, such as gold or silver.

To illustrate the potential of the project, the designers produced a sample ring using a section of cow bone with an inset silver band inscribed with the words *ab intra*, meaning "from within" (right).

Bio Jewellery is an example of a radical new branch of design called Critical Design, which focuses on producing objects that respond to social, ethical or intellectual needs rather than purely physical ones.

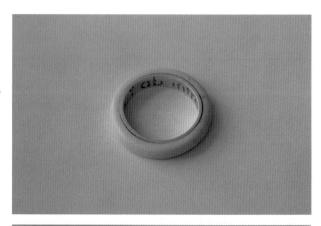

Visual Communication

Graphic designers over the past few decades have been almost too successful: the polished sophistication of advertising, media and packaging is threatening to drown consumers in an avalanche of messages. At the same time, consumers are becoming increasingly adept at filtering out such exhortations to buy and are becoming cynical about brands' attempts to communicate with them. In particular, the rise of the Internet has facilitated new methods of two-way communicating that make the traditional, one-way messages from brand to consumer seem antiquated.

The desktop publishing boom of the late twentieth century made the creation of seductive visuals relatively easy and now, in the twenty-first century, cutting-edge designers are exploring new ways of communicating. Many are pioneers of a new type of visual media that is complex, decorative and – initially at least – almost impenetrable. Arguing that messages have become too easy to decipher and are therefore ignored, the work of these designers demands effort to decode. Some are even questioning the morality of the work they do on behalf of brands: Jonathan Barnbrook's billboard for Adbusters, for example, is a heartfelt plea to the profession to think twice before taking on work that involves persuading consumers to buy things they don't need.

Other designers are taking their cue from developments in street art, such as fly-posting, graffiti and stickering. Ji Lee's Bubble Project subverts advertising by allowing passers-by to talk back at messages that, until now, they have simply had to endure. Meanwhile, street artist Banksy has become a counterculture hero, using the city itself as a billboard for imagery and messages that strike a chord with the public. In traditional advertising, brands are having to invent new ways of communicating with potential customers. Wieden + Kennedy's multi-award winning "Grrr" commercial for Honda is part entertainment and part global corporation laughing at itself.

Over the past few years, computers have allowed designers to create highly sophisticated imagery, but there are signs that both designers and the public are getting bored with this. Much of the more interesting contemporary illustrative work today involves using computers to create work that appears to be artisanal and folkloric, such as the pixel graphics of Delaware that resembles traditional cross-stitching. Similarly, Craig Robinson's Minipops and eBoy's pixillated landscapes perversely employ computer power to create imagery that recalls the crude visual style of early PCs. Others, such as Robert Ryan, are dispensing with computers altogether and producing beautiful, delicate works with traditional materials.

AIGA Detroit Lecture Poster

Date **1999**

Designer **Stefan Sagmeister**

This poster, consisting of a photograph of Austrian graphic artist Stefan Sagmeister's naked torso covered in words scratched into his skin, is one of the most memorable graphic images of recent years. With its DIY aesthetic, striking visual impact and macabre nihilism, the image recalls – in spirit at least – punk-era graphics, such as Jamie Reid's seminal artwork for the Sex Pistols. After studying in Vienna and New York and working with legendary graphic designer Tibor Kalman, this poster was the culmination of several years' work by New York-based Sagmeister – widely regarded as one of the most influential graphic designers of our time. In it he rejected the over-stylized, computer-generated look of most contemporary graphics and instead searched for something more raw and powerful.

The poster was created to advertise a lecture Sagmeister was giving at the Cranbrook Academy of Art, Michigan, during the annual conference of the American Institute of Graphic Arts (AIGA), held in Detroit in 1999. Featuring a variety of letter types and doodles, the typographic style of the poster resembles the inadvertent marks scribbled on a pad during a telephone conversation. Sagmeister's idea was to try to express the pain involved in producing good work and the entire text for the poster – down to the time, date, ticket prices and sponsors' credits – was scratched into Sagmeister's chest and arm with a scalpel. The process took several hours and "hurt real bad", according to Sagmeister.

Sagmeister Inc. has produced artwork for musicians, such as the Rolling Stones, Lou Reed and Talking Heads, and his work often features touches of humour, subversion and borderline obscenity. Previous posters include his 1996 Fresh Dialogue, an advertisement for a series of talks that showed hand-written text surrounding two cut-out photos of huge, extended tongues; and 1997's AIGA conference poster featuring a headless chicken running across a field, which was intended as a comment on the often directionless nature of much graphic design.

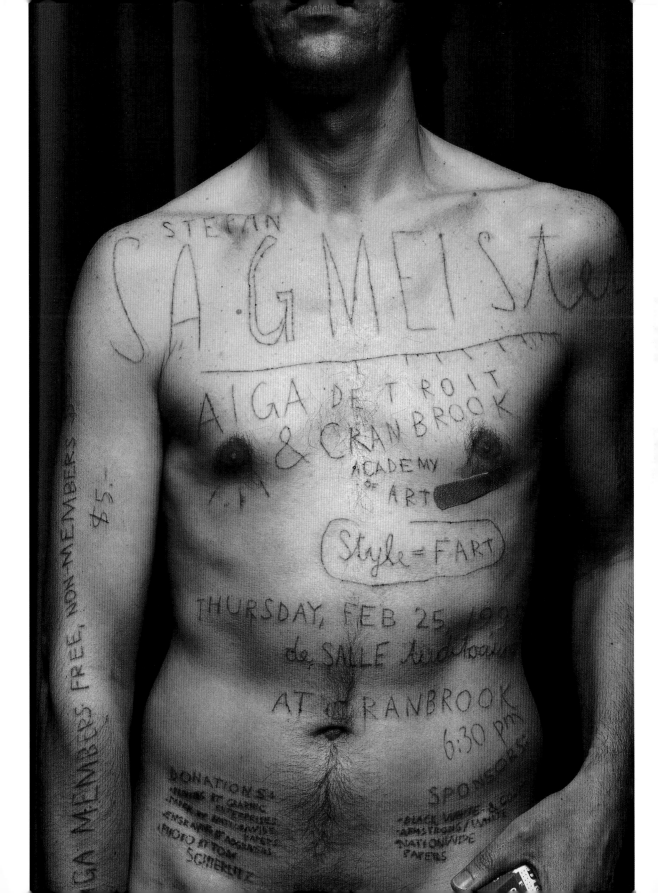

Stencils

Date **1999**
Designer **Banksy**

Bansky uses a technique developed by the graphic design industry – the stencil – but his work is variously described as art, graffiti and vandalism. Yet it is hugely influential, informing not only other designers but also challenging accepted notions of what constitutes art and design in an urban context.

His distinctive work, which is rich with social comment, pathos, irony and wit, began to appear on the streets of Shoreditch in East London around the turn of the millennium and he is now a highly successful counter-culture figure, publishing books, holding exhibitions and pulling off creative stunts around the world. But Banksy remains a shadowy figure, concealing his identity, rarely granting interviews and never allowing himself to be photographed. This is perhaps unsurprising as his work is essentially illegal.

Stencilling, which involves spray-painting over pre-prepared paper or card templates to build up images in layers, has in recent years replaced free form graffiti as the chosen mode of self-expression for underground artists.

Banksy's early stencils were predominantly in black and white, varying in scale from small designs sprayed on doorways or alleys to huge images covering sides of buildings and railway bridges. Many of these have become much-loved London landmarks, such as his image of John Travolta and Samuel L Jackson, taken from the movie *Pulp Fiction*, with their guns replaced by bananas (see opposite page); or an army of police officers in full riot gear, their helmeted faces replaced by giant yellow smileys.

More recently, Banksy has taken on more ambitious projects, including assaults on galleries and museums in London and New York in which he creates subversive "artworks" and glues them up alongside recognized canvases. Another project, undertaken in 2005, involved surreptitiously stencilling nine large murals on the giant 684 km (425 mile) security wall that now divides Israel from the Palestinian territories (see left, top to bottom). One mural depicts a giant hole in the wall through which a tropical paradise can be seen, and the other shows joyful children playing with a bucket and spade.

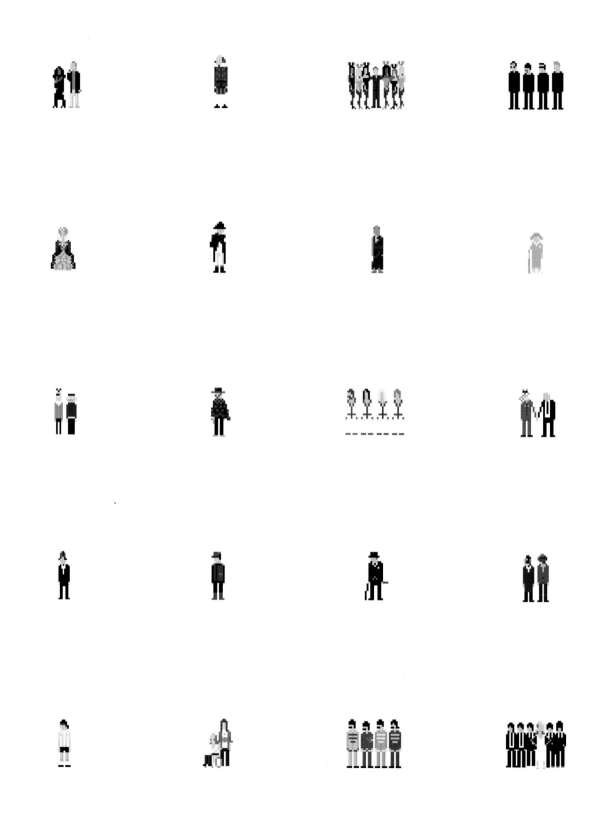

Minipops

Date **1999**
Designer **Craig Robinson**

Craig Robinson's Minipops started out as a quirky personal project for his website, but rapidly grew into an international graphics phenomenon. Consisting of tiny, pixillated drawings of pop stars and other celebrities, the series has expanded to over 7,000 drawings and is still growing – spawning a book, advertising campaigns and a host of imitators.

Minipops began on a Sunday afternoon in June 1999 when Robinson, an English-born artist, illustrator, designer and animator based in Berlin, was lacking inspiration. While watching trashy films on TV, he had the idea of drawing the five members of the Beach Boys – his favourite band – at the smallest possible scale that could be viewed on a computer screen yet still be recognizable. He built up representations of the band members using individual pixels, each character measuring no more than 8 by 2 mm ($^1/_3$ by $^1/_{16}$ in) and composed of just a couple of hundred tiny coloured squares with legs two pixels wide. He soon added the Beatles, Kraftwerk, Elvis and then hundreds of other characters, which he posted on his website, www.flipflopflying.com – the name of the site, which is also the name of his graphic design business, comes from the title of a Beach Boys' song "Loop de Loop (Flip Flop Flyin' in an Airplane)". Robinson has also created other series of characters including Normalpops – representations of generic characters, such as surgeons, cowboys and Guantanamo Bay prisoners.

The characters are now regarded as masterpieces of pixel art – a simple, naïve graphics style based on the manipulation of the smallest unit of digital composition, which is also pursued by designers including eBoy (see page 386) and Delaware (see page 393).

Robinson was born in 1970 in Lincoln, England, and studied in his home town and Derby before moving to London and later to Berlin. His self-taught digital style evolved after he bought his first iMac computer in 1998, which he used to build a website. He undertakes a wide range of commercial design work, but still dedicates hours to updating his site with new Minipops and other self-generated projects.

Design Museum Identity

Date **2002**
Designer **Kam Tang, Graphic Thought Facility**
Client **Design Museum, UK**

The new visual identity for London's Design Museum developed by illustrator Kam Tang and graphics studio Graphic Thought Facility is widely regarded as one of the most successful rebranding exercises of recent years. The museum was a rather dull and stuffy institution dedicated to industrial design when new director Alice Rawsthorn was appointed in 2001. She immediately set about revitalizing the institution to better reflect the diversity of contemporary design, and the following year commissioned GTF to develop and art direct a visual identity that reflected this. In turn, GTF brought in Kam Tang, a London-based illustrator renowned for his elaborately detailed and richly coloured vector graphics, to produce imagery to go with their typographic treatment.

Rather than create a single, pared-down icon to represent the museum, Tang developed a series of more than 50 complex black and white line drawings, each consisting of a different arrangement of intertwined objects. These objects are vaguely recognizable as domestic objects, products and so on and are intended to loosely suggest the wide variety of styles and movements in contemporary design. Yet, on closer inspection, it becomes clear that all the items are the fantastical product of Tang's imagination.

The concept has evolved each year to incorporate different materials and colours, and this highly flexible yet striking identity has been used to brand both the museum and its exhibitions as well as the museum's annual Designer of the Year award. The identity is used for print and screen applications as well as being applied directly to the walls of the Design Museum and, in 2006, the collage of objects also became a mobile, suspended in the museum's atrium.

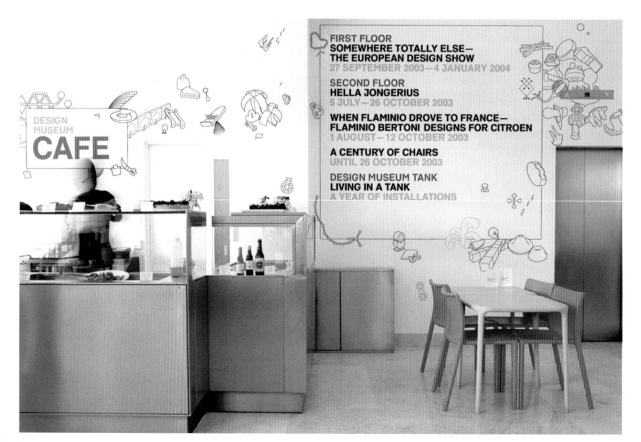

Honda Grr Commercial

Date **2004**

Animator **Nexus Productions**

Manufacturer **Wieden + Kennedy, UK**

Client **Honda, Japan**

Regularly described as one of the best television commercials of all time, Honda Grr is a fully animated spot commissioned to launch Honda's first-ever diesel engine. When briefed to create the advert, London advertising agency Wieden + Kennedy discovered that Kenichi Nagahiro, Honda's chief engine designer, hated diesel engines because they were dirty, noisy and smelly. Company legend has it that, when asked to design the brand's first diesel engine, he refused unless he was allowed to create a new, more environmentally friendly one from scratch. The result was the 2.2 i-CTDi engine, which Honda claims is one of the cleanest, quietest diesels on the market. Thus, Wieden + Kennedy deduced the engine was born out of hate. The ad's concept became about how hatred of something can be channelled creatively to replace the object of hate with something better.

The 90-second film, created by Nexus Productions using advanced computer animation software, is a psychedelic, colour-saturated fantasy that recalls the innocence and optimism of early Disney blockbusters. It features a fleet of diesel engines flying through a bucolic landscape of meadows, streams and gardens that are populated by endearing deer, rabbits and butterflies. The nasty, polluting diesel engines are shot down by the rabbits with bows and arrows while the clean, green Honda engines are greeted by friendly birds and animals as they float through their paradise garden without polluting the air. Meanwhile, a ditty is playing with the chorus "Love something/hate something" sung by American voice-over artist and author Garrison Keillor and featuring a catchy whistled hook. Wieden + Kennedy creatives pitched the idea to Honda executives while singing and whistling the tune themselves.

3 Logo

Date **2004**

Designer **Miles Newlyn**

Client **Hutchison Whampoa, Hong Kong**

The development of third generation (3G) mobile telephone networks in the early years of the twenty-first century created something of a gold rush in the UK, as businesses bid billions to secure national licences for networks that promised video and Internet access as well as voice calls. Hong Kong-based business conglomerate Hutchison Whampoa was among the most aggressive players in this market, securing licences around the world for its nascent network called "3". Choosing a number for the brand name rather than a word ensured that the title would be universally understood, and avoid the pitfalls created when a word in one language has a different meaning in another.

Created by British-born typographer Miles Newlyn in 2001, when the brand name was still secret, the 3 logo represents an attempt to reflect the universality of the name by creating a symbol that is understood in every country in the world without the need for translation or adaptation to local customs. London-based Newlyn, a graduate of St Martin's School of Art, went for the obvious option of using a number 3 rather than an abstract or conceptual design, making the figure three-dimensional to express the network's third-generation functionality. Keen to avoid colours associated with other mobile networks, he initially settled on violet, until he learned that this was the colour of death in Italy. Thus, instead of choosing just one corporate colour, he developed the idea of an animated logo that ran through all the colours of the rainbow. This makes the 3 logo perhaps the first dynamic corporate logo ever designed and appropriate for display on mobile phone screens.

Newlyn's completed design features a colourless shell in the shape of a highly stylized number 3 that has a molten, kaleidoscopic core, representing the notion of something that is cool on the outside and hot on the inside.

Grand Theft Auto: Vice City

Date **2002**

Designer **Rockstar Games**

When it was released in 2002, Grand Theft Auto: Vice City took computer games to a new level. Set in a city modelled closely on Miami, the game – that superseded Grand Theft Auto III – was the first to present a believable and realistically modelled environment. It was also the first with an open-ended narrative, where the gamer – rather than the game itself – decided what happened next. Designed with the same production values as movies, Grand Theft Auto: Vice City was also one of the first games marketed as a culturally relevant lifestyle product. The creators, Rockstar Games, designed the game as well as all the spin-off material, including advertising, posters and promotional material with the same attention to detail, creating a seamless and sophisticated brand.

This approach, borrowed from the fashion and music industries, was new to computer games. Previously, most games had been themed around children's cartoon characters, science fiction or fantasy genres, but Vice City drew on pop-culture memories of Miami that were drawn from the hit 1980s' TV series *Miami Vice*. With '80s fashion and music undergoing something of a revival at the time of the product's launch, this was a masterstroke: the game satirizes the clothes, hairstyles and attitudes of the era, presenting Miami as a sleazy, money-obsessed and crime-infested playground.

The game contains a hyper-realistic version of the city that gamers can navigate on foot or in a variety of vehicles including open-top sports cars, motorcycles and helicopters. The main character interacts, and even engages in conversation, with others along the way. The seductive power of the visuals and narrative disguises the game's technical innovation: sophisticated new streaming technology allows for high-speed action sequences and short loading times, while advanced modelling techniques were used to replicate the drive feel of the various vehicles. Following its launch in November 2002, Grand Theft Auto: Vice City became the world's bestselling computer game, selling 11.5 million copies.

In 2004, Grand Theft Auto: San Andreas was released – an even more realistic game set in three cities based on Los Angeles, San Francisco and Las Vegas in the early 1990s.

eCity

Date **2004**

Designer **Steffen Saurteig, Svend Smital, Kai Vermehr
and Peter Stemmler/eBoy**

Founded in Berlin in 1998 by Steffen Sauerteig, Svend Smital and Kai Vermehr, eBoy were later joined by New York-based Peter Stemmler. They now have offices in both cities, with the three Germans creating the pixel work and Stemmler working on a parallel series of vector graphics. This four-strong collective is the best-known exponent of the "pixel" style of illustration, which uses the basic digital unit as a building block for highly complex axonometric scenes that are reminiscent of computer games such as the Sims or Lego constructions. They draw much of their inspiration from images sourced in magazines and on Google, creating a database of toy-like individual elements, such as vehicles, buildings and advertising hoardings, all drawn in axonometric. They use these to build up their multi-layered compositions, which they create using PhotoShop image manipulation software.

They have worked for a huge range of clients, providing illustrations for magazines such as *Wired* and *Creative Review* and producing imagery for Coca Cola, Nike and Kellogg's. They have also staged numerous exhibitions.

In 2004, eBoy were commissioned by British fashion designer Paul Smith to create an addition to their eCity series based on London, which Smith used as a fabric print on elements of his collection such as bags, T-shirts and shoe linings. This series recreates fantastical, cartoon versions of real cities such as Venice, Miami and Berlin. They are brought to life with dramatic, but unrelated, scenes plucked from comics and action movies – police officers engage robbers in shoot-outs, while giant monsters rampage through streets and alien spacecraft destroy buildings. The four members of eBoy – who look remarkably similar with their cropped blond hair – are often to be found somewhere in their cityscapes, relaxing on rooftops or dancing in the street, and there are usually also a few nudes concealed among the mayhem.

Gorillaz

Date **1999**
Designer **Jamie Hewlett**

Underground comic culture burst into the mainstream with Gorillaz, a virtual band consisting of animated musicians created by the British cult illustrator Jamie Hewlett. Hewlett began his career in the late 1980s with *Tank Girl*, a cartoon strip about a punk character who had a mutant kangaroo for a boyfriend and drove around in a tank. The strip, featured in a British magazine called *Deadline*, became a cult classic and was later turned into a Hollywood movie.

Hewlett came up with the concept for Gorillaz with Damon Albarn, singer in the British group Blur, when the two shared a flat together in London. The band consists of four cartoon musicians: lead singer 2D, bass guitarist Murdoc Niccals, guitarist Noodle and drummer Russell Hobbs. While Albarn writes the music, Hewlett develops the band members' characters and fictional histories and produces the group's artwork, promo videos, website and animated performances. The runaway success of Gorillaz's first two albums – the eponymous *Gorillaz* sold six million copies worldwide and the

follow-up *Demon Days* sold even more – makes Hewlett perhaps the most visible graphic artist in the world. The gorillaz.com website – based around Kong Studios, the band's fictional home and studio – attracts around 10 million page impressions a month.

Since Gorillaz was formed in 1999, Hewlett's visuals have become increasingly sophisticated. Promo videos for songs from their second album feature ground-breaking combinations of traditional two-dimensional animation, computer-generated three-dimensional animation and live action. The videos are created in conjunction with Pete Candeland, animation director at Passion Pictures. Visually, the band is animated in a style that combines a number of influences: the small noses and large eyes recall Japanese Manga, but Hewlett also cites British cartoonist Gerald Scarfe and American artist Jean-Michel Basquiat among his influences. Hewlett still creates his characters and storyboards by hand, using pen and paper to set down ideas that are then used as the basis for artwork or animations.

Adbusters Billboard

Date **2002**
Designer **Jonathan Barnbrook**
Client **Adbusters, Canada**

"Designers, stay away from corporations that want you to lie for them," read the text on this 15 m (48 ft) high poster that was briefly displayed in Las Vegas in 2002. Designed by British graphic designer Jonathan Barnbrook, the poster coincided with the American Institute of Graphic Arts' conference that was taking place in the town, and was intended as a rallying cry for a more socially responsible approach to graphic design.

The initiative came about when Kalle Lasn – the founder and editor of Adbusters, a satirical Canadian anti-consumerist organization whose eponymous magazine was art directed by Barnbrook at the time – came across a magazine containing the original First Things First manifesto, issued by leading graphic designers in 1964. Together with legendary New York graphic designer Tibor Kalman, Lasn believed the ideas it contained had even greater relevance at the start of the twenty-first century. The stunt was intended to draw attention to

the launch of the reissued manifesto, initiated by Adbusters and signed by 33 of the world's leading graphic designers, which expressed disquiet at the way the profession had sacrificed its integrity by using its skills to help sell consumer products that nobody really needed. First Things First called on designers to put their communication skills to better use, stating, "The profession's time and energy is used up manufacturing demand for things that are inessential at best… Consumerism is running uncontested; it must be challenged by other perspectives expressed, in part, through the visual languages and resources of design."

London-based Barnbrook, who has created artwork for David Bowie and collaborated with the artist Damien Hirst created a poster that reads like a collage made up of the type of consumer advertising the manifesto decries and carries a quote by Tibor Kalman, who died in 1999 shortly after giving his backing to the First Things First initiative.

Pixel and Cross Stitch

Date **2001**

Designer **Masato Samata Aya Honda, Morhiro Tajiri and Yoshiki Watanabe/Delaware**

Formed in 1993, Japanese collective Delaware is both a graphics company and a music group whose slogan is "design rocks and rock designs". They describe themselves as "artoonists" – a hybrid of artists and cartoonists – and see no boundaries between their design, musical and performance work; there is no theory behind what they do beyond a child-like joy of creation. Their highly recognizable graphic images are often constructed of a pixillated "bitmap" texture as found on early computer games and low-resolution digital screens, yet it is also reminiscent of cross-stitching and embroidery. Their aesthetic is therefore a hybrid of technological and handicraft influences, combining two of the major trends in contemporary graphic design.

Using this idiosyncratic style, Delaware produce imagery for mobile phone screens, magazines, animations, websites and TV advertisements as well as a range of own-brand products such as T-shirts and publications. Their designs are often re-presentations of familiar images drawn from popular culture – their Obliquee series includes versions of rock album covers, while their Fun Fun Fun designs are inspired by the paintings of Keith Haring – and can be either realistic or highly abstract. In this way they sample the world around them and reformat it as whimsical, digitized symbols that are the contemporary equivalent of embroidery samplers. Their first major critical success came with their 2001 Mobile Gallery project – an online gallery of images that could be downloaded onto mobile phone screens.

As a band, they perform live and have released a number of CDs, beginning with: *Private* in 1996 and most recently *Delaware Strikes Back* and *Amen*, both released in 2004. Their songs are sparse, low-fi electronic ditties that often refer to their graphic work, as in the songs "Bitmap" and "Cross Stitch".

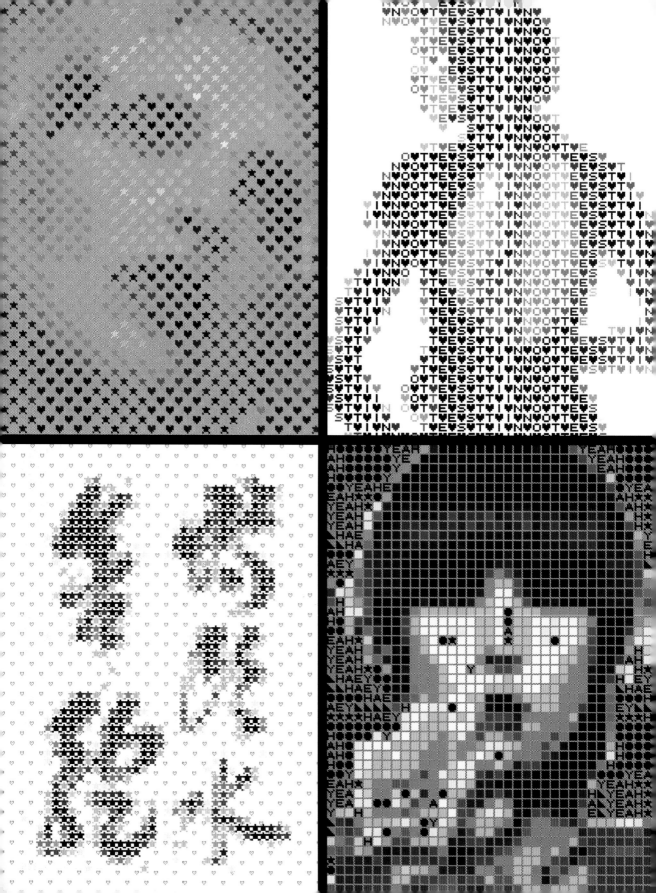

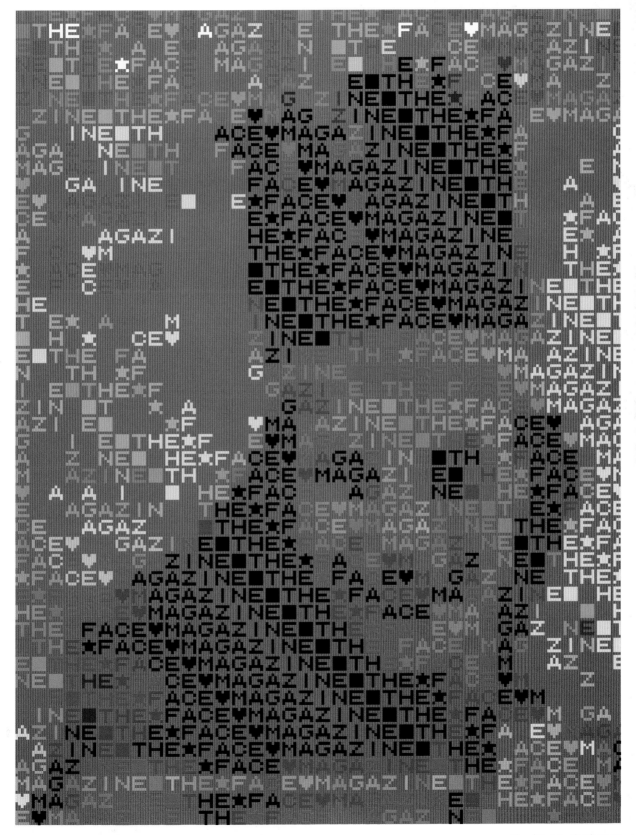

Shu by Ai
Packaging

Date **2003**
Designer **Ai Yamaguchi**
Manufacturer **Shu Uemera, Japan**

Ai Yamaguchi is a young Japanese graphic artist whose work combines influences from both classic Japanese art and contemporary pop and subculture references, such as Manga and children's cartoons. Yamaguchi trained as a textile designer and worked under leading Japanese graphic artist Takashi Murakami. She is one of the leading exponents of the Nouveau Japonisme movement, holding exhibitions of her paintings and prints around the world.

In 2003, Shu Uemura, founder of the eponymous cosmetics brand, sponsored an exhibition of her prints and paintings in Los Angeles, and so Yamaguchi's collaboration with the company began. Her first designs for the cosmetics company were illustrations for the Shu by Ai range of cleansers. The clear bottles were printed with delicate illustrations of young, partially clad Japanese girls surrounded by flowers and trees that recall traditional *ukiyo-e* ("pictures of the floating world") wood-block prints – a highly decorative and stylized art form that often depicted scenes with strongly sexual undertones. Like *ukiyo-e* prints, Yamaguchi's illustrations depict female courtesans working in brothels during Japan's Edo (1600–1868 AD) period – although Yamaguchi captures the girls during private moments of contemplation when off duty. Further limited edition cosmetic ranges followed, this time with illustrations of plants and flowers that represent the Japanese tradition of *hanakotaba* or "flower language," which assigns significance to each bloom – peony and bamboo, for example, represent calmness, while peach blossom stands for renewal.

Shu Uemura began as a make-up artist in Hollywood in the 1950s. His big break came when he replaced Shirley MacLaine's assistant, who had fallen ill. He transformed the star into a Japanese Geisha for the 1955 Paramount film *My Geisha* to great acclaim and became one of Hollywood's leading make-up artists. He launched his first cosmetics product in 1960 and opened his first store in Tokyo in 1983.

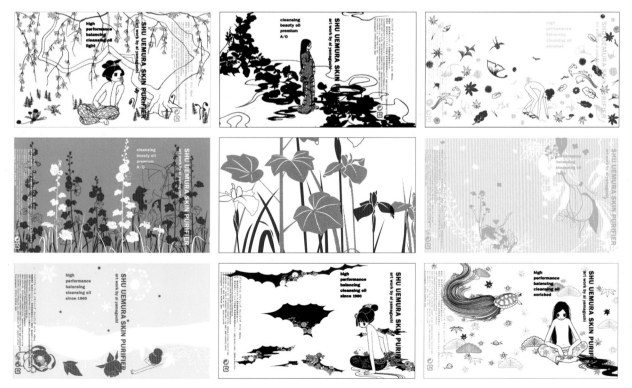

Museum of Us

Date **2005**

Designer **Robert Ryan**

British illustrator Robert Ryan has developed the art of paper cutting into a unique visual language that is simultaneously old-fashioned and highly contemporary. Ryan works entirely by hand, eschewing the computer and instead using the most basic palette of materials possible: a pencil, a sheet of paper and a scalpel. His intricate and highly personal illustrations are first drawn onto the paper and then painstakingly cut out. The delicate compositions are held together both visually and physically by decorative borders. Romantic, folkloric and somewhat naïve in style, they are full of images taken from nature, including birds, trees and flowers. This places him firmly at the centre of the recent revival of naturally inspired forms in design and his work has a strong affinity with that of lighting and furniture designer Tord Boontje, both in visual style and romantic content.

Ryan claims he strives to avoid making his work look contemporary and the figures that appear in his work tend to be dressed in styles more common in the '40s and '50s, yet it chimes strongly with the current rekindling of interest in craft, decoration and narrative. And while his influences tend to be British artists, such as Aubrey Beardsley and Eric Ravilious, as well as the English countryside, his work has global echoes with unintended similarities with Far Eastern shadow puppets or Central American folk art. Ryan's illustrations nearly always contain a narrative, featuring people and words to illustrate a particular conversation or situation of emotional importance to him. His Museum of Us series, for example, exhibited in London in 2005, tells the story of his relationship with his wife through images that form an album of memories.

Ryan studied at the Royal College of Art and is based in London. Besides his self-generated work, he has completed a number of commissions, including the cover artwork for the band Erasure's *Nightbird* album, which featured layers of paper cut-outs photographed in a studio to create a three-dimensional effect.

MY DARLING I HAVE NEVER DONE ANYTHING BRAVE IN MY LIFE. BUT ONE DAY 17 YEARS AGO IN BIRMINGHAM CITY ART GALLERY. I LEANT OVER AND KISSED A BEAUTIFUL GIRL. SHE WAS SO SWEET & KIND I LOVED THIS GIRL SO MUCH HER SMILE WAS SO DIFFERENT FROM ANY GIRL I'D EVER MET BEFORE.

YET SHE SEEMED SO MUCH LIKE ME... THAT IS TO SAY... ALONE. AND WE WERE SITTING ON A BENCH IN A ROOM FULL OF BEAUTIFUL PAINTINGS AND I THOUGHT NOW IS THE TIME. I AM SHAKING A LITTLE BIT AND IT SEEMS TO HAVE GONE VERY QUIET AND I LEANT OVER & KISSED HER ON THE LIPS AND TO MY SURPRISE SHE KISSED ME BACK AND MY HEART SOARED UP AND UP HIGHER AND HIGHER AND HIGHER UPWARDS INTO THE SKY WHERE IT EXPLODED LIKE A GIANT FIREWORK. THAT WAS YOUR MOTHER.

12   13

The Guardian

Date **2005**

Designer **Mark Porter and The Guardian design team**

The 2005 redesign of British newspaper *The Guardian* is one of the most radical and comprehensive ever undertaken. Faced, like most other quality daily papers, with a declining circulation as readers switched to the Internet, *The Guardian* decided to completely rethink the way it looked. Led by creative director Mark Porter, it decided to replace the "broadsheet" format – the large-size pages that were notoriously hard to turn and read – with the smaller "Berliner" size common in continental Europe. The change was part of a revolution in British newspapers. Rival papers including *The Times* and *The Independent* had already switched from broadsheet to the tabloid format traditionally favoured by populist titles, although the switch was not accompanied by any major design changes. Besides changing its size, *The Guardian* also became the first UK newspaper to print in colour on every page – a development made possible by the introduction of new digital printing presses. Graphically and typographically, the paper changed radically too. Rather than compete with the ever-larger headlines and sensationalist front cover imagery of other titles, it opted for a calmer, quieter look, with a lower-case masthead set in a blue band and smaller headlines set in serif type. Instead of the free-form layout increasingly adopted elsewhere, it adopted a rigorous five-column grid.

A new family of fonts called Guardian Egyptian was specially designed by Christian Schwartz and Paul Barnes, combining the weight of modern sans-serif with the elegance and readability of old-fashioned serif fonts . "Egyptian" fonts are slab-like serif fonts, which were popular early in the nineteenth century. They were the precursors to the sans-serif fonts that are almost ubiquitous today and which were, initially, Egyptian fonts with the serifs chopped off.

The redesigned *The Guardian* was introduced on 12 September 2005 and resulted in a rise in sales, bucking year-on-year industry trends.

The Bubble Project

Date **2002**

Designer **Ji Lee**

In 2002, New York advertising art director Ji Lee was getting frustrated with the advertising industry. He felt that conservative clients and agencies were killing off the most creative ideas and instead over-running the city with bad advertising. Walls, bus stops, phone booths, subways and other spaces once considered the public realm were gradually being taken over by corporations trying to sell things that people didn't really need.

In response, he devised the Bubble Project – a way of allowing citizens to strike back at the adverts that surrounded them. Lee printed 15,000 stickers in the shape of speech bubbles and travelled around New York adhering them to adverts.

This act of creative vandalism – defacing adverts is against the law – turned a corporate monologue into a potential public dialogue, and people soon started adding their thoughts to the bubbles. It took Lee two years to use up all 15,000 stickers; he then printed 15,000 more. He revisited all his stickering sites to photograph people's comments.

To date he has collected over 1,000 photos, the best of which he displays on his website, thebubbleproject.com and in a book published in 2006 called *Talk Back – The Bubble Project*.

The Bubble Project is an example of the recent explosion of subversive graphic design initiatives in which designers use stencilling, stickering or postering and which combine the visual sophistication of advertising with the immediacy – and illegality – of graffiti to get across messages that cannot be expressed using conventional design techniques. Graffiti artist Banksy (see page 376) and Jonathan Barnbrook's billboard (see page 392) are also examples of this trend.

Lee was born in Korea and brought up in Brazil before moving to New York, where he studied Communication Design at Parsons School of Design. He has worked on advertising campaigns for brands including Nike, Coca-Cola and Samsung.

Urban and Landscape

Urban and landscape design have taken on an unprecedented degree of importance in recent years as rapid urbanization – the need to regenerate former industrial land and fears that urban sprawl is destroying the countryside – have combined to galvanize architects and designers to invent new ways of making cities more habitable.

Urbanization is one of the most profound phenomena of our age. Within the next few years, researchers predict that more than half of all people will live in cities for the first time in history, as people abandon rural poverty in search of a better life in concentrated urban areas. This, together with a renewed cultural acceptance that these areas can be desirable places to live, is forcing architects and designers to consider not just the individual buildings that make up cities, but also the spaces between them. In many countries, notably the USA and the UK, the public realm has been

somewhat neglected in recent years, as urban development has increasingly been placed in private hands, with the resulting focus on spectacular set-piece buildings. However, there is now growing recognition of the role played by public spaces in improving the quality of life in a city.

The Spanish city of Barcelona was the global role model for enlightened public space strategies with its extensive makeover in the run up to the 1992 Olympic Games, which saw formerly derelict and dangerous areas of the city centre transformed into vibrant, desirable quarters, partially through the commissioning of high-quality public spaces and lighting schemes. However, designers are now beginning to question the Barcelona model – compact, hard-landscaped, Mediterranean-style squares surrounded by high-density construction – and invent models that are more sympathetic to other climates and urban typologies.

Catherine Mosbach's Bordeaux Botanical Garden, which brings the countryside into the city, is one good example of this, as is RMP Landscahftsarchitekten's Schloß Dyck project in Germany, which is decidedly agricultural yet also strikingly contemporary. EMBT Architects' Diagonal Mar park shows how this new interest in naturalesque landscapes can be applied in Barcelona itself. Located on former industrial land at the city's northern fringe, the park is partly a sculptural playground and partly an attempt to suggest how this formerly marshy coastal site might have looked before it was first urbanized. Not far from Barcelona, RCR Architects' Tussols-Basil athletics track is a complete inversion of most notions of urban design, placing a sports facility in a forested rural site with the minimum of disruption to the natural landscape.

As civic leaders rediscover the importance of the grand urban gesture, leading architects and designers are also increasingly being called upon to tackle infrastructure projects that would formerly have been the preserve of civil engineers or planners. Thomas Heatherwick's B of the Bang in Manchester and Rolling Bridge in London straddle the boundaries between urban design and sculpture while Foster & Partners' Millennium Bridge and Wilkinson Eyre Architects' Gateshead Millennium Bridge are every bit as iconic as many of the buildings that have been described in the architecture chapter of this book, but are of benefit – and freely accessible – to everyone, rather than just the fortunate minority of building users. The boundaries between art and urban design are also explored in two of the most remarkable architectural landscapes ever conceived: Zaha Hadid's tram station at Hoenheim, which is infrastructure disguised as conceptual art; and Peter Eisenman's Jewish memorial in Berlin, a 2 hectare (5 acre) maze of concrete obelisks that is both bewildering and powerfully evocative.

Hageneiland Housing

Date **2002**

Place **Ypenburg, Belgium**

Architect **MVRDV**

In recent years, the Netherlands has pioneered new approaches to urban design in order to provide modern housing and infrastructure in one of the most densely inhabited countries on earth. Simultaneously, a new breed of Dutch architects, led by Rem Koolhaas, emerged to reinvigorate Modernism and collectively became known as the "Superdutch" generation. Unlike young architects in other countries, this group was able to turn their ideas into reality, thanks to the forward-thinking policies of the Dutch government, who appointed practices such as Rotterdam-based MVRDV – led by Winy Maas, Jacob van Rijs and Nathalie de Vries – to design a string of public projects, most notably experimental housing developments. With extremely tight budgets and standardized materials to play with, these architects had to find ingenious ways of making their projects unique.

MVRDV's Hageneiland housing project, which was completed in 2002, is one of the best-known of these developments. A witty reinvention of a standard suburban layout, this consists of terraced and semi-detached houses set in gardens on a car-free estate, which has a grid of four parallel pedestrian alleys surrounded by an access road. The houses, which are fairly standard in many respects, are made extraordinary by the use of a limited palette of cladding materials – including timber shingles, pantiles, blue polyurethane and aluminium – that cover both walls and roof. Thus the archetypal pitched-roof house is transformed into something unique and unnerving.

The suburban typology is further subverted by the apparently random way the houses are arranged, with some terraces fronting onto the grid of pedestrian alleys and having gardens at the back, while others are set back and have their gardens at the front. This means that each house, while being superficially identical to all the others, features a unique combination of cladding material and orientation.

Federation Square

Date **2002**

Place **Melbourne, Australia**

Architect **Lab Architecture**

Melbourne is a gridded city laid out on the banks of the Yarra River, which – without landmark buildings or a large public square, and with the central business district cut off from the river by a railway yard and a fuel depot – had always lacked a civic heart. However, in the mid 1990s the vast Jolimont Rail Yard was rationalized, freeing up valuable land between the city centre and the river. In the hope of creating an architectural icon to rival Sydney's Opera House, Melbourne City Council launched an international competition for a new 3.2 hectare (8 acre) public square to be built over the remaining rail lines, which would serve as a focus for the city's cultural activity.

The competition attracted 177 entries. Lab Architecture – a hitherto unknown London-based practice founded by Peter Davidson and Donald Bates in 1994 – was selected as the winner. Lab's submission proposed a cluster of eight pavilion-like buildings that extended the city grid to the river's edge. The new galleries, restaurants, winter garden, performance spaces and other facilities are arranged around an informal and modestly scaled plaza. An exercise in urban design rather than gestural architecture, in plan it is reminiscent of the ad-hoc nature of European towns, where narrow twisting alleys feed unexpectedly into irregularly shaped market squares.

While relatively unadventurous in form, the pavilions are remarkable for their cladding, which is based on fractal geometry. Seemingly random, the glass, zinc and sandstone panels are in fact ordered in a highly mathematical system. Called a "pinwheel" grid. This consists of five identical right-angled triangles placed side by side to form façade panels. Five of these panels are then laid together to make larger mega-panels. By varying the cladding material the architects have created the illusion of randomness, which can be read as a metaphor for the balance of order and chaos required in any successful city.

Millennium Park

Date **2004**

Place **Chicago, Illinois, USA**

Architect **Various**

Chicago's Millennium Park project has been described as the biggest and most ambitious urban regeneration scheme ever undertaken in the USA. Completed in summer 2004, the 9.9 hectare (24 acre) site has been redeveloped with landscape design, architecture and artworks by leading international figures including Frank Gehry, Anish Kapoor and Kathryn Gustafson. The new park sits alongside Grant Park – the city's main park – in downtown Chicago, on land that was formerly occupied by railway tracks and a vast car lot.

The park is more of an urban pleasure garden than a naturalistic landscape and is made up of several different elements including a bridge and open-air concert venue, plus sculptures and fountains. The most popular feature is The Crown Fountain by Barcelona artist Jaume Plensa. This features two 15.4 m (51 ft) high rectangular towers made of glass bricks that face each other across a shallow reflecting pool of black granite. Enormous LED screens on the towers are programmed to display a random sequence of video footage of the faces of 1,000 different Chicago residents, each of whom stares, blinks and smiles for five minutes before a spout of water erupts from their mouth.

Other attractions include artist Anish Kapoor's Cloud Gate, a polished stainless steel form that is 18 m (60 ft) long, 9 m (30 ft) high and weighs 112 tonnes (110 tons). Nicknamed the "Jelly Bean" because of its bean-like form, the mirror-finished object reflects distorted images of the sky and surrounding skyscrapers.

Architect Frank Gehry produced the Jay Pritzker Pavilion, a huge bandstand with a canopy constructed in his trademark ballooning steel petals, and the BP Bridge, a meandering, snake-like structure with a timber deck and sinuous stainless steel sides that connects Millennium Park to Grant Park. Landscape architect Kathryn Gustafson's Lurie Garden is conceived as a secret garden containing 140 species of perennial plants and featuring the sort of timber decking that once kept the feet of Chicago's pioneer inhabitants clear of the swamps and mud of the Lake Michigan shore.

Millau Bridge

Date **2004**

Place **Tarn Valley, France**

Architect **Foster & Partners**

Opened in December 2004 after just four years of construction, this bridge was instantly acclaimed as a triumph of architecture and engineering. The monumental structure – 2.46 km (1 ½ miles) long and taller than the Eiffel Tower – strides across the beautiful Tarn Valley in central France. However, the elegance of its design means it enhances, rather than damages, the natural landscape. The bridge was built to relieve traffic in the picturesque town of Millau, a notorious bottleneck on a major route between northern France and the Mediterranean coast. An architectural competition was held in 1993 and, while most entrants proposed ways of bridging the narrow River Tarn at the base of the valley, Foster & Partners suggested bridging the entire valley with a single, cable-stayed viaduct slung between the high plateaux on either side.

Foster's winning proposal features seven equally spaced concrete masts, the tallest of which is 245 m (804 ft) high. These split into two when they pass through the road deck, creating a needle-like eye that flexes to accommodate expansion and contraction of the deck. The masts are profiled to appear as slim as possible when viewed from the side, reducing the bridge's impact on its surroundings. The concrete deck is suspended on steel cables 90 m (295 ft) below the mast tops, making it the highest road bridge in the world. The deck traces a shallow curve as it crosses the valley, allowing motorists to better appreciate the scale of the bridge as they drive across.

The project has been held up as an exemplar of how architects can work alongside engineers to produce more sensitive designs for major infrastructure projects. Unusually, the client (the Department of Transport and Public Works of France) insisted that engineering firms team up with architects to enter the design competition. Foster & Partners worked on the project alongside French engineering firm Eiffage, named after Gustav Eiffel who designed the Eiffel Tower.

Millennium Bridge

Date **2000**

Place **London, England, UK**

Architect **Foster & Partners**

Built to celebrate the Millennium, this 325 m (1,066 ft) long bridge was the first new river crossing in London since Tower Bridge opened in 1894, and the first-ever pedestrian bridge over the Thames in the City of London. It provides a direct link between the Tate Modern art gallery in Southwark on the river's South Bank and St Paul's Cathedral. Designed by Foster & Partners, with engineers Arup and sculptor Anthony Caro, the bridge was conceived as a "blade of light" crossing the water. It has an extremely flat profile to minimize its visual impact on the river and to maximize pedestrians' views.

The design, a radical feat of engineering, consists of a shallow suspension bridge with supporting cables slung in an arc six times shallower than on a normal suspension bridge. These are highly tensioned and dip just 2.3 m (7.5 ft) over the 144 m (472 ft) central span. Steel traverse arms, set 8 m (26 ft) apart clamp, the lightweight deck to the cables. Taut, expressive and masculine, the design eschews the organic sensualism of much contemporary architecture and design in favour of an aesthetic reminiscent of the high-tech style.

The bridge is in the daring tradition of British civil engineering as personified by Isambard Kingdom Brunel. But the design team encountered unforeseen problems when the bridge opened in June 2000. An estimated 80,000 to 100,000 people descended upon it on opening day. The sheer numbers caused the deck to sway alarmingly and forced the immediate closure of the bridge on safety grounds. The problem was down to a little-known phenomenon called Synchronous Lateral Excitation, under which groups of people subjected to lateral movement tend to fall into step with each other, shifting their weight in synch and thereby exacerbating the movement. Arup's engineers solved the problem by placing a series of specially made dampers under the deck, which counteract any lateral movement. The bridge reopened successfully in February 2002.

B of the Bang

Date **2005**
Place **Manchester, England, UK**
Architect **Thomas Heatherwick**

Thomas Heatherwick is at the vanguard of a new breed of young designers who work across many disciplines. His work merges art, design, engineering and invention and is characterized by a search for ingenious solutions to ordinary problems. He is regarded as one of the most gifted young designers in the world, and while he started out designing small-scale commissions, such as interiors and furniture, his work is becoming increasingly architectural in scale as clients entrust him to more and more ambitious projects.

Many of Heatherwick's greatest pieces are for civic spaces, making him one of the few leading designers whose work is accessible to the general public. His most famous work to date is B of the Bang, which at 56 m high (184 ft) is taller than the Statue of Liberty. It consists of 180 tapering steel tubes radiating from a single point and leans at 30 degrees to the horizontal. B of the Bang stands outside the City of Manchester Stadium and has no obvious function; it is not design in the traditional sense yet, as in all his work, practical considerations were foremost in Heatherwick's mind when conceiving the piece. Heatherwick approached it more as a piece of urban design than a sculpture, employing its towering height as a way of responding to the bulk of the stadium rather than being overwhelmed by it, and helping to give visual context to the stadium, which is out of scale with the residential streets that surround it.

The name B of the Bang refers to a remark once made by British Olympic gold medallist sprinter Linford Christie, who said he started a race "on the B of the Bang". Heatherwick's design represents both the retort of the starter's gun and the explosive force of a sprinter coming off the blocks.

Rolling Bridge

Date **2005**
Place **London, England, UK**
Architect **Thomas Heatherwick**

The Rolling Bridge, installed at Paddington Basin in West London in 2005, is a typical example of Heatherwick's ability to look at a problem from a new angle. Commissioned to design an opening pedestrian bridge over a narrow branch of the Grand Union Canal, Heatherwick decided to ignore the conventional approach of simply lifting or swinging the bridge structure out of the way. Instead, he set about developing a new typology that integrated the opening mechanism into the bridge itself, meaning that the structure would undergo a physical transformation as it lifted.

His solution was to invent a new type of mechanism that allows the flat bridge deck to curl up in a ball on one bank, rather like the way an outstretched palm is coiled into a fist. This is achieved by combining a system of hydraulic rams with the handrail. The deck of the 12.1 m (40 ft) long bridge is made up of eight hinged sections, the first of which is attached to one bank and the rest cantilevered over

the water. A hydraulic ram is positioned at each joint between the sections. When the remote controlled hydraulic system is activated, the deck sections gradually loop upwards until the last section comes to rest on the ground next to the first, forming a perfect octagon.

Thomas Heatherwick studied three-dimensional design at Manchester Polytechnic and then at the Royal College of Art, London, graduating in 1994. One of his first projects was a window display at Harvey Nichols department store in London that featured plywood scenery, bursting through the windows and wrapping itself around the building like a giant creeper. Other acclaimed projects by Heatherwick include B of the Bang (see page 422) and Bleigeissen, an installation at the headquarters of research charity the Wellcome Trust in London, and which is his most complex project yet. Consisting of 150,000 glass beads strung onto 27,000 tensioned wires, the 30 m (100 ft) tall installation hangs in the atrium.

Tussols-Basil Athletics Track

Date **2002**
Place **Olot, Catalunya, Spain**
Architect **RCR Aranda Pigem Vilalta Architects**

Set amid ancient woodland, close to a river, this athletics training facility in Catalunya, Spain, rejects the artificiality and grandiosity of most sports installations and instead creates an arena for sport that refers back to pre-industrial times. The controversial project was initially dogged by a battle between conservationists and the sports community: the former arguing against any tree-felling on the site, which is covered in stands of 100-year-old white oaks and littered with ancient volcanic rocks; the latter wanting the site to be cleared completely.

The resulting compromise from local architects RCR – a company whose work frequently responds strongly to the landscape – has created a facility that conjures images of ancient games when competitions were held in forest clearings. Walking through the woodland when the trees are in leaf it is difficult to see the track or grandstand, even at close range.

The facility is located at the edge of the town of Olot and is next to a recreation area that was designed by the same architects, who carry out much of their work in the town and surrounding rural area. The track, which sits in a clearing and loops around two groups of trees, has been placed to minimize damage to the landscape while still meeting regulations regarding sight lines for athletes and race officials. It is sited in a slight hollow, and grandstands for spectators have been provided by terracing the terrain around the track, creating irregularly curving banks with cast concrete walls that recall the terraced fields typical of the Mediterranean area. The facility is entered through an oxidized steel structure that both frames views across the site and accommodates a refreshments bar. When not in use, the façade of the bar folds away to close the aperture and the building becomes an abstract object in the landscape.

Paseo del Ovalo

Date **2003**
Place **Teruel, Spain**
Architect **David Chipperfield Architects and B720 Architects**

A huge, mysterious void punched into an ancient rampart and resembling the entrance to a lost tomb is the most visible element of this urban renewal project, which demonstrates how even the most historically sensitive site can be improved with intelligent contemporary design. The walled city of Teruel in southern Aragon, Spain, is designated a World Heritage Site for its unique collection of *Mudéjar* architecture – a style developed by Muslim craftsmen who remained in Spain after the Christian reconquest.

Working with Barcelona practice B720 Architects, British architect David Chipperfield won a competition to remodel the Paseo del Ovalo – a broad promenade lined with historic buildings that sits atop a 17 m high (56 ft) high section of the ramparts. One of Chipperfield's main priorities was to create a new link between the high-level parts of the city and the low-level railway station located at the foot of the ramparts. Previously, the only direct route between the two was a steep flight of ornate neo-*Mudéjar* stairs built in 1921.

The solution involved inserting two large-capacity public elevators into the ramparts and linking the two levels. At the lower level, Chipperfield created a dramatic, 15 m (49 ft) high cave-like incision, which is lined with preoxidized Corian steel. At the upper level, the elevators arrive on the Paseo de Ovalo within a simple steel-framed box clad in square glass bricks.

Elsewhere, the architects improved paving, lighting and street furniture and planted trees, but it is the restraint of this project that makes it exceptional: save for the entrance to the lift shaft, it is all but invisible.

Car Park and Terminus, Hoenheim North

Date **2002**

Place **Strasbourg, France**

Architect **Zaha Hadid**

This tram terminus on the northern outskirts of Strasbourg, France, is as much a work of land art as a piece of transport infrastructure. Like much of Zaha Hadid's work, it merges architecture and terrain, the station literally peeling away from the ground and the car park, pathways and tramlines treated as elements in a landscape composition. The station was commissioned to relieve congestion in the historic centre of Strasbourg. Located close to the motorway in the suburb of Hoenheim, it allows commuters to park their cars and take a 20-minute tram ride into central Strasbourg instead of driving.

Hadid took the movement of cars, pedestrians, cyclists and trams as her organizing principle, laying out the station and circulation routes as tangents to their trajectories, while the lines of the station's cast white-concrete canopy follow "materialized vectors" – the architect's term to describe the way paths of movement are made solid. The canopy emerges from the ground on the far side of the tracks, ramping and folding upwards to create a soaring roof supported by clusters of randomly angled steel columns. A white apron of concrete extends the form of the canopy into the car park, and double as a pedestrian route.

The 700-space car park is perhaps the most dramatic element of the project. It is laid out as if it were affected by force fields emanating from the tram tracks, the white markings painted in ripple patterns. The recessed strip lights in the canopy and the cast concrete benches on the platforms continue these lines into the station itself.

Hadid has explored this theme of architecture emerging from terrain before in projects such as the LF One pavilion for the Landesgartenschau garden festival at Weil am Rhein in Germany, in which a series of paths cut from the landscape rose and parted to form the roof. Also the Rosenthal Center for Contemporary Art in Cincinnati (see page 26), which featured an "urban carpet" – a term that describes the continuous concrete surface that enters the building's ground floor from the street before curving up to form the back wall.

Gateshead Millennium Bridge

Date **2002**

Place **Gateshead, England, UK**

Architect **Wilkinson Eyre Architects**

Of all the projects built in the UK to celebrate the Millennium, Wilkinson Eyre Architects' Gateshead Millennium Bridge is perhaps the most original. Providing a link for pedestrians and cyclists between Gateshead and Newcastle on either side of the River Tyne in the north-east of England, it lifts to allow ships to pass in a movement inspired by the way an eyelid opens and closes, earning it the nickname the "blinking eye".

The bridge, built as part of a wider arts-led regeneration programme in Gateshead, consists of two steel arches: a curving, 120 m (394 ft) long deck carrying a footpath and a cycle lane and a soaring, impossibly thin 50 m (164 ft) high parabolic arc from which the deck is suspended on cables. When the bridge is opened, the entire structure tilts parallel to the river on huge bearings that are located at the landing points on either side. The slenderness of the bridge's structure is a result of cutting-edge engineering techniques used to reduce weight to a minimum and contrasts with the heavy engineering of the other bridges on this stretch of the Tyne, which include the famous 1928 Tyne Bridge – modelled on Sydney Harbour Bridge – and Robert Stephenson's High Level Bridge of 1849.

London-based architects Wilkinson Eyre, led by Chris Wilkinson and Jim Eyre, have developed a reputation for adventurous bridge design and work on large-scale commissions around the world.

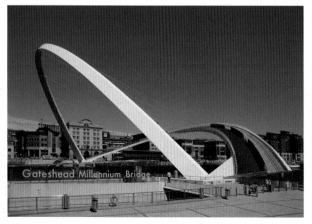

Gateshead Millennium Bridge

Duisburg-Nord Landscape Park

Date **2002**

Place **Ruhr Valley, Germany**

Architect **Latz and Partners**

The Ruhr Valley is Germany's industrial heartland, but recent years have seen the decline of much of its heavy industry, resulting in a legacy of abandoned factories and contaminated brownfield land. The Duisburg-Nord Landscape Park, developed on the site of a former iron-making plant, is a highly imaginative solution to the problem of what to do with such areas.

Peter Latz of German landscape architect, Latz and Partners was invited to propose ideas for turning the 200 hectare (494 acre) Thyssen Steelworks into a public park after its closure in 1985, but rather than propose the demolition of the monolithic blast furnaces, engine houses, ore bunkers and other structures, he suggested retaining and reusing them to create both a multi-purpose activity park and a museum of the area's industrial heritage.

Although begun in 1990, Latz's plans took more than a decade to implement, and involved allowing nature to seep back into the once-forested site, creating a series of tranquil green oases in what was once a place of infernal noise, fire and smoke. He has given inventive new uses to many of the plant's industrial relics, including the creation of children's playgrounds and rock-climbing walls in old ore bunkers, cherry orchards in former sintering (metal-melting) bunkers and a public square called Piazza Metallica at the heart of the plant. New bridges and stairways allow visitors to explore the various levels of the plant, while the once-contaminated network of sewage channels has been restored to both irrigate the park and create water features.

In general, however, Latz has left the plant intact and created a long-term strategy for its return to nature: as the steel rusts, so "pioneer" species such as birch trees, wildflowers and grasses will gradually improve the quality of the poor soil, allowing other species to take root.

Parc Diagonal Mar

Date **2003**

Place **Barcelona, Spain**

Architect **Enric Miralles Benedetta Taliabue (EMBT)**

Part of a major urban expansion of Barcelona on former industrial land, this 14 hectare (35 acre) park lies to the north of the existing city centre at the point where Avinguda Diagonal, one of Barcelona's main traffic axes, meets the Mediterranean. The park, which opened in 2003, provides one of the few car-free links between the city and the sea and was conceived as a green lung, akin to Central Park in New York, at the heart of the new urban district.

The architects, Barcelona-based practice Enric Miralles Benedetta Tagliabue (EMBT), have designed the park in a narrative way so that people walking through it towards the sea experience a gradual sense of leaving a manmade world and entering a more natural environment that approximates how the area would have looked before it was developed. In plan, the park resembles a tree – its roots in the sea and a series of paths spreading inland like branches. The hard, urban surfaces at the entrance gradually give way to softer, more rounded forms nearer the shore. The most significant ingredient is water: a lagoon – manmade and hard-edged with artificial fountains and spraying machines at one end, and organic and reed-fringed at the other – is set between low hills. With its mixture of architectural and natural forms, Diagonal Mar is reminiscent of Parc Güell, the famously surreal landscape created by the great Catalan architect Antoni Gaudí.

EMBT often use landscape design as a way of telling stories. Their 2001 remodelling of Utrecht town hall in the Netherlands created a new public square in which patterns in the paving traced the foundations of ancient buildings that once occupied the space. At their Scottish Parliament building in Edinburgh, a series of raised paths fan out from the main entrance and head towards the Highlands, tracing the routes that clan chieftains would have followed when attending gatherings (see page 36).

A13 Artscape

Date **2004**

Place **London, England, UK**

Architect **Various with masterplanning by Tom de Paor**

The A13 is a major arterial road that heads eastwards from central London and slices through a blighted and depressed urban corridor north of the River Thames. In 1996, to coincide with improvements to the road such as new junctions, cycle lanes and drainage systems, Barking and Dagenham Council embarked on an environmental project to improve the congested road and its environs by commissioning leading architects, designers and artists to transform wasteland alongside it into public art installations. Masterplanned by Dublin-based architect Tom de Paor, the project was conceived as a piece of theatre that could be enjoyed through the windscreen of a car. The diverse projects – not all of which were completed – are unified by their use of lighting schemes made up of points of light and arranged in grids, and bold, geometric forms that can be easily read by passengers driving past at speed.

The Pump House (right), designed by de Paor, marks one end of the project. This 6 m (20 ft) high concrete box contains the electronic system that controls the road's pumps. The cast concrete surface of the box is punctured by 512 clear acrylic rods, which contain LED lights that turn on and off in sequence. Other completed projects include Holding Pattern (below), a light installation by artists Graham Ellard and Stephen Johnstone, which consists of a field of 76 light columns, measuring 5.5 m (18 ft) high, topped by a blue airport taxiway luminaire. Set on wasteland beside the road, the lights give drivers the impression of coming in to land as the A13 descends from the elevated section.

Thomas Heatherwick designed Twin Roundabouts – a pair of volcano-shaped sculptures made of steel mesh attached to and sprayed with black concrete. They sit on two new roundabouts on either side of the A13 at the Goresbrook Interchange. Named Scylla and Carybdis, after the treacherous rocks that guarded a narrow sea passage in Classical mythology, they represent the epic voyages that travellers make along the A13.

Copenhagen Harbour Bath

Date **2004**

Place **Copenhagen, Denmark**

Architect **Plot**

Located in the up-and-coming Islands Brygge district of Copenhagen, this floating swimming pool is a contemporary take on the open-air baths that were popular in the early twentieth century. The project, which opened in 2004, was designed by Danish architects Plot and is part of a wider scheme to bring life back to the city's vast harbour district, many parts of which are no longer used by industry.

Conceived as a playful landscape clad entirely in timber decking, the project extends a strip of waterfront park out over the water itself. It consists of three irregular shaped pools: a large L-shaped one for competent swimmers, a smaller rectangular one for learners and a paddling pool. The pools are separated by a series of decked walkways, while the perimeter of the pontoon accommodates sunbathers. At one end of the floating pontoon is a large stepped timber structure resembling the prow of a ship, from which bathers can dive or jump into the larger pool. The wide steps double as a seating area. A red and white striped tower resembling a lighthouse gives lifeguards a view of the entire bathing area.

Plot was formed in Copenhagen in 2001 by architects Julien De Smedt and Bjarke Ingels and was considered one of Europe's most promising practices until the partners broke up the office and went their separate ways in 2006. A second waterfront regeneration project in Copenhagen by the same duo, the Maritime Youth House, is part architecture, part urban design and provides facilities for a sailing club and a youth organization. The former required boat storage space, while the latter needed play space, so the architects created an undulating landscape of timber decking that rises in places to create storerooms beneath, while the upper terraces provide a playground for children. Built on heavily polluted land, Plot saved the money earmarked for decontamination by lifting the structure clear of the ground on a grid of stilts.

Bordeaux Botanical Garden

Date **2002**
Place **Bordeaux, France**
Architect **Catherine Mosbach**

Created on a long, narrow strip of reclaimed industrial land leading down to the bank of the River Garonne, this is a strikingly contemporary interpretation of the traditional garden close to the heart of the French city of Bordeaux. Located in the La Bastide industrial district across the river from the historic city centre, the botanical garden is both a public park and a biodiversity research facility. The project is part of a wider, ongoing regeneration scheme for the derelict district of warehouses and railway yards on the riverfront.

Paris-based landscape architect Catherine Mosbach's design divides the 600 by 70 m (1,968 by 230 ft) site into three distinct zones: the water garden, the Environment Gallery and the Field of Crops. These recreate the environmental conditions in different parts of the countryside surrounding Bordeaux. Each zone has strong sculptural qualities.

Located closest to the river, the water garden consists of a large, square pond edged by a series of quadrilateral pools, each home to different water plants and separated by geometric paths set just a couple of centimetres above water level. The Environment Gallery takes a more naturalistic form and consists of 11 separate micro-landscapes, representing different natural habitats including sand dunes and limestone hills. Each habitat is set in a raised bed resembling an island and is surrounded by wide gravel paths, giving the impression that a slice of real countryside has been dropped into the park and allowing visitors to wander between habitats.

The third zone, Field of Crops, represents the cultivated parts of the region. A series of long, narrow irrigated strips are filled with different types of soil. These are furrowed and sewn with various crops, resembling ancient strip-farming landscapes. The fields are separated by narrow, turfed paths and each features a rectangular water trough.

Memorial to the Murdered Jews of Europe

Date **2005**
Place **Berlin, Germany**
Architect **Peter Eisenman**

Consisting of more than 2,700 concrete monoliths – up to 5 m (15 ft) tall, spaced about 1 m (3 ft) apart and arranged in a regular grid over a 2 hectare (5 acre) plot – this landscape, by the hugely influential New York architect Peter Eisenman, was commissioned by the German government as a national memorial to the Jews murdered by the Nazis. It is Germany's largest monument to the Holocaust and is conceived as an abstract space through which visitors are able to freely wander and contemplate. In contrast to Daniel Libeskind's Jewish Museum in Berlin (see page 40), which sets out to express the horror of the Holocaust, Eisenman's memorial offers the visitor a blank canvas that is intended to serve as a trigger to their own feelings.

The charcoal grey, concrete columns undulate across an entire vacant city block close to the Reichstag and the Brandenburg Gate in the centre of Berlin. Eisenman's inspiration came from his memory

of getting lost in a field of waving corn in Iowa – an experience he describes as being disorientating and frightening.

Born in Newark, New Jersey, in 1932, Eisenman has pioneered the Deconstructivist style that is practiced by such architects as Zaha Hadid, Frank Gehry and Daniel Libeskind. He studied architecture at Cornell University and took his masters at Columbia and a PhD at Cambridge University in England. He later formed a close friendship with French philosopher Jacques Derrida, whose Deconstructivist ideas Eisenman began to apply to architecture.

For much of his career, Eisenman's influence came through his teaching (he founded New York's Institute for Architecture and Urban Studies in 1967) and writing, although he now has a number of significant projects underway, notably his stadium for the Arizona Cardinals football team and his Cultural Centre in Santiago de Compostela, Spain.

Asphalt Spot

Date **2003**

Place **Tokamashi, Japan**

Architect **R&Sie**

Set amid farmland in rural Japan, this small project is a bizarre hybrid of landscape art and infrastructure. It consists of a square, 20-space car park that looks as if it has been struck by an earthquake – its corners have been lifted into the air, its surface is rippled and buckled and a great gash has been torn in its black asphalt surface. Asphalt Spot was completed in 2003 as part of the Echigo-Tsumari Art Triennial 2003 – a cultural festival that saw 157 artists and architects from 23 countries produce 224 artworks in the Shinano Basin of Niigata Prefecture. The area has experienced severe depopulation in recent years and the triennial was intended to attract visitors to the region.

Designed by Parisian architects R&Sie, Asphalt Spot was commissioned by the Art Front Gallery in the nearby town of Tokamashi as an exhibition venue with integrated visitor facilities and parking. Yet the architects treated the project itself as an art installation, designing a structure that mimics the bumpy terrain around it and merges seamlessly with the surrounding landscape. The building straddles a steep incline between a road and the lower-lying fields, creating a new topography linking the two levels. The undulating surface is even crisscrossed by fences similar to those used to divide fields. Beneath one corner of the car park is a 300 sq m (3,229 sq ft), open sided exhibition hall, which is used as a venue for art exhibitions. The hall is punctuated by a forest of leaning concrete columns that hold up the car park above and which have been covered in canvas sleeves, as has the underside of the ceiling.

Led by François Roche and Stéphanie Lavaux, R&Sie is firmly situated on the conceptual, experimental wing of the contemporary architecture scene. Their architecture often appears to have emerged from the landscape, consisting of forms that appear to drift or that mutate and clone elements found nearby.

Stortorget Public Square

Date **2003**
Place **Kalmar, Sweden**
Architect **Caruso St John Architects**

For 300 years, the people of Kalmar on Sweden's Baltic coast have cleared stones from the surrounding fields to construct walls, buildings and streets. With the remodelling of the town's main square, Caruso St John Architects have referred to this tradition using locally collected stones to repave the space, removing the granite slabs and kerbs that separated cars and pedestrians. This apparently simple gesture, commissioned to coincide with the pedestrianization of the square, is in contrast to most recent urban design projects, that tend to result in a clutter of street furniture and unnecessary design gestures. Instead, the project gives the square – surrounded by historic buildings including the town's Baroque cathedral – a sombre dignity.

Yet there are many subtle nuances in Caruso St John's scheme. The square is paved in three different types of surface: rough stones, which represent the "fields of stones" that existed in the area before farmers cleared them; smooth stones, representing the fields once

they had been cleared; and pedestrian walkways constructed of tiny stones set in concrete slabs. These smooth passages suggest routes across the square and link the streets that feed into it, channelling pedestrians between the rougher patches of stone, which are more uncomfortable to walk on. These three surface types are ordered in a geometric patchwork that resembles the fields that once went right up to the edge of the town. Parallel stripes of different coloured stones refer to the drystone walls that farmers laid using stones removed from the fields.

Thanks to a series of grilles set in the paving, water flowing through channels below the square can be heard, reminding people of the town's proximity to – and former dependence on – the sea. Ruby-red lights set on surrounding buildings atop slender masts and dotted randomly across the square create a datum in the sky when illuminated at night.

Landesgartenschau
Schloß Dyck

Date **2002**

Place **Dusseldorf, Germany**

Architect **RMP Landschaftarchitekten**

This 30 hectare (74 acre) park, set in countryside close to the River Rhine near Dusseldorf in Germany, represents a new movement in European landscape design. Rather than the hard-edged, urbanistic approach to public space that has dominated for the last two decades, the New Gardens in the Dyck Field are defiantly rural, and even agricultural, in their approach.

Designed by Bonn-based landscape architects RMP Landschaftsarchitekten, the gardens form part of a wider project to convert Schloß Dyck, a Baroque castle set amid flat farmland, into a centre for garden design and landscape culture. The bow-shaped site is bordered on one side by a straight avenue of horse chestnut trees that leads to the castle, and on the other by a curving road. RMP have created an irregular network of paths bordered by lawns across the park – long, broad ones radiating from the castle and shorter ones set at 90 degrees to each other that create a series of plots similar to allotments.

The spaces between the paths are planted with *miscanthus giganteus* – giant Chinese silver grass – a species that forms a dense, sculptural mass and that also is a useful crop used to make insulation material and as a fuel for bio-energy plants. As the grass grows over the course of a year, the park is transformed from an exposed series of fields into a maze, the colour of the grass changing from green to gold and then brown as it matures, until the grass is harvested in the autumn. Thus the park is both a public garden and a working field, uniting recreation and agriculture in a way that has rarely been attempted before. The park is also notable in its restraint, with the landscape architects holding back from the kind of over-design that afflicts so many urban design projects.

The tall banks of grass conceal 24 small theme gardens scattered around the field, which the visitor discovers almost by chance. Each of these was created by a different landscape designer and showcases a different variety of species or planting concept. Cargo Garden, for example, replicates the conditions found in disused railway sidings, while Heron's Grove features an irregular-shaped pond excavated among trees and which is designed to attract water birds.

Index

Resources

Ai Yamaguchi: www.ninyu.com
Adam Whiton and Yolita Nugent:
    www.no-contact.com
 Alexander Taylor: www.alexandertaylor.com
Alfredo Häberli: www.alfredo-haeberli.com
American Apparel: www.americanapparel.net
Atelier Jean Nouvel: www.jeannouvel.com

Banksy: www.banksy.co.uk
Barber Osgerby: www.barberosgerby.com
Behnisch, Behnisch & Partner:
    www.behnisch.com
Bertjan Pot: www.bertjanpot.nl
Bouroullec Brothers: www.bouroullec.com

Campana Brothers:
    www.campanabrothers.com
Caruso St John: www.carusostjohn.com
Chris Kabel: www.chriskabel.com
Committee: committee@gallop.co.uk
Concrete Architectural Associates:
    www.concreteamsterdam.nl
Constantin Boym: www.boym.com
Craig Robinson: www.flipflopflyin.com

Daniel Brown: www.danielbrowns.com
Daniel Libeskind: www.daniel-libeskind.com
David Adjaye: www.adjaye.com
David Chipperfield Architects:
    www.davidchipperfield.co.uk
Delaware: www.delaware.gr.jp
Demakersvan: demakersvan.com
Design Q: www.designq.co.uk
Diller, Scofidio & Renfrew:
    www.dillerscofidio.com
Doshi Levien: www.doshilevien.com
Dunne & Raby: www.dunneandraby.co.uk

eBoy: hello.eboy.com
Elena Manferdini: www.ateliermanferdini.com
EMBT Arquitectes:
    www.mirallestagliabue.com
Erick van Egeraat Associated Architects:
    www.eea-architects.co

Fabio Novembre: www.novembre.it
Foreign Office Architects: www.f-o-a.ne
Foster & Partners:
    www.fosterandpartners.com
Frank Gehry: www.frank-gehry.com
Frank Tjepkema: www.tjep.com
Freedom of Creation:
    www.freedomofcreation.com
Front: www.frontdesign.se
Future Systems: www.future-systems.com

Gorillaz: fans.gorillaz.com
 Graphic Thought Facility:
    www.graphicthoughtfacility.com

Hella Jongerius: www.jongeriuslab.com
Henry Kloss/PAL radio: www.tivoliaudio
Herzog & de Meuron: hdm.walkerart.org
Hussein Chalayan: www.husseinchalayan.com

Ilse Crawford: www.studioilse.c
Industrial Facility: www.industrialfacility.co.uk
Ineke Hans: www.inekehans.com
Inflate: www.inflate.co.uk/oiab
Inga Sempé: www.ingasempe.fr
Issey Miyake: www.isseymiyake.com

Jaime Hayon: www.hayonstudio.com
Jakob + McFarlane:
    www.jakobmacfarlane.com
Jamie Hewlett: www.jamiehewlett.co.uk
Jasper Morrison: www.jaspermorrison.com
Jerszy Seymour: www.jerszyseymour.com
Jess Shaw: www.jessshaw.com
Ji Lee: www.thebubbleproject.com
Jonathan Barnbrook: www.barnbrook.net
Joris Laarman: www.jorislaarman.com
Julia Lohmann: www.julialohmann.co.uk
Jurgen Bey: www.jurgenbey.nl

Kam Tang: www.kamtang.co.uk
Karim Rashid: www.karimrashid.com
Klein Dytham Architecture:
    www.klein-dytham.com

Konstantin Grcic: www.konstantin-grcic.com
Kram/Weisshaar: www.kramweisshaar.com

Lab Architecture: www.labarchitecture.com
Latz and Partners: www.latzundpartner.de
Lionel Theodore Dean:
    www.futurefactories.com

Maarten Baas: www.maartenbaas.com
Mansilla + Tuñón: www.mansilla-tunon.com
Manuel Torres/Fabrican: www.fabricanltd.com
Marc Newson: www.marcnewson.com
Marcel Wanders: www.marcelwanders.com
Martí Guixé: www.guixe.com
Matali Crasset: www.matalicrasset.com
Matthias Megyeri:
    www.sweetdreamssecurity.com
Max Barenbrug: www.bugaboo.ws
Meyer en Van Schooten:
    www.meyer-vanschooten.nl
Miles Newlyn: www.newlyn.com
Mixko: mixko.co.uk
Mosley meets Wilcox:
    www.mosleymeetswilcox.com
MVRDV: www.mvrdv.nl

Naoto Fukasawa: www.naotofukasawa.com
Nexus Productions: www.nexuslondon.com
Nicholas Grimshaw & Partners:
    www.grimshaw-architects.c
Nicolas Roope: www.hulger.com
Niels van Eijk: www.ons-adres.nl

Ora Ito: www.ora-ito.com

Patricia Urquiola: www.patriciaurquiola.com
Patrick Jouin: www.patrickjouin.com
Paul Cocksedge: www.paulcocksedge.co.uk
Pearson Lloyd: www.pearsonlloyd.co.uk
Peter Eisenman:
    www.eisenmanarchitects.com
Peter Traag: www.petertraag.com
Philippe Starck: www.philippe-starck.com
Piet Hein Eek: www.pietheineek.nl
Plot Architects: www.plot.dk
Priestman Goode: www.priestmangoode.com

R&Sie: new-territories.com
Rachel Kelly: www.interactivewallpaper.co.uk
Rachel Wingfield: loop.ph
RCR Aranda Pgiem Vilalta Architects:
    www.rcrarquitectes.es

Rem Koolhaas/OMA: www.oma.nl
Richard Hutten: www.richardhutten.com
RMJM: www.rmjm.com
RMP Landschaftarchitekten:
    www.rpm-architekten.de
Robert Dawson:
    www.aestheticsabotage.com
Robert Ryan: www.misterrob.co.uk
Robert Stadler: www.robertstadler.net
Rockstar Games: www.rockstargames.com
Ron Arad: www.ronarad.com
Ross Lovegrove: www.rosslovegrove.com

Sam Buxton: www.sambuxton.com
SANAA/ Kazuyo Sejima & Ryue Nishizawa:
    www.sanaa.co.jp
Scott Kochlefl/Ideation: www.takbrand.com
Seymour Powell: www.seymourpowell.co.uk
Shigeru Ban: www.shigerubanarchitects.com
Simon Conder Associates:
    www.simonconder.co.uk
Softroom: www.softroom.com
Stefan Sagmeister: www.sagmeister.com
Stuart Haygarth: www.stuarthaygarth.com
Studio Job: www.studiojob.nl
Sybarite: www.sybarite-uk.com

TAK pushpins by Ideation: www.TAKbrand.
    com; info@TAKbrand.com
Thom Mayne/Morphosis: www.morphosis.ne
Thomas Heatherwick:
    www.thomasheatherwick.com
Timorous Beasties:
    www.timorousbeasties.com
Tobie Kerridge and Nikki Stott:
    www.biojewellery.com
Tokujin Yoshioka: www.tokujin.com
Tom Dixon: www.tomdixon.ne
Toord Boontje: www.tordboontje.com

Weiki Somers: www.wiekisomers.com
Werner Aisslinger: www.aisslinger.de
Wilkinson Eyre Architects:
    www.wilkinsoneyre.com
Wokmedia: www.wokmedia.com
WonderWall/Masamichi Karayama:
    www.wonder-wall.com

Yves Behar: www.fuseproject.com

Zaha Hadid Architects: www.zaha-hadid.com

Picture Credits

The publishers would like to thank the following sources for their kind permission to reproduce the pictures in this book.

Endpapers, front and back: Courtesy of eBoy.

Introductory pages:
1 Courtesy of Stuart Haygarth; 2 Top Left–© Rafael Vargas, Right – Courtesy of Kartell; 3 Top Left – Courtesy of This Is Real Art, Bottom Right – Courtesy of Jamie Hewlett; 4 Top – © Charlie Koolhaas, Bottom – Courtesy of Droog; 5 Top Left – Courtesy of Normann Copenhagen, Top Right – Courtesy of Matthias Megyeri, Bottom – Courtesy of www.maartenbaas.com; 6 Left – © Maarten Van Houten/Courtesy of Marcel Wanders, Right – Courtesy of Marcel Wanders, Bottom Right – © Inga Powilleit, styling Tatjana Quax/Courtesy of Marcel Wanders; 7 Both – Courtesy of Marcel Wanders; 8 Bitter Bredt; 9 Top – Peter Jordan/PA/Empics, Bottom – Courtesy of Toord Boontje; 10 Courtesy of Campana Design; 11 Courtesy of Ineke Hans; 12 Left – © Peer van de Kruis/Courtesy of Niels Van Eijk, Right – ©Janne Kyttanen/Courtesy of Freedom of Creation; 13 Left – © Ronan Bouroullec/Courtesy of Ronan & Erwan Bouroullec, Right – © Frank Tjepkema/Courtesy of Tjep.

Architecture:
14 Ted Soqui/Corbis; 15 Top – Joe Klamar/AFP/Getty Images, Bottom – © Hiroyuki Hirai; 16 Top – Edmund Sumner/VIEW, Bottom – Courtesy of Toyo Ito; 17 Edmund Sumner/VIEW; 18 Top & Bottom – Joe Klamar/AFP/Getty Images; 19 Richard Gardner/Rex Features; 20 Left & Right – © Charlie Koolhaas; 21 Top – Jose Pedro Fernandes/Alamy; Bottom Left – © Charlie Koolhaas, Bottom Right – © AMO Nicolas Firket; 22 Sipa Press/Rex Features; 23 Top – Sipa Press/Rex Features, Bottom – © Philippe Ruault; 24 –25 All – Paul Raftery/VIEW; 26 Nick Guttridge/VIEW; 27 © Roland Halbe; 28 –29 All – Nick Guttridge/VIEW; 30–31 Both – ©Werner Huthmacher; 32 Top – Rainer Viertlboeck/Artur/VIEW, Bottom Left – Franz Marc Frei/Corbis, Bottom Right – Action Press/Rex Features; 33 Top – Courtesy of Foster and Partners, Bottom – Eddie Mulholland/Rex Features; 34 Courtesy of Foster and Partners; 35 Paul Hardy/Corbis; 36 –37 © Christine Ottewill;37 Top Left – Roland Halbe/Artur/VIEW; 38 –39 © Roland Halbe; 40 Bottom Right – Bitter Bredt; 41 Top – Action Press/Rex Features; Bottom Left & Right – Bitter Bredt; 42–43 © Steffen Jaenicke; 44 Left & Right – David McNew/Getty Images; 45 Hufton & Crow/VIEW; 46–47 Rufus F Folkks/Corbis; 48 © Rob 't Hart; 49 All – © Hiroyuki Hirai; 50 Sam Tinson/Rex Features; 52 Top – Dave Penman/Rex Features, Centre & Bottom – Peter Cook/VIEW; 53 Edmund Sumner/VIEW; 54 Left – R Bryant/Arcaid/Rex Features, Right – Cesar Rangel/AFP/Getty Images; 55 Lluis Gene/AFP/Getty Images; 56 –59 All – © Katsuhisa Kida; 60 Top – Sue Barr/VIEW Bottom – © Margherita Spiluttini; 61 –63 All – © Christian Richters; 64 Roland Halbe/Artur; 65 Top & Centre – Chris Gascoigne/VIEW, Bottom – © Stephen Ambrose; 66 Edmund Sumner/VIEW; 67 All – © Satoru Mishima; 68 © James Haig Streeter; 69 Top – Sue Barr/VIEW, Bottom – © Satoru Mishima; 71 © Richard Davies; 72 Top – Arcaid/Alamy, Bottom – Ted Soqui/Corbis; 73 Top – Ted Soqui/Corbis, Bottom – Arcaid/Alamy; 74 –75 Arcaid/Alamy.

Interiors:
76 © Rafael Vargas; 77 Top Left – Paul Raftery/VIEW, Bottom Right – © Jeroen Musch; 78 –79 All – © Albert Ferrero; 80 –81 All – Courtesy of Comme des Garçons; 82 Courtesy of Studio Ilse; 83 All – Courtesy of Soho House; 84 Top – Courtesy of Studio Ilse, Centre Upper – Courtesy of Studio Ilse, Centre Lower – Courtesy of Soho House, Bottom – Courtesy of Studio Ilse; 85 Courtesy of Soho House; 86 –87 All – © Jeroen Musch, 88 © Rafael Vargas; 89 Top – © Rafael Vargas Bottom – Courtesy of Silken Hotels; 90 Top Left – © Rafael Vargas, Top Right – © Rafael Vargas, Bottom Left – Courtesy of Silken Hotels, Bottom Right – © Rafael Vargas; 91 Both – © Rafael Vargas; 92 Both – © George Terberg; 93 Top Left – © Alberto Ferrero, Top Right – © George Terberg, Bottom Left – © Alberto Ferrero, Bottom Right –

Both – Courtesy of Konstantin Grcic; 172 ©
Ashley Cameron/Courtesy of Tom Dixon; 173
Courtesy of Tom Dixon; 174–5 All – Courtesy
of Ineke Hans; 176–7 Both – Courtesy of
Peter Traag; 178–9 Courtesy of Edra; 180–1
Both – Courtesy of Patrick Jouin; 182 Top
– Courtesy of Zaha Hadid Architects,
Bottom – Courtesy of Established &
Sons; 183 Courtesy of Established & Sons;
184–5 Both – © Frank Stolle/Courtesy of KW;
186–7 Both – Courtesy of Studio Job; 188–9
Courtesy of Piet Hein Eek.

© Inga Powilleit; 94 Imagekontainer; 95
Top & Centre – © Philippe Ruault, Bottom
– Paul Raftery/VIEW; 96–97 All – © Vivien
Chen/Courtesy of Michael Young; 98 Left
& Top Right – Directphoto.org/Alamy,
Bottom Right – Nick Guttridge/VIEW; 99
Directphoto.org/Alamy; 100–101 © Jean
François Jaussaud; 101 Bottom Right
– © Vagelis Paterakis; 102 Left – Chris
Gascoigne/VIEW, Top Right & Bottom
Right – Courtesy of Jurgen Bey; 103–105
All – Courtesy of Fox Hotel; 106 Both
– © Hélène Binet/Courtesy of Caruso St
John; 107 Top – © Hélène Binet/Courtesy
of Caruso St John, Bottom – © Ioana
Marinescu/Courtesy of Caruso St John;
108 © Roberto d'Addona/Courtesy of Marc
Newson; 109 Top – Neil Setchfield/Alamy,
Centre Upper – Sue Barr/VIEW, Centre
Lower – Neil Setchfield/Alamy, Bottom – Sue
Barr/VIEW; 110 Top & Bottom – Gregoire
Korganov/Getty Images, Centre – Courtesy
of Hotel du Petit Moulin; 111 Both – Dennis
Gilbert/VIEW; 112 Christian Michel/VIEW;
113 Courtesy of Hi Hotel; 114 Top – Christian
Michel/VIEW, Bottom – Courtesy of Hi Hotel;
115 Courtesy of Hi Hotel; 116–9 All – © Kozo
Takayama; 120–1 All – Courtesy of www.
pearsonlloyd.co.uk; 122–3 All – Courtesy
of Priestman Goode; 124–5 All – Courtesy

of Sybarite; 126–7 All – Courtesy of Afroco;
128–9 All – Courtesy of Hitoshi Abe; 130–1
Both – Courtesy of Concrete Architectural
Associates; 131 Courtesy of Concrete
Architectural Associates.

Furniture:

132 Top Right – Courtesy of www.
maartenbaas.com, Bottom Left – © André
Huber/Courtesy of Magis; 133 © Frank Stolle/
Courtesy of KW; 134–5 Both – Courtesy of
Marcel Wanders; 136–7 Both – © Henk Jan
Kamerbeek/Courtesy of Moooi; 138–9 Both
– © Paul Tahon/Courtesy of Ronan & Erwan
Bouroullec; 140–1 All – Courtesy of IKEA;
143 Courtesy of Studio Morozzi; 144–5 All – ©
Vitra/Courtesy of Ronan & Erwan Bouroullec;
146 © Anna Lonnerstam/Courtesy of Front;
148–9 All – Courtesy of Front; 150–1 All
– Courtesy of www.maartenbaas.com; 152
–3 All – © André Huber/Courtesy of Magis;
154–5 Both – Courtesy of Magis; 156–7 Both
– Courtesy of Moooi; 158–9 Both – Courtesy
of Moroso; 160–1 All – © Nacasa & Partners
Inc/Courtesy of Tokujin Yoshioka Design;
162–3 Courtesy of Jurgen Bey; 164–5 Both
– Courtesy of Demakersvan; 166–7 Both
– © Tom Vack/Courtesy of Ron Arad; 168–9
Both – Courtesy of Fredrikson Stallard; 170–1

Lighting:

190 Courtesy of Committee; 191 Top
– Courtesy of Mixko, Bottom – © Loop.pH
Ltd;193–4 Both – Courtesy of Toord Boontje;
196–7 Both – ©Janne Kyttanen/Courtesy
of Freedom of Creation; 198–9 Both
– © Loop.pH Ltd; 200–1 All – Courtesy of
Committee; 203 © Richard Brine/Courtesy
of Paul Cocksedge; 204 Courtesy of Jurgen
Bey; 205 Giuseppe Cacace/Getty Images;
207 Courtesy of Yves Behar; 208 © Andrea
Ferrari/Courtesy of Paul Cocksedge; 209 ©
Richard Brine/Courtesy of Paul Cocksedge;
211 Courtesy of Moooi; 212–3 Both – © Peer
van de Kruis/Courtesy of Niels Van Eijk; 214
Courtesy of Normann Copenhagen; 216–7
All – Courtesy of Flos; 218–9 Both – Courtesy
of Kartell; 220 Courtesy of Moooi; 221
Courtesy of Established & Sons; 222
Courtesy of Tom Dixon; 223 © Gideon Hart/
Courtesy of Tom Dixon; 225 © Patrick Gries/
Courtesy of Robert Stadler; 226 Courtesy of
Mixko; 227 Courtesy of Fredrikson Stallard;
228–9 Both – Courtesy of Stuart Haygarth;
230–3 All – Courtesy of Jerszy Seymour;
234–5 Courtesy of Materialise. MGX; 236–7
© Carlo Draisci/Courtesy of Jess Shaw;
238–9 Both – Courtesy of Wokmedia ; 240–1
Both – Courtesy of Yves Behar; 242–3 Both
– Courtesy of Julia Lohmann.

Homeware:

244 Courtesy of Timorous Beasties;
245 Top – Courtesy of Robert Dawson,
Bottom – Courtesy of Rachel Kelly;
246–9 All – Courtesy of Jongerius
Lab; 250–1 All – Courtesy of Timorous
Beasties; 252–3 Both – Courtesy of
Missoni; 254–5 All – © Anna Lonnerstam/
Courtesy of Front; 256–7 All – Courtesy
of Rachel Kelly; 258–61 All – Courtesy
of Royal Tichelaar Makkum; 262 Both
– Courtesy of Daniel Brown; 263 © Luis
Silva Campos/Courtesy of Daniel Brown;
264 Courtesy of Cor Unum; 265 © Marek
Novotny/Courtesy of Maxim Velcovsky;
266–7 Both – © Ronan Bouroullec/
Courtesy of Ronan & Erwan Bouroullec;
268–9 All – Courtesy of Marcel Wanders;
270–1 Both – © Frank Tjepkema/Courtesy
of Tjep.; 272–273 Both – Courtesy of
Ineke Hans; 274–275 Both – Courtesy
of Tom Dixon; 277 Courtesy of Richard
Hutten; 278–279 All – Courtesy of Robert
Dawson; 280–1 Both – Courtesy of Iittala;
282–3 Both – Courtesy of Fernando
Brizio; 284–5 All – Courtesy of Constantin
Boym; 286–7 Both – Courtesy of Mosley
Meets Wilcox.

Products:

288 © Maarten van Houten/Courtesy of
Marcel Wanders; 289 Left – Courtesy of
Scott Kochlefl/Ideation Designs, Top Right
– Courtesy of Matthias Megyeri; 290 Both
– Courtesy of Apple; 291 Courtesy of Muji; 293
Courtesy of Priestman Goode; 294 Courtesy
of HULGER Ltd; 295 Both – Courtesy of Paolo
Ulian; 296–7 All – Courtesy of KDDI; 298
Courtesy of Industrial Facility; 299 Courtesy
of Droog; 300–1 Both – Courtesy of Ruark
Acoustics; 302 Both – Courtesy of Dunne
& Raby; 303–5 All – Courtesy of Matthias
Megyeri; 306 Both – Courtesy of Luis Eslava
Eloy; 307 Both – Courtesy of Heineken; 308
Courtesy of Scott Kochlefl/Ideation Designs;
309 Courtesy of Ineke Hans; 310–311 Both
– Courtesy of Ty Nant; 312–3 All – Courtesy
of Sam Buxton; 314–5 All – © Maarten
van Houten/Courtesy of Marcel Wanders;
316–7 Both – © Christoph Kicherer/Rowenta/
Courtesy of Jasper Morrison; 318–9 Both
– Courtesy of Demakersvan; 320–1 Courtesy
of Bugaboo; 322–3 All – Courtesy of Doshi
Levien; 324–5 All – Courtesy of Inflate;
326–7 Both – Courtesy of Barber Osgerby;
328 Courtesy of Hayon Studio; 330–1
Both – Courtesy of Seymour Powell;

332–4 Both – Courtesy of BMW; 335 Top –
Courtesy of BMW, Centre – Sion Touhig/Getty
Images, Bottom – Phil Noble/PA/Empics; 337
H Gousse/AP/Empics; 338–9 All – Courtesy of
Priestman Goode.

Clothing and Accessories:

340 Courtesy of Starck Network; 341
Top – Courtesy of Freedom of Creation,
Bottom – © Deborah Bird/Courtesy of
Elena Manferdini; 342–3 All – Siemoneit
Ronald/Corbis; 344–5 Both – © Miyaki
Design Studio 2006; 346 Reuters/Corbis;
347 Both – Peter Jordan/PA/Empics; 348
Courtesy of Yves Behar; 350 Both – Sipa
Press/Rex Features; 351 Reuters/Corbis;
352–3 All – Courtesy of Adam Whiton;
354 Both – © Adam Parker; 355 Courtesy
of American Apparel; 356 Courtesy of
American Apparel; 357 Top Left & Top
Right – Courtesy of American Apparel,
Bottom – David McNew/Getty Images; 358
All – © Deborah Bird/Courtesy of Elena
Manferdini; 359 Top & Centre – © Deborah
Bird/Courtesy of Elena Manferdini, Bottom
– © Robert Robert/Courtesy of Elena
Manferdini; 360–361 All – Courtesy of Marc
Newson; 362–3 Both – Courtesy of Freedom
of Creation; 364–5 Courtesy of Campana
Design; 366–7 All – Courtesy of Starck
Network; 368–9 Both – © Frank Tjepkema/
Courtesy of Tjep; 370–1 All – Courtesy
of Tobie Kerridge.

Visual Communication:

372 Courtesy of Graphic Thought Facility;
373 Top Right – Courtesy of Craig Robinson,
Bottom Left – Courtesy of This Is Real Art;
375 Courtesy of Stefan Sagmeister; 376
All – Courtesy of Banksy; 377 All – Marco Di
Lauro/Getty Images; 378–9 Courtesy of
Craig Robinson; 380–1 Both – Courtesy
of Graphic Thought Facility; 382–3 All

Every effort has been made to
acknowledge correctly and contact
the source and/or copyright holder
of each picture and Carlton Books
Limited apologizes for any unintentional
errors or omissions, which will be corrected
in future editions of this book.

Publisher's notes:
On entries for furniture, lighting, homeware
and products where no manufacturers
names are provided, these items have been
manufactured by the designers themselves,
are in prototype or have been produced in
a limited-edition run only. As many of these
items may go into wider production in the
future, it is best to contact the designer for
further information.

Sketch by Front is sold via the Barry Friedman
Gallery in New York: www.barryfriedmanltd.
com. For more details on the VKB virtual
keyboard, contact Nick Thompson at Avenir
Telecom UK: +44 (0)20 8731 4412.

The dates given for the entries throughout
are for completion dates, and every effort
has been made to verify these. We apologize
for any errors, which will be corrected in
future editions of this work. Several 1999
designs that are groundbreaking and
influential examples of design in the twenty-
first century have been included in this book
in order to avoid ignoring any seminal works
that characterized the new century but
which were completed before the year 2000.